LF

Simone de Beauvoir and
the Limits of Commitment

Simone de Beauvoir and the Limits of Commitment

Anne Whitmarsh

Cambridge University Press

Cambridge

London   New York   New Rochelle

Melbourne   Sydney

Published by the Press Syndicate of the University of Cambridge
The Pitt Building, Trumpington Street, Cambridge CB2 1RP
32 East 57th Street, New York, NY 10022, USA
296 Beaconsfield Parade, Middle Park, Melbourne 3206, Australia

First published 1981

Printed in Great Britain by
Western Printing Services Ltd, Bristol

British Library Cataloguing in Publication Data
Whitmarsh, Anne
Simone de Beauvoir and the limits of commitment.
1. Beauvoir, Simone de – Criticism and
interpretation
I. Title
843'.9'12   PQ2603.E362Z/   80–41567
ISBN 0 521 23669 x

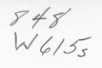

Contents

Preface

The structure followed in this work is part-thematic, part-chronological: a broadly chronological pattern is followed, but within each chapter significant themes are explored both forward and backward in time, as indicated by the chapter titles. The one partial exception is chapter 4 where the thematic structure predominates.

Any translations of quotations from works without a published translation are the responsibility of the author, as are certain revisions to published versions (indicated in each instance). The references in the notes are to the published English translation of the work in question if one exists; details of both the original and the translation used are given in the bibliography. In order not to burden the reader, page references have wherever possible been grouped together at the end of a paragraph or section.

I am particularly grateful to Professor Richard Coe for giving me the benefit of his wide-ranging scholarship and his skilled advice. My thanks are also due to the following people for their help: Dr W. D. Redfern, Professor Margaret Stacey, Dr Susan Bassnett-McGuire, Dr Veronica Beechey, Mr Peter Larkin, and Mrs Marilyn Wilkins; and to my husband, without whose encouragement tempered with salutary criticism this book would never have been written.

Biographical notes

The four volumes of Simone de Beauvoir's autobiography, although conspicuously lacking in dates, provide a full and detailed account of her life. The reader is also directed to the very complete chronology in *Les écrits de Simone de Beauvoir*, compiled by Claude Francis and Fernande Gontier, although there is occasionally confusion over dates. The following chronology is designed to help the reader to locate the most important episodes and events, including the writing and publication of her books and the most significant journeys abroad. Historical events have been included where relevant.

1905   21 June: Jean-Paul Sartre born in Paris.

1908   9 January: Simone de Beauvoir born in Paris, Boulevard Raspail.

1913   Becomes a pupil at a private school, the Cours Désir, where she spends all her schooldays.

1917   Elizabeth Mabille (Zaza) joins the school.

1925   Leaves school after taking the second part of her baccalauréat – Joins the course in Latin and literature at the Institut Sainte-Marie at Neuilly, at the same time attending lectures in mathematics at the Institut Catholique.

1926   Continues her studies in philosophy and literature at the Sorbonne while still attending philosophy lectures at Neuilly.

1928   Starts to prepare for the philosophy agrégation at the Ecole Normale Supérieure concurrently with the final year of her licence at the Sorbonne.

1929   Meets Sartre, also at the E.N.S. taking the agrégation for the second time; Sartre comes first in the examination and she comes second – Moves away from home into a room in her grandmother's flat – Death of Zaza – For two years lives on a part-time teaching post and private pupils – Sartre starts his eighteen months' military service.

1931   First teaching post in Marseille – Sartre appointed to Le Havre.

1932   Appointed to lycée in Rouen.

1933   Olga Kosakiewicz enters their lives – Sartre in Berlin for a year as research student at the Institut Français.

1936   Appointed to Lycée Molière in Paris – Sartre appointed to Laon – Popular Front government elected (in power until 1938) – Start of Spanish civil war (until 1939).

1937   Sartre to Lycée Pasteur in Paris.

1938   Munich agreement 29 September.

1939   War declared 3 September – Sartre joins up immediately – She starts teaching at the Lycée Camille-Sée and the Lycée Henri VI.

1940   Sartre taken prisoner – Paris occupied – Defeat of France and armistice.

1941   Sartre released and back in Paris.

1943   Simone de Beauvoir dismissed from teaching service – *L'invitée* (written 1938–41) – Established as a writer.

1944   Liberation of Paris – *Pyrrhus et Cinéas* (written in three months 1943) – Reinstated as a teacher but never teaches again.

1945   *Les bouches inutiles* (written in three months 1944) – Visit to Spain and Portugal – End of war in Europe (May) and the Far East (September) – *Le sang des autres* (written 1941–3) – First issue of *Les Temps Modernes* – First performance of *Les bouches inutiles*.

1946   *Tous les hommes sont mortels* (started 1943) – 'Pour une morale de l'ambiguïté' published in *Les Temps Modernes* December–January 1947.

1947   First visit to U.S.A. – Meets Nelson Algren; her affair with him lasts four years – Further visit later in year – *Pour une morale de l'ambiguïté* published as a book – Height of 'existentialist' vogue in Saint-Germain-des-Prés.

1948   Rassemblement Démocratique Révolutionnaire founded – *L'existentialisme et la sagesse des nations* (collection of articles first published in *Les Temps Modernes*) – Visit to Algren in U.S.A. and trip with him to Mexico – *L'Amérique au jour le jour*.

1949   *Le deuxième sexe* (started in 1946) – Algren in Paris – Sartre resigns from R.D.R. – Existence of Soviet labour camps breaks on the world.

1950 Visit to Africa – Start of Korean war (until 1953) – Visit to Algren in U.S.A.

1951 Visit to Algren in U.S.A. – End of their relationship.

1952 Simone de Beauvoir and Claude Lanzmann decide to live together.

1953 Begins to spend most summers with Sartre in Rome.

1954 *Les mandarins* (written 1950–3) – Receives the Prix Goncourt – Start of terrorism in Algeria.

1955 World Peace Congress in Helsinki – Visit with Sartre to China – *Privilèges* (collection of articles first published in *Les Temps Modernes*).

1956 Hungarian uprising.

1957 *La longue marche* (written 1955–6).

1958 *Mémoires d'une jeune fille rangée* (written 1956–8; covers the years 1908–29) – Return of General de Gaulle to power and start of Fifth Republic – Simone de Beauvoir and Lanzmann separate.

1960 Visits to Cuba and U.S.A. with Sartre – Publication of the *Manifeste des 121* – Visit to Brazil with Sartre – *La force de l'âge* (covers the years 1929–44) – *Brigitte Bardot and the Lolita syndrome* (written 1959) – Campaign on behalf of Djamila Boupacha (1960–1).

1962 Evian agreement ends Algerian war – Visit with Sartre to U.S.S.R. and Poland – Winter spent in U.S.S.R.

1963 Visit with Sartre to U.S.S.R. for Communauté Européenne des Ecrivains congress – *La force des choses* (covers the years 1944–62) – Visit with Sartre to Czechoslovakia – Death of her mother.

1964 Visit with Sartre to U.S.S.R. – *Une mort très douce* (written 1963–4) – *Clarté* debate: 'Que peut la littérature?'.

1965 *Que peut la littérature?* published as a book – Start of U.S. offensive against North Vietnam.

1966 Visits with Sartre to U.S.S.R. and Japan – *Les belles images* (written 1965–6).

1967 Visit with Sartre to Middle East just before six-day war – Russell Tribunal.

1968 *La femme rompue* (written 1966–7, luxury edition published October 1967) – Visit with Sartre to Yugoslavia – The May 'events' – Russian invasion of Czechoslovakia – Visit with Sartre to Czechoslovakia.

1969   Elected to consultative committee of the Bibliothèque Nationale.

1970   *La vieillesse* (written 1967–9) – Affair of *La Cause du Peuple* – Becomes nominal editor of *L'Idiot international* – Joins in Mouvement de Libération des Femmes marches and demonstrations for free abortion on demand.

1971   Publication of the *Manifeste des 343*, campaigning for abortion.

1972   Joins in demonstrations protesting about crimes against women – Becomes President of Choisir – *Tout compte fait* (covers the years 1962–72, but thematic, not chronological).

1973   First issue of *Libération* – Start of feminist column in *Les Temps Modernes*.

1974   Becomes President of the Ligue des droits des femmes.

1975   Awarded the Jerusalem prize for writers who have promoted the cause of the freedom of the individual – End of Vietnam War.

1979   Film on her life (largely shot spring 1978) – *Quand prime le spirituel* (written 1935–7).

1980   15 April: Death of Sartre.

Introduction

Simone de Beauvoir's name evokes images of belles-lettres, politics and women's rights. Currently she is probably best known to the general public for her involvement in the women's movement but in truth this is only the latest manifestation of a long-standing existentialist commitment. She is firmly established as the doyenne of existentialism – the nearest it ever got to a high priestess. Likewise she is seen as a lifelong member of the intelligentsia of the French left who have always uncompromisingly denounced capitalism as a system and the established social *mores* of bourgeois society. In short she is among the most renowned of those who personify what she and others have labelled *engagement*.

Simone de Beauvoir accepted Sartre's contention that commitment must necessarily be political, specifically to the cause of the revolutionary left, and that the committed writer had a social and political role to play. This study focusses upon the ethical, social and above all political implications of this commitment both in her work and in the way she has led her own life. It discusses the justification for her reputation and the extent to which the notion of *engagement* was restricted in theory and practice. It offers detailed analyses of her literary œuvre and significant *ex cathedra* statements and activities in so far as any of these can be categorised, however loosely, as manifestations of her commitment. Estimations are made of the extent to which she can reasonably be said to have created effective strategies and in practice to have advanced any of the causes to which she has, or is reputed to have, devoted herself.

In the nature of things the time scale, from the 1930s to the present, encompasses great changes in European society in general and French society in particular. Consequently the developments in her attitudes and opinions are set against changing circumstances – even though Mme de Beauvoir herself has changed less than the society within which she lives. It may well be that she has been much influenced by the relative continuity of the restricted milieu of Parisian intellectuals from which she has never detached herself.

Within this closed circle Sartre was intellectually the dominant personality, and she regarded him as such. In order fully to understand the points of view, the theories and the actions of Simone de Beauvoir, it is essential to see them in relation to those of Sartre. Their thought processes were always interactive, arising out of a dialogue between them, and are often inseparable. That is not to say they were always identical, and this study attempts to demonstrate the differences in their thinking as well as indicating the similarities, especially where this can prove a useful *point de repère* for the reader.

Partisan judgments on the work of Simone de Beauvoir are the norm, tending to the extremes of either virulent attack or uncritical admiration. It is hoped that this work will achieve a balance which is often missing, and that it will do justice to a figure who, together with Sartre, has become a French national institution.

I

From apoliticism to involvement

Simone de Beauvoir's name, like that of Sartre, is inextricably associated with politics, the politics of the left. Her public image is that of someone who has always been politically active. She has many times elaborated her political views in public statements, in books, articles and reviews; in interviews she uses the language of revolution. People often make the assumption that Sartre was at one time a member of the Communist Party,[1] and as Sartre's lifelong companion her name is linked by this association with all his political actions, whether or not she participated actively. Credibility is given to this image by a few well-publicised incidents in recent years, such as when they have both been photographed selling banned *gauchiste* newspapers.

Even so, the paradoxical truth is that until the second world war both Simone de Beauvoir and Sartre eschewed political action and indeed that, although they believed themselves to be situated on the left, they felt no commitment to politics, only to literature. The attitudes of these early years, the apoliticism which characterised their life together in the thirties, and their fairly abrupt conversion brought about by the advent of war, are recounted in the first two volumes of Simone de Beauvoir's autobiography.

Here a caveat must be entered. We depend almost entirely on her autobiography for an analysis of herself and her views during the period before any of her writing had been published. It was written from a wealth of detailed personal documentation, research into the public events of the time, and a remarkable memory, and Sartre has vouched for its accuracy regarding everything that is said about him.[2] However, in *Mémoires d'une jeune fille rangée* she is going back up to fifty years, and in *La force de l'âge* up to thirty-one years. Historians regard the personal memoir as a type of historical evidence to be used with great caution, although it is excellent evidence of the way people think at the time of writing, and of the way they see, and want others to see, events. It cannot be denied that she always attempted to be totally honest and dispassionate about herself in her

3

writing and was frequently critical of past attitudes. Nevertheless as historical evidence about herself, her autobiography must be regarded with some circumspection.

Simone de Beauvoir was born in 1908 into a bourgeois family. The background of these early years explains to some extent her later attitudes. At first she had a very stable and contented childhood, living in Paris with her parents and younger sister, and spending her happiest times on the long family holidays at her grandfather's estate in Lomousin. Her father came from a wealthy family; prevented by the conventions of his class from taking up acting as a career, he had become secretary to a lawyer but used his personal fortune to enable him to mix with actors and frequent fashionable circles where he indulged in amateur acting. Flamboyant, cultured, a man of the world, he was idolised by his elder daughter. He became her intellectual mentor and was able to satisfy her perpetual thirst for knowledge, and it was he who opened up the world of books to her. He was an unbeliever and a firm supporter of the far right. Her mother, brought up in the provinces and educated in a convent, was very different in character. Devout, quiet and lacking in self-assurance, physically inhibited, conventional in the extreme, she was warmly affectionate towards her children and took very seriously her duties as a mother, in particular her responsibility for their spiritual upbringing. The difference in her parents' religious views could have caused her agonies: like her mother, she believed absolutely in the existence of God, yet her father, whom she admired so much and who was always right, was a sceptic. In fact she adopted her mother's attitude, which was to accept this as quite natural. She rationalised it by separating the spiritual world embodied by her mother and the intellectual world of her father. She claims, indeed, that this had a profound effect on her later thinking; it taught her to question matters which might otherwise have been taken for granted. She believes that this largely explains why she became an intellectual.

The contrast between Christian values and bourgeois values proved more difficult to reconcile. Christian precepts about charity evaporated when it was a question of German children benefiting from it; telling lies was an offence – except that Colonel Henry's forgery of a letter in the Dreyfus affair was in the national interest; murder was a sin, but the death penalty was essential; the Pope, elected by the Holy Spirit, was wrong to meddle in social questions. So there was, apparently, a distinction to be made between the affairs of this world

and the next. She was more puzzled than tortured by the inconsistencies she noticed, and usually accepted her parents' explanation.
It was easier to take refuge in their unquestioned authority. She still
felt certain reactions to injustice and inequality, although always
without drawing any political conclusions. She had been taught that
all men were created equal by God and was therefore scandalised by
attitudes that she discovered from time to time in her own family
that seemed inconsistent with this belief. Her own view was quite
firm: 'I believed in the absolute equality of human beings.' She
readily accepted, however, that the middle classes were more intelligent than, and therefore different from, the lower orders, and was
thus able to feel superior to the mass of ordinary children and quite
happy to belong to an elite. Similarly, while believing that being rich
did not automatically confer any rights or merit on anyone, and
remembering that the New Testament extolled poverty, she nevertheless thought that property was a sacred right. Although some of
her reading led to enthusiasm about a democratic society that would
guarantee equal rights and freedom to all, she confesses: 'That was
as far as I went.'[3]

It was during her teens that she began seriously to question the
accepted values of her upbringing, and to rebel against her parents.
For some time her rebellion was silent but the easy *entente* which
had existed between her and them had disappeared. The first positive
step away from her background was an outright rejection of religion.
Encouraged by her mother and by the devout ladies who taught her
at the Cours Désir, the Catholic establishment where she spent all her
schooldays, she was as a child excessively pious. She even decided at
an early age that the spiritual life and the everyday life of the world
were so irreconcilable that the only way to gain salvation was to
become a Carmelite nun. God, it seemed, had nothing to do with
human endeavours, politics, business, the society we live in. By the
time she was twelve she began to yearn for some reward for her
piety – a sense of spiritual progress, some mystic revelation or ecstasy
as a result of her prayers, meditations and attempts at physical
mortification. Nothing happened. These self-regarding spiritual exercises earned praise from all around her, but it was a role she was
playing, and eventually she saw it for the masquerade it was.
The feverish piety suddenly seemed sterile. Moreover the way she
had conceived religion meant that the spiritual life and the worldly
life were mutually exclusive; never able to compromise, she character-

istically abandoned her religious beliefs totally at the age of fifteen and opted firmly for this world, there being no way in her eyes of reconciling the two. She stopped believing in God quite suddenly, and for ever: 'My incredulity never once wavered.'[4]

The rejection of her bourgeois background was more gradual. By the time she was fifteen she was resolute in her determination to devote her life to intellectual pursuits and had already decided that the life of a *mère de famille* was not for her – the idea of maternity appalled her as did the bourgeois acceptance of the marriage of convenience. It was unheard of for a girl of her milieu to go into higher education or to take a job, and the later decision to pursue an academic career was only accepted because of her family's somewhat reduced circumstances. She began to refuse to participate in the various social activities expected of her by her parents, for she had no interest in social success or status. Her father lost interest in her and she suffered from his disapproval. But gradually she was realising that it was possible to hold other opinions than his: she was beginning to question, for instance, his outright support of the far right, his view that children should not criticise their parents even if the criticism was justified, his conception of woman's place as being in the home in the role of model wife (only if she belonged to high society was she allowed to be witty and intelligent, though she must be charming and beautiful also). Alienated now from both her parents, she at first kept her views largely to herself and outwardly conformed, though often with bad grace. Once she became a student at the Institut Sainte-Marie at Neuilly and thereafter at the Sorbonne, it was relatively easy to free herself gradually from parental control, though not without frequent attempts by her parents to prevent her emancipation. The final break with the family environment came when she moved out at the end of her studies at the Ecole Normale Supérieure in September 1929 and rented a room of her own in her grandmother's flat. Thereafter she remained totally independent of her parents in every way.

During this whole period of adolescence and estrangement she had derived consolation from two things. The first was her love of reading. This was encouraged by her father but was strictly censored by him and even more so by her mother, although she soon took to clandestine reading of books from her father's large library. Her taste was further widened by her cousin Jacques, whom she greatly admired during her teens for his intellectual superiority over her, even believing for a time that she was in love with him; he introduced her to many new authors of whom her father much disapproved. By the time she was seventeen she was reading everything she wanted, irrespective of her parents' wishes. The other way of escape was friendship for a schoolfriend, Elizabeth Mabille, known as Zaza. It was through Zaza that she first learned that it was possible to be independent and disrespectful, but Zaza's rebellion was much more superficial than her own. Zaza was torn between love of her mother and respectful obedience to parents as prescribed by her religion on the one hand, and a loathing of the tyranny, the conformity and the conventions of life as a dutiful daughter of the bourgeoisie. She wished to marry one of Simone de Beauvoir's fellow students but, convinced that her parents would never agree to a marriage that they had not arranged, she succumbed to a sudden illness, supposedly meningitis. Simone de Beauvoir saw her death symbolically as an assassination for it epitomised the crushing effect of the bourgeois family upon a young girl. She herself had narrowly escaped, but she believed that she had paid for her freedom with the death of Zaza.

She never forgave the bourgeoisie. The theme of bourgeois morality and attempted emancipation from it is taken up in several of her fictional works as well as in her autobiography, notably in *La femme rompue, Les belles images*, and the set of five interconnected short stories, *Quand prime le spirituel*. The latter, written between 1935 and 1937 although unpublished until 1979, includes one of several attempts to tell the story of Zaza's tragedy in fictional form. Already here, in her first work, we see Simone de Beauvoir's rejection of the family as a valid institution and her equation of parenthood with tyranny, both of them judgments that she has never retracted and that have been further developed and elaborated throughout her life. Her major concern in the stories is to indicate the powerful hold on these children of the bourgeoisie of the moral and spiritual absolutes inculcated from the cradle onwards. She casts an ironic eye on the way the young women upon whom they are centred either find it impossible to give up their religious beliefs or, believing they have done so, have in fact replaced their religion with some other 'spiritual' activity. Simone de Beauvoir is honest enough to recognise that for her the practice of literature filled the gap left by loss of faith, and it will be seen that writing was itself a spiritual exercise. Whether she is sufficiently conscious of the other legacies she retains from the bourgeoisie is a matter of debate.

Her conversion to the politics of the left is recounted in less detail in her autobiography, although the literary way to it was opened by her wide reading. Her first foray into 'political' activity, during her first year as a student, seems to have acted as a powerful deterrent to further experiments of that sort. She was inspired by the personality and missionary zeal of Robert Garric who lectured to her on French literature at the Institut Sainte-Marie. He was a Catholic who believed in dispensing culture to the underprivileged and in breaking down class barriers. To this end he had founded the Equipes Sociales movement, an experiment in bringing together teams of students and working-class youths, which had spread throughout France. His message seemed entirely new to her. Her Catholic upbringing had taught her in theory that everyone, however underprivileged, was important and had a right to fulfilment, but in practice devotion to others had been strictly limited to the family circle; as for the workers, they were a dangerous species. Excited by Garric's belief that there were no class barriers, she felt for the first time that all men were her brothers; inspired by his example, she would serve humanity. She joined his Equipes Sociales and attended evening meetings at which she attempted to bring culture and enlightenment to young workers. These were patently unsuccessful. Disillusioned by their futility Simone de Beauvoir decided that action was of little use, not imagining that there could be any other field of activity. Although this experience gave her the illusion that the working classes were pleasant, deferential and ready to cooperate with more fortunate people like herself, she found it impossible to communicate with them with any degree of reciprocity or friendship. It is possible that this sense of distance and of being, in spite of herself, unable to escape from her class or from her intellectual milieu was one of the constraints on her political action later, and prevented her from engaging in physical labour or missionary activity among the working classes of the sort that Simone Weil attempted. At all events, her admiration for Garric faded with her faith in his works. Her only other actions as a student that could be considered in any way political were to sign a petition against a bill proposing the mobilisation of women, because she had been persuaded that such a step would lead to 'a general mobilisation of freedom of conscience', and another in favour of the pardon of two people she had never heard of, because she was against the death penalty. She confesses that her political activities did not go any further.

The Sorbonne at the time was not notably left wing. Simone de Beauvoir asserts that those who lectured to her deliberately ignored Hegel and Marx, but it was there that she had her first contact with students like Pierre Nodier. He was a member of the *Philosophies* group of Marxist students at the Sorbonne and the Ecole Normale Supérieure to which Nizan, Friedmann, Lefèbvre, Morhange and Politzer also belonged. The title comes from the periodical which they produced, later replaced by a journal called *L'Esprit*, of which he lent her copies.[5] Their frequent conversations, during which she plied him with questions, made her more aware and open-minded, but her ideas remained very hazy. She was still very muddled about her attitude to social problems, particularly after her experience of the Equipes Sociales; neither history, which seemed like a series of anecdotes, nor the present day, which she gathered from hearing her father talk consisted of gloomy financial and other equally distant matters, concerned her in the slightest. All she was really sure of was that she hated the extreme right and yet, as she saw later, this period marked the awakening of her political consciousness. Confused though her ideas still were she was charmed by the idea of Revolution and 'slid leftwards'. Her enthusiasm was negative: she wanted society to be turned upside down, without any real idea of the complexity of its workings or of what kind of alternative should be established.[6]

There was a large section of opinion, among both the students and the staff at the Ecole Normale Supérieure, that tended towards the left or the far left.[7] Whether or not this had any effect on Simone de Beauvoir during her year there, she certainly must have been influenced by the political attitudes of Maheu (given in her autobiography the pseudonym of André Herbaud) and then of Sartre and Nizan when he finally introduced her to them. In fact we hear at first very little about their politics, and it seems to be their philosophical views that interested her most. She merely notes that 'They made fun of bourgeois law and order', and that Nizan was a member of the Communist Party. As for Sartre: 'He was interested in social and political questions; he sympathized with Nizan's position; but as far as he was concerned, the main thing was to write and the rest would come later.'[8] These three, all the same age, three years older than Simone de Beauvoir, formed a select little band. They kept their distance from the other students and had a formidable reputation, both moral and intellectual, inspiring awe in their contemporaries. It was René Maheu who first became friendly with her and then drew her into the group, when she started meeting with them to work for the oral of the agrégation. One of the things she notes about him was that, to her surprise, he seemed to attach considerable importance to social success. He failed the examination and almost faded from their lives after that. He became a philosophy teacher, and then changed careers to work with U.N.E.S.C.O., eventually becoming director from 1961 until 1974. Paul Nizan went on to establish an early reputation during the thirties with his pamphlets and novels. He was the only one of them who was already politically committed. He remained a member of the Communist Party until 1939, when he resigned in protest at the volte-face of the party's support for the Nazi-Soviet pact and went to serve as a soldier. He was killed at Dunkirk in 1940 and subsequently had his reputation systematically destroyed by the party. Jean-Paul Sartre, equally critical of society as it existed, was not disposed to take an interest in politics; it was to be many years before he reached that stage, and the evolution of his political thought will be traced below, together with that of Simone de Beauvoir.

By the time she and Sartre parted for the summer, Simone de Beauvoir had decided that here was the man with whom she would be able to share everything and who would never go out of her life. He was, she discovered, superior to her in intellectual terms, but their views were almost identical. When, many years later, she recalls that she chose Sartre because he led her where she wanted to go, she declares that she would never have been influenced by anyone who did not share certain of her attitudes: 'I could only have become attached to a man who was hostile to all that I loathed: the Right, conventional thinking, religion.'[9] It seems therefore that by the time she met him her ideas had crystallised around these three main areas, although we never really learn how she came to see herself as being left wing. It is interesting to note that these attitudes are all negative, and that together they represent an apparently total rejection of the values of her parents: her father's support for the causes of the far right, her mother's devout Catholicism, and the bourgeois values of both. Certainly left-wing inclinations were the natural correlation of this bid for personal liberation from the ties of her family and class. Whether she ever really freed herself from the conditioning of her upbringing is another matter. Her austere morality and her devotion to the work ethic undoubtedly had a religious basis and, while rejecting the outward forms of religion, she was deeply influenced by her mother's rigid moral attitudes. Similarly, her intellectual rejection of the bourgeoisie still allowed her to retain those elements of bourgeois thinking and life-style that suited her.

Irrespective of how she arrived there, both she and Sartre located themselves firmly on the left by the time their lives became bound up together in the autumn of 1929. She frequently refers to 'the whole of the French left', including themselves therein; yet this was a rhetorical stance, intellectualised and very distant from reality. As Georges Hourdin puts it, 'she was satisfied with being sentimentally and instinctively on the left without seeing what this entailed'.[10] They were against society in its present form, that is, capitalist society, and they despised people like Raymond Aron for being a socialist because reformism was repugnant to them: 'Society, we felt, could change only as a result of sudden cataclysmic upheaval on a global scale.'[11] Aron, born like Sartre in 1905, had been at the E.N.S. with them and later became an academic and a writer with a particular interest in politics and sociology. Simone de Beauvoir admired his solid cultural grounding and sympathised with his idealistic viewpoint in the philosophical arguments he used to have with Sartre and which he tended to win – or thought he did. It was he who introduced Sartre to the work of Husserl, the German phenomenologist philosopher. They never discussed politics. At that time Aron was a member of the S.F.I.O., the French socialist party. He later became virulently anti-communist and when Sartre had become politically active Aron was one of the most outspoken and devastating critics of his espousal of the revolutionary cause. At this earlier stage Sartre and Simone de Beauvoir were not themselves concerned with bringing about the revolution. Their view was that they did not need to take any positive action because the collapse of capitalist society was inevitable. Indeed the world economic crisis following from the Wall Street crash in 1929 seemed to prove that it could not last much longer. They were filled with optimism for a future that would fulfil all their wishes and she says that this optimism was shared by all the French left. The nearest either of them came to committing themselves politically was between 1929 and 1932 when Sartre was several times tempted to become a member of the Communist Party – he felt a certain responsibility that she did not feel, in spite of his taste for independence. When this was mulled over between them they decided that if they had belonged to the proletariat they would have had to join, but that since the struggle of the working classes was not their struggle, their only duty was to give support. Besides, his ideas and temperament were against it, she says. Their main contribution was to be through their books, although she does not specify how.

They were writers first and foremost. Sartre lived for his writing: it concerned him above all else. Simone de Beauvoir had never envisaged any other future than one in which she would write, except for a brief period as a child when she saw herself as a teacher. Through their conversations, their teaching, and above all their writing, they would make a personal contribution, but it would be 'critical rather than constructive'. Herein lies the essence of their attitude to the revolution, which interested them only in its negative aspects. They wanted the destruction of the bourgeoisie, and Trotsky's idea of the permanent revolution appealed to their anarchic tendencies. On the other hand she admits, 'We still were not actively for anything', on the grounds that man and the world, as they saw it, still had to be remoulded, 'created anew'. The construction of a new socialist society to replace the present one was not their concern; they merely assumed that its realisation was certain and that in some way their criticism would help to mould this future society. She claims that this anarchic attitude was absolutely in tune with the times and that most intellectuals felt the same way they did. She is supported in this by Pierre-Henri Simon who, reviewing Nizan's *Aden–Arabie* in *Le Monde* of 27 July 1960, suggests that 'the fault of our generation was its inability to construct'. Likewise, Raymond Aron sees the intellectuals' condemnation of the 'désordre établi' ('the established disorder'), their systematic criticism of Western society, as being totally biassed, unrealistic and cowardly because 'In criticising one evades responsibility for the unpleasant consequences entailed by a measure which may be desirable on the whole.'[12]

Besides, this reliance on the inevitability of the future new society has a slightly hypocritical ring about it. First of all, she confesses that the society that was being constructed in Russia ('une civilisation d'ingénieurs' – 'a technological culture' – as Sartre deprecatingly called it) was not the sort of place in which they as writers would have felt at home. And then there is evidence of a certain enjoyment of *contestation*. Sartre even went as far as claiming that his 'opposition aesthetics' needed such objects of attack for without them literature would not be very important. So as a writer he did not mind the continued existence of this detestable society and it could be said that he came close to implying that if the bourgeoisie did not exist it would have to be invented. Simone de Beauvoir in later life is certainly hard on her earlier views about literature. She seems now to dismiss the idea that she really had any intention of helping the cause of revolution by her writing: 'Theoretically I was on the left in those days, but in practice my attitude was right wing; I believed that writing should be apolitical.' This attitude was to last right up to the war. She also sees the role they gave themselves as writers as being an excuse rather than a valid substitute for political action. In a sarcastic comment, years later, she writes: 'Two *petits bourgeois* invoking their unwritten work as an excuse for avoiding political commitment: that was the truth, and indeed we had no intention of forgetting it.'[13]

Not only was the whole of the period up to the war spent by them in avoiding political *engagement*, but Simone de Beauvoir, and to a lesser degree Sartre, actually took no interest in contemporary political events in France or elsewhere. Time and again she repeats: 'public affairs bored us', 'public events touched us scarcely at all'. The world around them was just a background for their own private lives. This attitude lasted longer with her than with Sartre. By 1933 their viewpoints diverged. She was still claiming that she was bored to tears by political articles, while Sartre insisted on reading the newspapers far too much for her liking. When she protested about this he claimed that there was no need to live in ignorance in order to maintain one's independence of thought, but she remained unconvinced. When Sartre left for Berlin, where he was to spend the year at the French Institute, she lapsed even further without his influence: 'I lost all interest in public affairs.'

Political action was quite another matter, for here they were in agreement: 'nothing could shake us out of our apolitical attitude'. They both remained steadfast in their view that their role was not an active one. There was at that time no question of her joining a political party even though they both felt sympathy for communism. Circumstances sometimes arose which might have led to some action on her part, for instance when there was a teachers' strike in 1934, but she did not join in because she was 'such a stranger to all practical political activities'.[14] In part it was also because of a reluctance on her part to identify with her role as a teacher, but it does demonstrate an enduring aversion to participation in any kind of mass manifestation of opinion. She also remained indifferent when women were

agitating for the vote: she would not have used it even if she had had
the right, and on this matter, too, she has not changed her mind.
Sartre did not use his, even in 1936 for the Popular Front.

The triumph of the Popular Front is a characteristic example of
the way they remained 'restricted... to the role of witnesses', even
when excited and delighted by what was going on. The consequence
of an attempted *coup* of 6 February 1934 by the fascist leagues
(extra-parliamentary political groups of the far right) had been to
rally the French left into collaborating against them. This happened
only gradually, and the first sign of success was a great Bastille Day
procession on 14 July 1935 and a meeting of three or four thousand
socialists, communists and radicals, addressed by their leaders.
Simone de Beauvoir and Sartre shared the enthusiasm of the crowds
on this occasion, but would never have dreamt of joining in the
marching, singing and shouting: 'This more or less represented our
attitude at the time: events could arouse strong emotions in us,
whether anger, fear, or joy, but we did not participate in them.
We remained spectators.' Eventually a common programme was
agreed by the three parties, and this alliance, known as the Rassemblement Populaire, was coherent enough to win the elections of May
1936. She tells of their impatience at the time with those left-wing
intellectuals who exhausted themselves in useless agitation: 'Talk,
declamations, manifestos, propaganda – what a lot of painful fuss!'
She finds, retrospectively, an excuse for their attitude on this occasion:
their inactivity came from a sense of impotence. If they had found an
effective means of action they would have acted, she is sure, and she
cites as proof of this the fact that when the strikes came they contributed to funds for the strikers. In spite of this she admits that
another factor was involved: 'our individualism hampered our more
progressive instincts'.[15]

The first stirrings of social conscience in both of them can be
detected in their reaction to events in Spain. When Franco landed in
Spain in July 1936 they were not worried that the Republic which
had replaced the monarchy in 1931 was in any danger for the
country had chosen republicanism and the rebels would be defeated.
Simone de Beauvoir and Sartre packed their bags and went off on
holiday with a light heart. It was only when they returned to Paris
that they became caught up in the drama of the Spanish civil war,
which thereafter impinged on their lives for two and a half years as
nothing else had yet done. Even when the army and the administra-

tion had gone over to Franco's side, they did not think that he would win. They believed in the inevitability of a Republican victory, and she claims that 'nobody in our camp' thought otherwise. The heroism of the Spanish people fighting a disciplined army against all odds moved them deeply: 'It was an astonishing and epic struggle, in which we felt ourselves directly involved.' When writing about it many years later (1972) she confirms the emotional involvement, but apparently draws the line there: 'I was stirred by the war in Spain, but did not think it had anything to do with me personally.'

It seems there was a distinction to be made as far as they were concerned between action and the emotional response of sympathy and anger. What, then, could they have done? As far as direct action was concerned, there were many idealist intellectuals from various countries who unselfishly went off to Spain and joined the International Brigades in order to save the Republic and fight fascism. Many of them died there. The largest national group of volunteers, the French, included several of their friends and acquaintances, André Malraux, Simone Weil, Colette Audry, for example. In contrast, there was no question of *their* going off to Spain: 'nothing in our previous background inclined us to such headstrong action'. According to Sartre, looking back over this period in the film made in 1972 which constitutes a sort of self-portrait, he did not feel himself to be needed and was never tempted to join the International Brigades; she confirms that she would vigorously have opposed any such suggestion. They were not yet *engagés*, of course, but it has to be said that the unwillingness to take physical risks did not materially alter with the years. In the thirties they were not even ready to act in ways that were riskless. Their indignation was particularly aroused by the non-intervention policy of Léon Blum, then Prime Minister of the Popular Front government, and his refusal to send arms and planes to the Republicans,[16] and one of the things they might have done was to speak and write in favour of French intervention. As more towns fell to Franco's troops, they became more and more wretched at not being able to do anything. So why did they *not* act in the one way that as writers they might have seemed competent to use? Because, according to her, their words would have had no effect since their names were not known and therefore carried no weight.

This was an interesting new development in her thinking. For the first time she expressed the notion that one could and should exert influence by making public statements, verbal or written, provided one is well known. In effect she was establishing a theory which she never discarded, about the nature of French public opinion and its susceptibility to influence by writers. As widely read authors in later years Simone de Beauvoir and Sartre frequently used this tactic, and also lent their names to collective undertakings by signing protests and manifestos in order to add weight to them. This was certainly successful in terms of publicity; the actual influence exerted as a result will be discussed later.

At the same time there is another aspect of their concern about the war in Spain that is of considerable significance. This is that it can be seen as a turning-point in their apoliticism. Throughout the Spanish war their doubts about their own responsibility for the collapse of the Republic had been growing; soon, she claims, they were no longer looking for excuses for inaction but were frustrated by their inability to help: 'For the first time in our lives, because the fate of Spain concerned us so deeply, indignation per se was no longer a sufficient outlet for us: our political impotence, far from furnishing us with an alibi, left us feeling hopeless and desolate.' In spite of what she says, their political impotence was still being used to some extent as an excuse, even if at the same time it grieved them to do nothing. Gradually a new element could be distinguished which showed a further evolution. By the time Barcelona and then Madrid fell to the nationalists in 1939, she was beginning to feel her own guilt in the affair: 'I was coming to realise that my political inertia did not guarantee me a certificate of innocence'. With the final victory of Franco's troops and the establishment of the fascist dictatorship in the same year, this guilt was to remain on her mind for a long time to come.[17]

The Spanish tragedy was something that involved them personally. They knew and loved the country and its people, they had friends who were ardent Republicans, and they identified with the hopes and promises of the new regime. This explains their initial hope and subsequent distress at the fascist victory. There was another area, however, with regard to which Simone de Beauvoir's optimism, shared at first by Sartre and many others, persisted in the face of reality. This was the rise of fascism in Europe and the growth of nazism in Germany, leading eventually to the second world war. Just as they were convinced that the Spanish Republic, supported by the people of Spain, could not be threatened by the rebels, so they refused to believe (together with the German Communist Party while it was still allowed to exist) that Hitler could ever have the full support of the German people; fascism was only a passing phenomenon and it was bound to fail before long. They were indignant at the things that were going on in Germany but, 'like everyone else on the French Left, we watched these developments quite calmly'.

By 1934 Sartre had already become aware, as a result of his stay in Berlin, that fascism could not be so lightly dismissed. He had been unable to escape the fact that it was spreading across Europe. In 1935 Simone de Beauvoir was still convinced that this did not mean war, for Hitler would not lead his country into war against the combined forces of the U.S.S.R. and France (the Franco-Soviet pact had been signed in 1935), and the German people would in any case refuse to follow him. The successes of the Popular Front in 1935 and 1936 meant that fascism appeared to have suffered an irreparable blow in France, so at least there was no internal danger, but she seems to have spared little thought for events in Germany during this period. By 1937 Sartre had no illusions: the chances of peace were becoming slighter every day. She, on the other hand, would not admit that war was imminent or even possible, and persisted in her ostrich-like behaviour even in the face of the failing Popular Front and the growing fascist influence in France. All the same she felt that her future was somehow slipping away, 'a sick feeling akin to real anguish'. This grew with Germany's annexation of Austria and the crisis in Czechoslovakia, but still she refused to believe the evidence that war was inevitable. Suddenly the cloud that had been hanging over her was swept away by the Munich agreement in September 1938, and she was filled once more with optimism: the concessions made to Germany might not have pleased the Czechs but they seemed to herald peace, and anything was better than war. Sartre disagreed. This optimism, which consisted in maintaining her serenity, her private world of eternal peace, allowed her for a time to go on believing that the war would not happen but in the face of the terrible events which were taking place she soon began to feel shame. Sartre did not accept her argument that one could not condemn a million Frenchmen to death for the sake of humanity, that anything was better than war, even a nazi France. He was adamant that war was preferable to fascism and that if Frenchmen did not fight against Hitler they would probably one day find themselves fighting for him. She was eventually convinced by him, but this conversion took place over a period of time. She pinpoints spring 1939 as the crucial moment. It had taken her some time to gain control of herself and of her own reactions, principally that of fear. For a few weeks she had lingering hopes that the war, although inevitable, would not happen to *her*; moreover, instead of accepting what she now knew must happen, she revolted against the notion that innocent young people might lose their lives because people like herself had been guilty of inaction.

This marked a clear turning-point in her attitudes. One could say that this was the moment at which she became *engagée* in her own terms. This does not mean that she immediately became a political activist. It was simply that, facing reality at last, she recognised that she could no longer live her life in isolation, insulated from the outside world and her fellow men, to whom she had responsibilities because of their mutual dependence: 'I learned the value of solidarity.' The decision to act upon this realisation came later, but first it is necessary to attempt to decipher the reasons for her previous apoliticism.[18]

From earliest childhood Simone de Beauvoir dedicated herself to the pursuit of happiness: 'I have never met anyone, in the whole of my life, who was so well equipped for happiness as I was, or who laboured so stubbornly to achieve it.' She is of the opinion that her happy childhood predisposed her for this, but however that may be she devoted a large part of her early life to what she calls 'une vocation'. She believed in 1929 that she would kill herself rather than put up with extreme unhappiness. Sartre was very different, according to her; he attached little importance to his happiness and would have continued to live and to write through all adversity. She describes her dedication as 'a long and exacting undertaking, to which I devoted myself without stint for years'. Happiness consisted in living her life in total freedom, with no outside constraints; in enjoying life to the full, attempting 'to embrace all experience and to bear witness concerning it', especially through reading and travel; and in pursuing her chosen vocation as a writer.

It is worth looking more closely at the way she set about the rich and rewarding pursuit of experience and happiness. The ten years between 1929 and 1939 were like a perpetual holiday. There was so much to learn, so many new experiences to enjoy: 'everything enriched and delighted me'.[19] For two years she lived on part-time

in the school
alter radically.
taurants, with
se friends and
they came to
quented their
as travelling,
neighbouring
ere unknown
exhilarating
er education
d, of course,
y and other
nd Russian,
Dos Passos,
derstanding
hazard and
In the mid-
e of history,
imposed on
nd, like the

that earliest
e calls both
lared inten-
business of
he ten years
rience, she
something
had begun
ently repri-
a pleasant
danger of
nd lack of
to write,
that for a
ng because
at she had
artre, and
a teaching

post in Marseille in 193

was convinced that the

craft which had to be lea

later that this was not th

was directly threatened

her vocation. First cam

provided the subject-ma

the book), and then the

posed. Thus the inabilit

hand in hand with her

only became possible as

commitment.[20]

Any doubts about th

but luckily she was fill

said so – in peace, pro

she need do nothing to

part her inaction. It als

blind herself to unplea

and she admits that thi

really indulging in esca

guard my peace of mi

could never be disturb

it for a considerable ti

optimism as to the f

Events in Germany th

used every pretext in o

change. This explains

Munich: 'decidedly, I

war with Germany w

own future was in jeo

at last to confront t

happiness now filled

apprehend the world

changed, happiness

longer important to

that she had discarde

meant but, looking ba

that she ever escaped

while looking confide

never regain her for

post in Marseille in 1931. As for writing, she was not impatient and was convinced that the time would come, and that writing was a craft which had to be learned through trial and error. She recognised later that this was not the only reason: it was not until her happiness was directly threatened that she was able to commit herself fully to her vocation. First came the personal threat of the 'trio' (which provided the subject-matter for *L'invitée*, but also the need to write the book), and then the war and the more general threat which that posed. Thus the inability to produce anything worth publishing went hand in hand with her apoliticism, and true commitment to writing only became possible as a result of events that led also to her political commitment.[20]

Any doubts about the future would have tarnished her happiness but luckily she was filled with optimism: 'In 1929 I believed – and said so – in peace, progress and a glorious future.' This meant that she need do nothing to alter the course of events, and so it explains in part her inaction. It also meant that as time went on she had often to blind herself to unpleasant facts in order to preserve her happiness, and she admits that this blindness had been partly deliberate: 'I was really indulging in escapism, putting myself in blinkers so as to safeguard my peace of mind.' She wanted to believe that her happiness could never be disturbed. We have seen that she was able to preserve it for a considerable time with regard to the war in Spain, when her optimism as to the final outcome lasted almost until the end. Events in Germany threatened to affect her more directly and she used every pretext in order to continue believing that nothing would change. This explains her overwhelming sense of relief at the time of Munich: 'decidedly, I thought, I was born lucky'. It was only when war with Germany was declared that she finally recognised that her own future was in jeopardy. In those last few months she had learned at last to confront the facts and her former preoccupation with happiness now filled her with guilt. She had seen it as a means to apprehend the world and mould it to her wishes. Now the world had changed, happiness was no longer the key to it and therefore no longer important to her. She thought in the early years of the war that she had discarded completely her selfish conception of what it meant but, looking back on this assumption later, she is not convinced that she ever escaped from it entirely. Yet at the end of the war, while looking confidently at the future, she recognised that she could never regain her former optimism. Too much had happened and she teaching and private pupils, only taking up a career in the school system in 1931, but even then her way of life did not alter radically. Much of her free time was spent in cafés, bars and restaurants, with Sartre when that was possible, but in any case with close friends and a wide circle of acquaintances. In the course of time they came to know many writers, artists and theatre people who frequented their milieu. During this period one of her greatest joys was travelling, and over the years she and Sartre visited all the neighbouring European countries as well as parts of France which were unknown to them. She particularly liked to go on exhausting and exhilarating walking tours. Another pleasure was the extension of her education through art exhibitions, the theatre and the cinema and, of course, books. She read omnivorously: Claudel, Saint-Exupéry and other modern French writers, translations from English and Russian, and with particular enjoyment American writers like Dos Passos, Faulkner and Hemingway. She read Marx without understanding him very well. For the most part this reading was haphazard and she read for pleasure only, as she had done when a child. In the mid-thirties she attempted consciously to extend her knowledge of history, but there was still no evidence of the discipline she later imposed on her reading when she had a particular purpose in mind, like the research for a book.

Indistinguishable from her admiration for writers and that earliest passion, her love of reading, was the wish to write. She calls both 'the great passion of my life'. From adolescence her declared intention was to become a writer, but for a long time the business of writing seems in practice to have taken second place. In the ten years after finishing her studies, while gaining richly in experience, she covered many sheets of paper in a vain attempt to write something worthwhile. At first she did not even do that. Her family had begun to suggest she was incapable of writing. Even Sartre gently reprimanded her for giving up her ambitions and vegetating in a pleasant but unproductive existence and warned that she was in danger of becoming a mere housewife. Tiring of her indolence and lack of purpose and constantly prompted by Sartre, she started to write, though without much conviction or success. The fact was that for a time she no longer felt the need to express herself in writing because she was so satisfied by life with Sartre. She began to see that she had nearly betrayed her ideals by surrendering autonomy to Sartre, and it was to reassert independence that she finally took up a teaching could no longer run away: 'Henceforth I took reality at its proper weight and valuation.'[21]

The refusal to face reality was only part of the problem. She and Sartre (although he was certainly more aware than she was) both suffered from almost total ignorance of life outside their immediate circle. Their political blindness arose from this ignorance which shielded them from most of the problems that ought to have been troubling them. They knew nothing of what she calls 'the weight of reality', the reality of human suffering. A protected bourgeois up-bringing, which promised her 'a happy life in a happy world', had shielded her from the horrors of war, of starvation, of oppression, of death. Her existence with Sartre from 1929 onwards corresponded exactly to their mutual wishes, and because they enjoyed this good fortune they did not see the adversity that afflicted others. They happily travelled the world unable to see what lay behind appear-ances. Simone de Beauvoir recalls a visit to Italy: 'When I looked at the Umbrian landscape, it gave me a unique unforgettable moment; but in fact Umbria itself eluded me. What I contemplated were mere tricks of light and shade, what I told myself was the old myth: I failed to see the harshness of the soil, and the joyless lives of the peasants who work it.'

This sheltered life was shattered by the war, which was her first real encounter with the brutality of the world and with the power of politics. But it was only a first step. Francis Jeanson claims that only when she visited the United States in 1947 did she become fully aware of social phenomena that until then were something she only knew about second-hand in the setting of her life in France. According to him, this visit was the start of her political education,[22] although she herself says that her eyes were not fully opened until her later travels and finally the Algerian war. In various interviews she explains the pessimistic ending of *La force des choses*, and in particular this statement: 'The promises have all been kept. And yet, turning an incredulous gaze towards that young and credulous girl, I realise with stupor how much I've been cheated.' She is not refer-ring, as so many critics were quick to assume when the book appeared, to failures in her private life. All she wanted of life had been fulfilled, but in the course of time she had found that realisation of her adolescent vision of life was no longer possible. Experience had revealed the world as it really was, not a beautiful place but one where there was suffering, oppression and hunger for most people.

Her discovery of the misery that exists in the world was a very gradual process, but by the time she came to write *La force des choses* she had already travelled a long way from the optimism of the thirties. Although she now despairs of what can be achieved by an individual when the whole world needs to be changed, she still claims that she is not a pessimist. In spite of that cry of despair at the end of *La force des choses* the message of her work is that even an unsuccessful struggle is worthwhile, provided one accepts that the results can only be partial, since there can be no final solutions or fixed values in this inconsistent life.[23]

The process was slow, but it was the brutal experience of the war that first taught her that she could not ignore the rest of humanity and its problems and that it was impossible to be happy in isolation. The other thing she and Sartre learned from the war was that the freedom and independence in which they had lived for so long was not only morally indefensible but impossible to sustain. The craving for independence was to be seen in her even as a child. In those days she did not look at herself in the context of the world around her and she never compared herself to others; in her own eyes she was 'the One and Only'. Her sense of individuality was such that she did not like to be called a child: 'I was not "a child": I was me, myself'. Even as a child she always remained her own master, refusing to submit to the will of others. She wrote in her diary in 1927: 'I don't want life to obey any other will but my own'. This sense of separation from others continued until she was thirty years old. That, at least, is when she began to feel the constraints of the outside world on her own life, but it might still be said that she has succeeded more than most people in fashioning her own life independently of the will of others.

Between 1929 and 1939 she and Sartre lived a life which they believed to be absolutely free from all outside limitations. Because the life they were able to lead coincided so exactly with their wishes, and because no obstacle had ever prevented them from doing what they wanted, they had the impression that they had chosen this life and controlled it absolutely. It was their assumption that having thrown off the constraints of their backgrounds and having no binding ties, they belonged to no particular place, country, class, profession or generation. They depended on nothing and on nobody: 'we believed ourselves to consist of pure reason and pure will'. This independent existence that they forged for themselves was an entirely selfish one which required them to be able to cut themselves off from the outside world: 'We had no external limitations, no overriding authority, no imposed pattern of existence. We created our own links with the world, and freedom was the very essence of our existence.'

This shared sense of freedom and independence was in many ways misplaced. First of all, they might have rejected their background but this background still affected them. Simone de Beauvoir was perceptive enough to see this later: 'Our open-mindedness was bound up with a cultural background, and the sort of activities accessible only to people of our social class. It was our conditioning as young *petit bourgeois* intellectuals that led us to believe ourselves free of all conditioning whatsoever.'[24] Moreover their indifference to money was a luxury they could allow themselves simply because they had enough to sustain the way of life they had chosen and therefore did not need to do any work which was uncongenial. Secondly, they did not realise to what extent they depended on outside circumstances being favourable to them, for often other people made decisions that fell in with their wishes and allowed them to believe that they had real control over their lives.[25] The war taught them that outside forces, whether they liked it or not, could affect their lives and thwart their wishes. The possibilities of freedom turned out to be limited: their fault had been not to see these limits.

The realisation that their lives depended on other people and could not be led in complete isolation was a turning-point in Simone de Beauvoir's life. Suddenly she saw that life was not merely 'une belle histoire' constructed for oneself in complete indifference to the world at large. Freedom is circumscribed by the presence of others, and this relationship is reciprocal. She already knew instinctively that she depended on other people: 'now I was learning that this dependent condition carried a complementary burden of responsibility'. Again and again she uses the word 'lié' to describe her new relationship with others: 'I knew then that my destiny was bound to that of all other people; freedom, oppression, the happiness and misery of men was a matter of intimate concern to me.' This involved her in a complete revision of her conception of how life should be lived: 'I ceased to regard my life as an autonomous and self-sufficient project, I was obliged to rediscover my links with a universe the very face of which I had forgotten'.

As the significance of this dawned, she was filled with a sense of guilt at the previous pursuit of happiness and independence. She realised not only that the war would bring suffering and that other people's suffering was her concern, but also that if she had not been so blind she might perhaps have affected the course of events. Even if that was too much to expect, the fact remained that she had not lifted a finger to prevent it. Overcome with remorse she realised that Nizan had been right to declare that you cannot avoid political commitment: 'to abstain from politics is itself a political attitude'. She saw her individualism, her previous rejection of *engagement*, as being an *anti-humanisme*. Her change of attitude reflected this: she was now intellectually, idealistically committed to the rest of humanity though it was some time before this led to any action on her part.[26]

There seems to be little doubt that Simone de Beavour's blindness and rejection of political commitment was in part the result of living in a very limited intellectual circle. Her contention that many intellectuals possessed similar attitudes is probably defensible, although it was equally true that large numbers of them had seen things very clearly and had therefore chosen the path of commitment. She does not seek to excuse herself by this, but she certainly suffered from the disadvantage of moving only among like-minded people.

It might be thought that the Ecole Normale Supérieure opened up for her a whole new circle, totally different from the bourgeois one of her family. Yet there were limits here also. According to Raymond Aron, up to 1939 the students at the *grandes écoles* rarely came from working-class or peasant backgrounds, and only occasionally from the lower middle class. Even today only 5.8% of students at the E.N.S. are working class, although it is noted for its 'democratic' intake as compared with the other *grandes écoles*.[27] Not only was the E.N.S. unable to provide the possibility of contact with other classes than her own, it also brought her into a circle that was restricted in another way: the *normaliens* were an intellectual elite. In this 'hothouse severed from and insulated against external reality... a largely verbal universe', a premium was put on the training of the mind. Nizan believed that it was this cult of pure thought that led to political abstention, but ignorance was also a factor. The products of the school emerged with no knowledge of the real world: 'A whole wide world of suffering lies, largely unseen, beyond this intellectual hothouse.' This ignorance, which was partly the result of a deliberate flight from reality, continued for many of them up to 1939. Simone de Beauvoir herself admits that 'our life, like that of all *petits bourgeois* intellectuals, was in fact mainly characterised by its *lack* of reality', and believes that this explains her blind optimism.[28]

If there were French intellectuals in the thirties who had already been moved by events to come out of their isolation and look for practical solutions to contemporary problems, this clearly was not the case with Simone de Beauvoir's immediate entourage. According to Michel Burnier in *Les existentialistes et la politique,* until 1939 the attitude of the existentialist writers to politics was accurately mirrored in that of Mathieu Delarue in Sartre's trilogy *Les chemins de la liberté*: 'a spontaneous sympathy for the proletariat, a distant admiration for the Russian Revolution, a certain attraction for the Communist Party, but totally inactive and freed for no reason, with lots of abstract ideas but at bottom disinterested'. Sartre describes himself as he was in 1939 in similar terms: 'apolitical, stubbornly refusing any commitment, my heart, of course, was with the Left, as was everyone's'.[29] There was nevertheless no clear political activity to be pursued at the time. After all, even those who had been actively committed like Nizan or Colette Audry (a colleague of Simone de Beauvoir's and a close friend, member of a Trotskyite splinter group and frequently critical of the point of view expressed by her and Sartre) were feeling disorientated. It was the war that finally put an end to their deliberate isolation and made them conscious of their collective responsibility. They began revising their attitudes after the Munich agreement in 1938, by which time most of the intellectuals had abandoned, in theory at least, the ivory tower.

Living in this restricted milieu, Simone de Beauvoir always had the impression that her views were shared by the whole of the French left – general optimism in 1929, equanimity about the rise of fascism in the thirties, political blindness during the whole period 1929–39, and a tendency to be critical rather than constructive. She claims, probably with more accuracy, that she was only one among many who felt nothing but relief at the time of Munich, and by August 1939 she was defending in the same terms her change of view: 'my reversal of attitude coincided with nearly everybody else's'.[30] What is surprising is the way in which Simone de Beauvoir and Sartre, even though surrounded by intellectuals whose attitude was apparently so like their own, failed to be influenced by the few among them who were already politically or socially active in the

twenties and thirties. Simone Weil, for instance, had that contact
with reality that was missing in their lives. Born in 1909, she entered
the E.N.S. at the same time as Simone de Beauvoir. While still a
student she was involved in the trade-union movement and the Ligue
des Droits de l'Homme (a liberal–democratic body founded in 1898
as a result of the Dreyfus affair by a group of intellectuals to combat
offences against human rights), taught at a working-men's college,
and worked as a farm labourer in the vacations. Later, as a teacher of
philosophy, she caused a scandal by her activity in local trade-union
groups, fighting for the rights of the unemployed, spreading culture
to the workers, and attempting to reform the unions themselves.
In spite of very poor health she worked in factories in 1934, briefly
joined in the Spanish civil war in 1936, and did farm labouring
again during the war. She eventually joined the Free French in
London, and died in 1943 of tuberculosis aggravated by a hunger
strike when she could not bring herself to eat while her compatriots
were starving in France. Her collected articles, essays and notebooks
bear witness to her gifts as a writer. She was *engagée* in practice long
before *engagement* became fashionable, and although she was very
conscious that her contact with the workers was bound to be superficial she felt morally obliged to subject herself to the same experiences as they suffered. But it seems that her world was miles apart
from that of Simone de Beauvoir, who used to see her at the Sorbonne
occasionally and admired her from a distance. They only once had
contact and Simone de Beauvoir tells this story against herself:
'[Simone Weil] declared in no uncertain tones that only one thing
mattered in the world today: the Revolution which would feed all
starving people of the earth. I retorted, no less peremptorily, that the
problem was not to make men happy, but to find the reason for their
existence. She looked me up and down: "It's easy to see you've never
gone hungry," she snapped.'[31] That was the end of their relationship.

Then, of course, there was Nizan and his close friendship with
Simone de Beauvoir and Sartre. Sartre comments on Nizan: 'this
revolutionary lacked blindness'. So why did the example of Nizan
not affect them, since they were so close? It seems to be the case that
Nizan realised that they were far more interested in literature than
in social or political action. They took his political views too lightly
and misunderstood him so completely that he must have decided to
communicate with them on a superficial level only and to keep from
them his deeply held political convictions: 'We never had discussions

with Nizan: he refused to approach serious subjects directly . . . As a result our differences were passed over in silence.' When Nizan left the Communist Party, he wrote to Sartre that he could not (or would not) at that time explain to him his reasons for resigning. Their apparent agreement was based on fundamental misunderstandings which they allowed to persist. Sartre confessed later that he was at fault in not seeing the real Nizan; their ways had diverged since they had left the E.N.S. and it was a long time before Sartre reached the point at which he would have been able to communicate with Nizan had the latter still been alive. The example of people like Nizan and Colette Audry could have had little influence on their philosophy and consequent political stance, according to Burnier, because 'the weight of tradition and the bourgeoisie was too strong'. In fact it was a little more complex than that, as we have seen. In the end history had to intervene in the form of the war to jolt them out of their indifference. Simone de Beauvoir describes it as a sudden, brutal awareness: 'Then, suddenly, History burst over me, and I dissolved into fragments. I woke to find myself scattered over the four quarters of the globe, linked by every nerve in me to each and every other individual. All my ideas and values were turned upside down.'

War was finally declared and Sartre was called up. When he returned on leave in February 1940 his thinking had already changed. According to Simone de Beauvoir, his new ethical stance based on the notion of 'authenticity' was that man should 'assume' his 'situation', that is recognise the circumstances in which he finds himself, become master of them and transcend them through action, instead of running away from them. Any attitude other than *engagement* would be a flight from responsibility and would be an example of *mauvaise foi*.[32] He had therefore decided not to stand aside from politics after the war. She sees this as an important change in him, one with which she was instantly in agreement: 'I rallied to his point of view immediately'.[33] The solidarity that she had begun to feel in 1939 was intensified by the occupation. All were suffering the same deprivations and difficulties, which put everyone on the same level. More seriously, people all around her lived in constant fear for their lives; merely by breathing she was a consenting party to the oppression which she witnessed every day. She could not escape by suicide because her salvation could not be separated from that of the whole country. Her inactivity meant implicit support for what was going on, but she could envisage no practical solution and she simply went on existing, waiting for things to change. It took Sartre, as so often, to precipitate her first political action, participation in the Resistance when he returned from prison camp in 1941.

Looking at Simone de Beauvoir's attitudes up to 1939, one is struck by an almost total consistency in her life. All the threads of her later life were there already. Her life has been unusually stable in practical terms: she has always lived in Paris, or so near that she has been able to spend half her time there, in similar surroundings (a hotel room or a studio room), even in the same district; her interests are still the same – books, records, art, the cinema; many, though not all, of her close friendships have lasted into her old age, including her relation-ship with Sartre; and she has always had the same ambitions. She herself sees the unity in her life as being due to the last two factors: 'the place that Sartre has always had in it, and my faithful-ness to my original design: that of knowing and writing'.[34] Similarly, her views have evolved and been modified but only within a frame-work of continuity, and her life has exemplified with little change the remarkable persistence of the attitudes and values that had been established by the time war broke out. As stated above, however, in a reconstruction of this kind we cannot know to what extent a con-sistency which was missing or only partially in evidence at the time has been imposed later with hindsight.

What are these elements in her thinking which were apparently already present before the war? Her opposition to the political right and to the bourgeoisie has never altered, nor has her rejection of religion, although a certain puritanism is clearly evident both in her philosophy and in her way of life. Her support for revolution has remained as strong as ever, but her political interest, awakened by the war, has only led to a minimum of action. She has never completely abandoned her vocation as a writer, even though she has not written a major work since 1972. Her pursuit of freedom, her wish to control her own life, her refusal to lose her own identity in the mass of humanity, her striving after happiness – none of this has gone, but it has become circumscribed. She began to realise that freedom was restricted by the presence of others, for one cannot control one's own life completely, as if living in a vacuum. But she learned to fight just as passionately for the freedom of others as for her own. The dis-covery brought by the advent of war of her ties with other people, of her dependence and her responsibility, led to a revised notion of freedom. Life, she now saw, was a compromise between herself and the world; she no longer revolted against the adversities which thwarted her wishes but sought ways of getting round them. Similarly she now envisaged a new sort of happiness through commitment to other people, without whom it is impossible to lead an authentic existence.

So in spite of all the manifold changes in the European world since 1939 and the traumas of France itself, Simone de Beauvoir has experienced no major transformation in belief or attitude apart from the sudden and brutal realisation at the beginning of the war of her close and inescapable relationship with other people, and the moral and political commitment that she felt was the logical consequence of this realisation. Since that point there have been elaborations, variations, which are explored in detail in later chapters, but essentially the limits of her *engagement* had already been reached and were not significantly to be extended later. It was a point of arrival, rather than a point of departure.

2

Freedom and responsibility

The notion of personal freedom is basic to Simone de Beauvoir's way of life and to all her thinking. Its development led first to the philosophical idea of commitment to action in the shaping of one's own life and secondly to the philosophical but ultimately political idea of commitment to others. The second makes the first possible and both are inextricably bound up with the fierce struggle to win or to preserve one's own freedom and that of other people. Hence the political and social implications which will be studied below, and which are manifested in her stance against the exploitation of the working classes, colonialism, racialism, anti-feminism, and all forms of oppression which she believes deny the freedom and dignity of man.

Existentialism – and it must be remembered that it was a label which Sartre and Simone de Beauvoir accepted unwillingly when it was first applied to them – was a philosophy that corresponded exactly with the mood of the postwar period in France. The intellectual world was in tumult: the experiences lived through during the war brought a reaction against prewar philosophies of non-involvement as well as aspirations to replace the now discredited established morality with a more socially orientated ethic, firmly rooted in the contemporary world. The austerity and pessimism of existentialism seemed realistic and courageous; there was hope in its humanism, its teaching of freedom of choice and its appeal to man's responsibility for fashioning himself by his own action. Sartre, whose key work *L'être et le néant* had appeared in 1943, was the undisputed leader of the movement, which had an extraordinary success. Unfortunately it also became fashionable in a popularised version among a large group of young people who understood little about the philosophy although they used its vocabulary extensively. They affected disenchantment and nausea, and took its exaltation of man's freedom to mean that complete moral licence was allowable. Bearded and unkempt, sporting black T-shirts, they frequented the cafés and night-clubs of Saint-Germain-des-Prés. Their outrageous behaviour caused many a scandal which reflected upon Sartre and Simone de Beauvoir by association, and discredited their status as exponents of a philosophy.

Simone de Beauvoir did not consider herself to be a creative philosopher; as she put it, she knew her limitations. What she meant was that she was not an original thinker in the sense that Sartre was. It was this very lack of originality that enabled her to grasp and assimilate so quickly and surely the philosophical doctrines of others, just as Sartre's own hypotheses always got in the way when he attempted to interpret other viewpoints. She was not capable of or interested in constructing a total philosophy. For her there was no need, since Sartre provided this for her. He was so much better at it than she was and always took the initiative: 'it was through him that these problems. . . presented themselves to me'. When asked to contribute a philosophical essay for a collection of works representing the ideological trends of the time, she at first refused on the grounds that there was nothing to add to *L'être et le néant*. It must be stressed that this does not mean a blind submission to his ideas. First of all, she never accepted any idea or decision of his without first criticising it and making it her own, thereby – in her view – preserving her independence and taking full responsibility on herself. From time to time, when she was unable to do so, their ideas diverged, as will be seen. The divergence was never very great, and indeed she sometimes attempted to reconcile their points of view. According to Sartre, she was always one of his most penetrating critics, because she understood so exactly what his objectives were; her ability to analyse and explain his work showed a complete understanding of his philosophy which stemmed from a near-identity of viewpoints. This brings us to the second point, which is that although she did not do the original thinking, Sartre's philosophy corresponded with and seemed to explain her own views. Even when she first met him it was already the case that they thought alike: 'I followed him joyfully because he led me along the paths I wanted to take'.[1] Because all her previous life had prepared her for it, it was quite natural to her later to adopt the ideas of Kierkegaard (whom she read with some excitement in 1940) and of Sartre, to become what was to be known as an 'existentialist'. From earliest childhood she had always had confidence in her own wishes and decisions: 'In reality I refused to submit to anybody: I was, and I would always remain, my own master.' By the time she was nineteen she was convinced that it was

up to every man to make his own life meaningful, without recourse
to outside help. Already, without knowing it, she was an existentialist. When she was asked in 1943 whether she was one, the question
embarrassed her. She was not quite sure what was meant, and anyway
she objected to being thus labelled on two grounds. First, she was not
important enough, and second, her ideas reflected the truth and not
some arbitrary doctrinal viewpoint. She sees a certain arrogance in
this second reaction but it remains true that her philosophical stance
was not constructed on an *a priori* basis but grew out of her developing views of life and her personal experience: 'I had written my
novel [*Le sang des autres*] before I had even encountered the term
Existentialist; my inspiration came from my own experience, not
from a system.'[2]

For Simone de Beauvoir the activity of writing was the re-creation,
exploration and communication of the meaning of personal experience. All her work is to some degree autobiographical even though
events and people are often re-worked into the form of fiction; however, she herself insists that her novels should not be regarded as
romans à clef. Before she ever started writing, she had a very clear
idea of what it would mean for her: she was going to live her life to
the full and preserve her experiences by committing them to paper.
It became more than that later, but it is true to say that she always
considered that her main concern was to present to the reader herself
and her ideas. Of course this is rather a simplistic explanation of her
work,[3] but it is the case that all her writing was a reflection, and
sometimes the mode of development, of her ideas. It is probably a
mistake to draw too sharp a distinction between her formal statements of philosophy and social theory and their fictional counterparts.
The latter are as much as the former the occasion for the transmission
of these theories and, more important, they offer the possibility of the
exploration and exemplification of ideas in action. Believing that
literature can bridge the gap between the wish or possibility and the
reality, she often presents her characters as going much further than
she towards the realisation of the sort of action she would have
wished to undertake. It is therefore essential for an understanding of
her notions of freedom and responsibility to refer to her play and her
first three novels in particular, as well as to *Pyrrhus et Cinéas* and
Pour une morale de l'ambiguïté which are her major philosophical
works.[4]

The concept of freedom underwent considerable revision with the passage of time and as the result of experience, but always remained basic to the thinking of both Sartre and Simone de Beauvoir. It is therefore essential to look at it in detail, following its evolution, in order to have an understanding of the philosophy and the dependent political attitudes of both. What does this concept mean? It means that man is free to construct his own life, his own essence, for existence precedes essence. This is the basic tenet of existentialist philosophy. 'Man is nothing else but that which he makes of himself', writes Sartre.[5] Man is thrown into this world and must forge his own destiny, without any ready-defined aims to support him. It is for man himself to establish these, as Blomart tells Hélène in *Le sang des autres*: 'I think that where you go wrong is that you imagine that your reasons for living ought to fall on you, ready-made from heaven, whereas we have to find them.' Simone de Beauvoir defends atheist existentialism against the criticism that if God does not exist then nothing is immoral and everything is permissible. The absence of God does *not*, she says, lead to anarchy. Far from allowing complete licence, the absence of God puts full responsibility on to man. Existentialism, therefore, is far more demanding than any religion for there is no prescribed set of rules, neither is the world the creation of some supernatural power but of man himself. Man carries total responsibility for it, and if he fails he has no excuses, and no one to wipe out his sins. Sartre's position is exactly the same, but he adds that man is quite free to invent a God to dictate his essence if he wishes to abdicate his own responsibility. This, however, is an example of *mauvaise foi*.[6] Man's responsibility for constructing his own life means that to be free and to be a moral being are one and the same thing. Man cannot escape the fact that he is free (that is what Sartre means when he says: 'man is condemned to be free'). About this he has no choice and therefore no moral quality attaches to it. The bridge between freedom and morality is made when man wills his own freedom and uses it positively to construct the venture which is his life. Freedom is the mainspring of action, and man must commit himself to decisions, to choices, and act upon them. 'We only exist if we act', as Blomart finally discovers; only by concrete action can we make our lives fully meaningful, 'authentic'.[7]

So the supreme exercise of human freedom is for man deliberately to choose to make something of his life even though he is always acting within limits. If there is no way of transcending these limits in positive action, there is no point in the negative pursuit of banging your head against the wall – you should choose another way out which is *not* closed.[8] The true existentialist does not allow things to happen to him, he wills them. Even death freely chosen is better than having it inflicted upon you. Clarice in *Les bouches inutiles* refuses to be reduced to a state of slavery by having death forced on her by someone else's decision to throw her outside the city walls to starve or be killed by the enemy. She decides to kill herself: 'They have not allowed me to live. But they will not steal my death from me.'[9] In more favourable circumstances man's choice leads him forward into the future (the 'avenir ouvert' of which Simone de Beauvoir talks so often) through his various projects and ventures. Thus man can surpass himself by transcending the normal constraints on the human condition. Sartre is saying the same thing when he describes freedom as the only source of human greatness.

The choice is not made once and for all but is a constantly recurring process. Man can never sit back and contemplate what he has achieved, and this is why Simone de Beauvoir is critical of people displaying aesthetic attitudes towards the past when these imply a rejection of the modern world and an unwillingness to be committed to it and its future improvement. The venture is never completed; the achievement of one's original aim is only the starting point for the next. So there can be no paradise at the end of the road, because the struggle never ends. There is only 'a goal which constantly recedes'. At least, this is what it seems like; in fact you have a goal, reach it, and then go beyond it, impelled towards new objectives. In this constant renewal, this refusal to allow your freedom to become ossified, there lies a certain optimism: if there is no paradise, at least there is a future to believe in. It opens up fresh horizons and allows man constantly to transcend himself: 'Every subject plays his part as such specifically through exploits or projects that serve as a mode of transcendence; he achieves liberty only through a continual reaching out towards other liberties. There is no justification for present existence other than its expansion into an indefinitely open future.' The optimism of this ever-present impulse comes alive in the words of Pyrrhus: 'In spite of everything my heart beats, my hand is held out, new projects are born and urge me on.'[10]

This faith in the future is absolutely essential to man. No matter if there is no progress, if man's attempts to improve the world can only have a minimal effect, action is always worthwhile. Seen through the eyes of Fosca, in *Tous les hommes sont mortels*, man's struggles are futile. The immortal Fosca has seen man's failures over the centuries. But his sights (man's infinite happiness in a totally ideal world, both of which are unattainable) are set too high and Simone de Beauvoir undoubtedly believes with Armand that however little can be achieved man should always attempt positive action and have faith in its efficacy. The question 'What use is it all?' that she asks in *Pyrrhus et Cinéas* and in *Tous les hommes sont mortels*, was in the forefront of her mind on 1943. Then, as now, her reply is the same: 'Against sluggish reason, and the void, and everything else, I set up the incontrovertible evidence of a *living affirmative*.' She holds, however, that both views (Fosca's and Armand's) are valid. It has to be said that her optimism has decreased somewhat with the years, and that by the end of the Algerian war she had become very disillusioned about progress and the improvement of man's lot. She has never lost her belief that all possible efforts must be made to this end, but she is clearly tempted personally by Fosca's view of the futility of action.

Man's venture not only has to be perpetually renewed; it also carries with it certain risks, in particular that of failure. She denies that this means existentialism is a philosophy of despair. It merely recognises the possibility of failure inherent in man's attempts to conquer freedom. Indeed she claims that without this possibility there would be no morality – what virtue is there in succeeding if there is no chance of failing? Thus we see, for instance, that Fosca cannot display courage because, being immortal, he runs no risk by exposing himself to apparent danger. In spite of this risk, man must act: 'He must consciously accept risk; by plunging himself heart and soul into an uncertain future, he builds a firm foundation for the present.' Failure is not a fault: the fault lies only in never trying.[11]

Simone de Beauvoir sees that the responsibility implicit in this freedom is too great for some people: 'Men dread responsibilities above all, they do not like to run risks, and are so afraid of engaging their freedom that they prefer to deny it. And that is the underlying cause of their dislike of a doctrine which gives pre-eminence to this freedom.' The responsibility of defining one's own values, for creating one's own life, the risk of failure, the 'receding goal', the effort required to sustain this perpetual venture, all these can lead to indifference and abstention, either because of fearfulness or because of laziness and a wish for an easy life. All sorts of excuses are used.

Some people, if they are Christians, maintain that they are only the instruments of God's will; some practise self-sacrifice, total abdication of their freedom in favour of others; for some the agony of making a decision which might turn out to be wrong is too much and they abandon themselves to quietism. For both Sartre and Simone de Beauvoir this sort of abdication, even for the best of motives, is always wrong. You cannot renounce your freedom, only hide it, and if you have recourse to any of these excuses for refusing to assume your own will, you are guilty of *mauvaise foi*. It is easy enough to be tempted into indifference. The characters in Simone de Beauvoir's novels often feel the desire to abandon their responsibility, and some of them succumb. Women in particular are prone to do this, for instance by playing a role instead of being authentically themselves, because they cannot face reality, or by deliberately deceiving themselves into believing that their traditional role of housewife is valid and satisfying because to break out of it would be too demanding.[12]

But is it just a question of laziness, cowardice or self-deception? It is sometimes objected that existentialism is a philosophy possible only for an elite of exceptionally rational people, and that taking the reponsibility for making a choice is far more difficult for ordinary beings. Simone de Beauvoir sees clearly that it is not easy for them but she asserts that it is quite *possible*. All choices are made in partial ignorance. It is just a question of degree, and even an elite does not have total knowledge. This does not mean that she is blind to the fact that some people are better placed than others. On the contrary she saw this well before Sartre, although the full significance of it was not clear to her until much later. She defines a specific role for the enlightened elite: it is to attempt to change the conditions in which action takes place. Thus freedom is no longer a privilege but a power to pursue it for others: 'An activity is good when you aim to conquer these positions of privilege, both for yourself and for others: to set freedom free.'[13] This at least saves the theory of all having the same possibilities open to them from the criticism that it seems to have quite extraordinarily close parallels (for a theory devised by people who considered themselves to be left wing) with liberal individualism and the bourgeois ideal of self-help and betterment being equally available to all.

Both Sartre and Simone de Beauvoir have continuously modified their notion of 'pure' freedom over the years. This evolution possesses two dimensions: one is the way in which man's freedom and his ability to use it to the full are circumscribed, and in some cases totally annihilated, by all kinds of factors outside his control, inherent in the circumstances of his environment, upbringing and outside events which affect his life. The existence of such restrictions on freedom first came home to them in terms of the practical reality of their own lives.

Having been convinced in the thirties that they were 'inconditionnés' and only realising later that it was their very background as middle-class intellectuals which made them what they were, they gradually saw more and more clearly the extent of this conditioning. Currently she regards the stability and happiness of her childhood as making her capable of becoming the sort of person she is today. Similarly he believed that he felt free in later life because he had experienced no early family conflicts. She even goes as far as to say that all is decided by the age of ten, or even two, and that these early experiences are fundamental and exert their influence for ever; it is open to some people to succeed or to fail, but there are others whose childhood is such that they can never win.[14] Oddly enough, put in terms of the 'nature' versus 'nurture' controversy, they at first had refused to recognise that anything was given in terms of nature (essence), while at the same time denying the effect of circumstances and upbringing on what can be achieved in personal terms. They came round eventually to the view that the situation in which people find themselves can be of vital importance.

Their realisation of the effect of this situation on an individual was reflected in the elaboration of their philosophy. Simone de Beauvoir saw fairly early the inconsistencies inherent in the idea of absolute freedom, given that everyone's life is lived within certain prescribed limits. In *Pour une morale de l'ambiguïté* she attempted to reconcile with Sartre's ideas her own less categorical view, which she had often maintained in discussions with him. Sartre at first asserted that, whatever the circumstances, man is given absolute freedom to master them.[15] Believing as they did that freedom was the only goal justifying human action, the question had to be asked, how can freedom be the goal if it is given already? She attempted to solve the problem by distinguishing two sorts of freedom: the freedom to dominate and use to the full the circumstances in which one finds oneself, which is given to all and which means that salvation is accessible to all; and the possibility of planning ventures which transcend these and lead beyond them to a new situation. The latter opportunity is not available to all in equal measure: 'actual concrete possibilities vary from one person to the next'. Only in favourable circumstances is true *dépassement* possible. This more realistic view, that the objective situation sometimes ensures the success of the enterprise and sometimes dooms it to failure by blocking all possibility of action, was not seen by Sartre at all at first and was only later adopted by him. Earlier, he believed that it was possible to exercise freedom however difficult the circumstances, to transcend a situation by internalising it, and so to give a meaning to it – as can a prisoner, for example, by not betraying his principles. In *L'existentialisme est un humanisme* he was still claiming that man cannot blame his failure on circumstances.[16] But Sartre's view changed: he confessed in 1977 that while as late as 1945 he had believed that whatever the situation man was always free to choose in and through that situation (his freedom being guaranteed by the simple fact that he was conscious of it), this notion now seemed to him to be absurd and he could hardly believe that he had ever thought that. Freedom is far more complex, possibilities are limited or opened up according to individuals and circumstances, and what a man makes of himself can only be based on what others have already made of him. Indeed Simone de Beauvoir herself realised only quite late in life *to what extent* it was true that freedom of action is limited by circumstances, for example in the context of women's liberation.[17] Her attempt to reconcile the basic conception of complete freedom, theoretically required by their philosophy, with the growing realisation that there was no such thing, is not totally convincing. It is clear that they themselves conceded this as the notion of absolute freedom became modified and in the end was virtually abandoned by both.

The second dimension in the development of the concept of freedom lies in the understanding of the way this freedom is restricted by other people (*autrui*), and this happened in three stages. At first it seemed to both Simone de Beauvoir and Sartre that the freedom to construct one's own life was limited only by other people's wish to do the same, and that the inevitable result was conflict: this view is exemplified in *L'invitée*. Then with the war, as it impinged on her life, came the knowledge that whether she liked it or not outside circumstances were going to affect her life and impose constraints upon her freedom which she had till then considered limitless.

With the war, too, but more gradually, came the crucial recognition that other people, whom she had earlier seen as limiting her freedom and posing a threat, were in fact essential to it. Separate entities could never be an adequate expression of 'human reality' because each one was bound up with all the rest.[18] This led to what she calls 'the "moral" period of my literary career', which began in 1943 with *Le sang des autres* and lasted several years. During this period she was trying to formulate her ideas, and she was having to force herself to accept a new concept of freedom and of man's relationship with man. Therefore to an extent she was passing on to the reader the lessons she was having to learn herself. At this point she believed she had escaped from her individualistic approach, but in fact, although she now thought others were essential to give the individual a fully human dimension, she still saw man as forging his own destiny by himself and only subsequently needing others to validate it. She deplores this subjective view which she set out in *Pyrrhus et Cinéas*, and claims it represented only a certain point in her development. It was only later that she saw it as being mistaken: 'In truth, society has been all about me from the day of my birth; it is in the bosom of that society, and in my own close relationship with it, that all my personal decisions must be formed.' It is not clear when this third stage was reached – probably soon after the war – but it certainly did not manifest itself in her writing until she had published her theoretical essays and her early novels. She is particularly critical of her purely abstract and moral approach in *Pour une morale de l'ambiguïté*, which she likes least among her books: 'I was in error when I thought I could define a morality independent of a social context.'[19] She was mistaken, she says, in attempting to define a theory of action without reference to the 'objective' conditions of the real world, and her answers to the questions raised were platitudinous and hollow. This does not mean that she rejects the fundamental views expressed in the book, merely the manner of expounding them in such abstract terms, unrelated to reality and the society in which we live.

L'invitée presents Simone de Beauvoir's early view of others, rather simple and distinctly pessimistic.[20] It was published in 1943, but she had started writing it in 1938 and it is located clearly in the context of her attitudes of the thirties. She had had in mind a study of *autrui* even before the formation of the 'trio' which directly inspired the novel. By the time it was published it belonged, she says, 'to past history'. This stage coincides very largely with Sartre's view of others as a threat to one's freedom and therefore to one's very existence: 'The essence of the relations between consciousnesses is not the *Mitsein*; it is conflict.' The very existence of other people in the world and the fact that they are 'conscious beings' as well is terrifying to Françoise. Others can steal the world from us. Merely by looking on the same scene they take possession of it and deprive us of it. Sartre quotes the man alone in a park which exists for him only until someone else arrives and steals it. Françoise possesses such a scene in the theatre because she is there alone but in a more fundamental way she realises that Xavière is stealing her whole world. Other people threaten our freedom too, with their critical gaze ('le regard') which possesses us and reduces us to objects by judging us, and so we act as they expect us to, thus losing our freedom. It is particularly menacing for women (both Anne in *Les mandarins* and Françoise in *L'invitée* suffer from it) because the notion of possession joins that of being treated like an object, a notion explicitly treated in *Le deuxième sexe*. This can only lead to conflict, because we must either destroy the other by treating him as an object, or be destroyed by him and abdicate our freedom and responsibility by behaving like an object. Simone de Beauvoir tells us that her own personal relationships as a child were dogged by this problem: 'Either I reigned supreme or sank into the abyss.'[21] At best the result will be alienation between individuals, at worst it will end in destruction. This destruction is epitomised by Simone de Beauvoir in the murder of Xavière by Françoise at the end of the novel, thus putting into concrete form the statement by Hegel quoted at the beginning: 'Each consciousness seeks the death of the other.' Françoise has gradually realised that the sole authentic human relationship is one of reciprocity and equality, but, unable to resolve the problem of co-existence by establishing such a relationship, she resorts to murder.[22]

It is evident that Sartre's view of others as expressed in *L'être et le néant* and Simone de Beauvoir's as expressed in *L'invitée* are very much the same. It is a pessimistic view of human relationships and offers little hope of their ending in anything but conflict. The views of both evolved after that, but not in the same way, and it is necessary to look at the development of each of their viewpoints separately. At the beginning of the war Sartre realised, as we have seen she did, the solidarity that links all men together, and he began to see a new aspect of their relationship. According to Colette Audry, 'Relations with the Other...are transcended: they become relations with others.' Although he still believed that on the strictly individual level all human relations were based on conflict, he now thought that by going beyond this solitary state to the level of working together with other men (for example in militant action for revolution), one could find salvation. Burnier maintains that Sartre's philosophical thinking lagged behind his political practice, and indeed it is not clear whether Sartre ever abandoned, as Simone de Beauvoir did, the notion of insoluble conflict between *individuals*. He certainly seems to have seen class conflict as only one manifestation of the 'conflit des consciences'.[23] Moreover in this revised view of relations with others the individual remains isolated, and although he can to some extent overcome this isolation in a common undertaking, yet there is a basic contradiction which Sartre found insoluble. This has its roots in a refusal to surrender his personal freedom. It is noticeable that while in Sartre's view man cannot will his own freedom without willing that of others,[24] there is not the intimate connection we see in Simone de Beauvoir's thinking between his freedom and that of others: they exist side by side. And while there is a social responsibility involved in choosing and constructing his own life, it is his responsibility to himself which is the basis of this: 'I am thus responsible for myself and for all men, and I am creating a certain image of man as I would have him to be. In fashioning myself I fashion man.' When describing the realities of freedom and responsibility in the Resistance, he talks of it as 'total responsibility in total solitude'. Each member of the Resistance had a duty to all and was responsible for their lives, but was alone. He could only rely on himself, but was free to be himself, 'and in choosing himself in freedom, he was choosing the freedom of all men'.[25]

Sartre was at first unable to make the step from individual salvation, which he now (after 1939) realised was impossible, to collective struggle, which he believed was the only way to transcend one's situation and the only way to improve man's lot. The transition was made in theory between *Les mouches*, ending as it does with Orestes pursuing his solitary way, and *Le diable et le Bon Dieu*, ending with Goetz staying with the people he wishes to liberate, a decision taken because of a commitment to collective responsibility. However in practice Sartre found the contradiction within himself too great: 'For my liberty implied also the liberty of all men. And all men were not free. I could not submit to the discipline of solidarity with all men without breaking beneath the strain. And I could not be free alone.' He never really resolved the contradiction, for although he pursued this political ideal within a limited framework by working with the Communist Party and later with *gauchiste* groups, he never gave up his freedom to the extent of joining a political party. His latest stance, however, showed him to have gone much further (in theory) in stressing the importance of the group. He now said that he was a revolutionary because the individual alone is impotent and can achieve nothing; in the group he becomes *fully free and individual* and is better off than on his own.[26]

For Simone de Beauvoir the problem did not pose itself in the same way. With the war and the consequent development of her views on *l'autre*, she came to believe that while other people's freedom restricts our own and appears to be a threat, man's initial reaction of hatred is naïve. Thus she makes the same point as Sartre: 'To will oneself free is also to will others free.' Others not only have the same right as ourselves to exist fully, but are even necessary for our own freedom and our own ventures. They give at the same time as taking, because it is through others that we realise ourselves: 'We need others in order to make our existence fully justified and necessary.' An individual defines himself only through his relationship with the world and with other individuals. He is not alone in the world and he must not live in isolation in an ivory tower because he can have no valid existence if it is limited to himself. Neither should he attempt to possess the world and other people totally. Man's first reaction to the threat of others should give way to a realisation that by their presence and their possession of the world they are in fact giving the world to him by allowing him to define himself. Therefore we need men who are free around us: 'Only the freedom of others keeps each one of us from hardening in the absurdity of facticity.' How can this be so? Because it is others who by existing or by acting create situations that necessitate his action. Without them there would be no new projects and he would be unable to exercise his own freedom to transcend himself. But this is reciprocal. Man can only be helped in this way by the freedom of others if in his turn his aims can serve as a point of departure for them: 'Therefore I must endeavour to create for men situations which will enable them to join me in my transcendence and rise above it; I need them to be free to make use of me and at the same time to preserve me by transcending me.'[27] Thus we reach others by affecting their situation and therefore their freedom, and they do the same for us. The direct relationship established in this way means that subjectivity (the way we see ourselves) and objectivity (the way others see us) are inseparable; other people are both subjects and objects and the two aspects are not mutually exclusive.[28]

The freedom of others, then, is not a threat but a challenge to man to conquer the difficulties and ambiguities involved in this complex relationship. If he accepts the challenge, then the future is opened up for him. We must understand that this is what freedom is all about: it is *not* to have the power to do anything we wish. If it were, then recognition of the freedom of others would indeed limit our own. On the contrary, to be free is to go beyond the present situation into a new future; it is others who enable us to do this and who are therefore the very condition of our freedom: 'my freedom, in order to fulfill itself, requires that it emerge into an open future: it is other men who open the future to me'. Although she personally had resolved this problem, a development mirrored in the transition from *L'invitée* to *Le sang des autres*, she concedes that this is not an easy task. How much of ourselves must be yielded up in the process? There is always the risk that in order to become integrated into the community we will have to sacrifice our individuality, to suppress all those things which make us different from each other. Moreover it is frightening to realise the distance which separates one man from another, and the existence of so many individual beings, each of them free: 'I am involved, not in the liberty of one man but in the liberty of many.' But somehow we must establish a relationship involving freedom on both sides.[29] Her very thesis in *Pour une morale de l'ambiguïté* is that it is possible for these separate beings and separate freedoms to be bound together with each other. But the existence of opposing freedoms means that although all men with whom we establish a relationship exist for us, they can exist either as allies or as enemies according to whether or not their aim is the same as ours, and if not conflict is bound to follow. We must fight anyone who prevents us from existing (for instance by stifling our voice or keeping us prisoner) and it follows from her views on the freedom of others that we must also fight for their right to exist. This is the paradox: action *for* men often implies action *against* men. Violence should be avoided as far as possible, but we must not hesitate to fight when it becomes necessary, and indeed it is our moral responsibility to do so.

Man's moral concern, then, although it comes from within himself, is not selfish, for just as he is the concern of others, they are his: 'we are all responsible to all for all'.[30] This implies a very delicate balance: while accepting our responsibility for others, we must take care not to infringe their freedom. People must be free to decide their own destiny and to attempt to help them by deciding for them is unacceptable. 'Servir' ('to serve') then becomes instead 'asservir' ('to subjugate'). She admits that this is often a difficult decision on a personal level: should we attempt to save someone's life against his will? We might be right to do so. On the other hand we might be saving him for a life which is not bearable. To know the will of others is difficult, so the choice of how to act for their benefit is risky. Moreover, self-sacrifice to this end is no such thing unless our aim is defined by the person for whom we are making the sacrifice – it is tyranny. The necessity of acting in someone else's interest is an argument that is used ruthlessly in support of colonialism and other forms of paternalism or even political oppression. On the whole she believes it to be indefensible to take decisions for others: 'To want to prohibit a man from error is to forbid him to fulfill his own existence, it is to deprive him of life.'

This is one of the main themes of *Tous les hommes sont mortels*. For Fosca all means are permissible in order to realise his aim of making men happy and bringing peace, but always he dictates to others the terrible crimes that must be committed, the suffering that must be inflicted in order to achieve this ever-receding goal on their behalf. On the personal level, he denies certain individuals the right to put their lives in danger; he decides what is best for them. But no man has the right to decide this for others. Controlling another person's life can only lead to that person's unhappiness or death, for in order to feel alive and to exist fully men must take risks, even if they achieve nothing. Fosca discusses this with Charles V: 'Nothing can be done for man; his good depends only upon himself.' He has wished to make them happy, but he learns late in his long life, from Armand, who seems here to represent Simone de Beauvoir's own view, that it is no use trying to achieve this for them: 'Men want to be free. Don't you hear their voices?'

This pessimistic message of being unable to do anything for others is most starkly put in the words: 'Nothing can be done either for them or against them . . . Nothing can be done.' It has, however, its positive side. It is perfectly possible to serve others without infringing their freedom, without acting on their behalf: 'For other people I can only ever create points of departure.'[31] In *Pyrrhus et Cinéas* she compares this action with Kant's image of the dove: the air which resists the flight of the dove, far from hampering it, actually supports it. It is an image which she used on another occasion to describe her personal realisation that she depended on other people and on outside circumstances that circumscribed her liberty, whereas she had wrongly believed herself to be entirely free. We are instrumental in helping others to create themselves, which they do by transcending what we give them, just as they open up for us future possibilities. The process is therefore reciprocal. The result is a relationship between individuals that is no longer threatening and inimical, as it had earlier seemed to her and still seemed to Sartre; moreover it is one that can be achieved on the individual level without recourse to group action for some common undertaking.

Man's responsibility to others is an unavoidable condition to which he is condemned, condemned because he cannot escape the fact that he is *engagé* in this world, committed to work to improve it and the lot of his fellow men. By a conscious choice he assumes this responsibility and makes his contribution to mould the course of history, and he does this in concrete action, because to will one's own freedom and that of others implies more than idealism, abstract wishes or a search for absolutes. Since such action is consciously chosen in an attempt to improve the society in which man lives, it leads almost inevitably to political commitment. The question of choice and responsibility assumed through *engagement* nearly always takes on a political complexion in Simone de Beauvoir's novels, since she regards action in its ideal form as being political.

Engagement is a willingness to make personal choices and it is also a recognition of responsibility both to oneself and to one's fellow men. But it must also be stressed that to choose nothing is still to choose: 'all refusals are choices, all silences speak'. We cannot *not* be *engagés*. Ife we ignore our responsibilities we are guilty of *mauvaise foi*, in Sartre's phrase; we are deceiving ourselves that we have not chosen, but in fact we have. We have chosen to let anything happen (to us or to others) rather than making a lucid and conscious choice: 'Your silence implied consent to any fate that might befall you.'[32] Abstention is not possible. If we opt out of difficult decisions we still influence the course of events, as Jean Blomart and Jean-Pierre Gauthier discover. Her characters often attempt to avoid responsibility by silence or inaction, to keep their hands clean by refusing to take decisions which might turn out to be wrong. What they learn in time is that by doing nothing they can still be guilty of influencing events, sometimes even of the death of others. Merely by existing, by breathing, man affects the lives of others and carries responsibility for what happens.

So man must take the risk of making a choice – not always simply a personal risk, because each time we make a choice we expose others as well as ourselves to possible dangers. It is not only the weak characters who through indifference are tempted to do nothing; it is also those who are conscious of all the risks involved, conscious of the possibilities of failure, who find the choice so difficult to make. These are sensitive, intelligent people who try to weigh the ends against the means, who see clearly the consequences of every action. They carry the weight of the world on their shoulders[33] and are riddled with guilt – for what they did not do through inaction, for what they might do through action. They are often moved to action through shame, but still have to bear the guilt for the consequences of their action. This is particularly true of those situations where personal *engagement* becomes political *engagement*, and the difficulty of making such decisions is one of the problems inherent in political action.

It has been remarked above that Simone de Beauvoir discarded the traditional religion of her family and regarded herself as being without a religion. Yet having rejected the outward forms of this religion, she retained the moral content. Her values and way of life are focussed upon an ethical stance that is entirely compatible with traditional religion. This is borne out by the detailed exposition of her views above. She freely admits that the moral discipline of her Catholic upbringing was at the basis of a puritanism that has always characterised her behaviour, and she believes that this characteristic was also common to Sartre and most of their friends. A certain reserve and lack of emotional spontaneity have always dogged her personal relationships, apart from that with Lanzmann whose own lack of inhibition infected her.[34] Her public image, based on her unconventional liaison with Sartre and on her treatment of a taboo subject in *Le deuxième sexe*, has often been a picture of depravity. Nothing could be further from the truth. She has led the austere life of one whose only extravagance was travel; as a writer she is immensely hard-working and self-disciplined, carrying her research to extraordinary lengths; she is not only hard on herself and self-critical but also morally unyielding on matters of principle. She distinguishes very insistently between her philosophy and Christianity, and has never apparently shown any awareness that the two have anything in common,[35] possibly considering that the differences are too fundamental to allow of comparison. Nevertheless when comparisons are made there are many similarities that are worth pursuing.

There is in particular a considerable affinity between Simone de Beauvoir's ethics and those of a certain kind of Catholicism, which is characterised by Mounier. Emmanuel Mounier (1905–50) passed his agrégation in philosophy a year before Sartre and Simone de Beauvoir, and then taught for four years. He then left full-time teaching in 1932 in order to start with a group of like-minded people the dual venture of a review, *Esprit*, and a political movement, the Troisième Force; both were concerned to find a middle way (*la troisième voie*) between bourgeois liberal democracy and Marxist totalitarian socialism. The movement, short-lived as it turned out, soon separated from the review, leaving Mounier as editor to pursue his own ideal of what a review should be. *Esprit*, dedicated to spiritual renewal without being an organ of the Catholic Church, and to social and political revolution without aligning itself to any political party, was concerned with a wide range of issues, political, spiritual, philosophical, social. Mounier continued to publish it in the Vichy zone during the occupation until it was banned in 1941; thereafter he joined the Resistance, was imprisoned as a suspect, during which time he wrote a major work, *Traité du caractère*, and was finally tried and acquitted. Returning to Paris in 1944 he launched *Esprit* once more and continued as its editor until his death.

Simone de Beauvoir makes almost no mention of Mounier in her autobiography and so it is difficult to assess whether his earlier work had any influence on the thinking that led to her writing of this period, but their views are quite remarkably similar. In *Le personnalisme*, Mounier sets out in a popularly accessible form his philosophy of personalism, but like his concept of *engagement* it was already formed and clearly enunciated in various of his writings dating from the thirties. His criticism of certain aspects of existentialism, in particular with regard to freedom and man's relationship with man, is very often answered by Simone de Beauvoir's work. Absolute freedom (the concept of which he attributes to Sartre) does not exist

in his view. First of all there *is* such a thing as human nature, otherwise there would be no history and no community, that is no unity of
humanity in time and space. For Mounier this is important because
this unity implies the equality of all members of the human race and
the absence of any differences of civilisation, race or caste. Secondly,
existence is given as well as created, that is, there are given situations
which put constraints on our freedom. As has already been demonstrated, these two limitations on freedom were eventually admitted
by Simone de Beauvoir, even if they were seen in a different light.
Mounier concedes, however, that the possibilities open to man to
forge his own destiny as a person are enormous; he does this by
transcending nature and overcoming the determinism of circumstances. This is possible because every situation leads to various
potential outcomes, and man uses his freedom to decide among them.
But he claims that Sartre is wrong in saying that freedom is a
necessity, because if it were, man would not be able to make it his
own, but would use it blindly. For Mounier freedom is a gift to be
accepted or refused. Here he puts his finger on the very contradiction
that Simone de Beauvoir had perceived in Sartre's thinking and
attempted to resolve in distinguishing two sorts of freedom in order
to explain the moral aspect of freedom. For the Christian this possibility of refusal explains the existence of sin: man cannot choose
what Mounier calls 'la valeur' ('values') if 'la non-valeur' ('non-
values') does not exist. God has not made a perfect creature, but has
allowed man freely to choose and to transcend his condition: 'the
ability to sin, that is, to refuse his destiny, is essential to the full
exercise of liberty'. The exact equivalent (except that God does not
enter into it) is seen in Simone de Beauvoir's thinking: man has the
right to refuse to use his freedom, to refuse to commit himself, but
this is wrong, and is the equivalent of Mounier's 'sinning'.

The aspect of existentialist freedom that Mounier seems to criticise
most strongly is the relationship with others and Sartre's contention
that each person's freedom can only have a relationship of dominance
or subservience to that of other people. Mounier sees this individual-
ised freedom, confronting a hostile world, as a self-defence mechanism and a block in communication leading to egocentricity and
alienation, whereas in his view 'individual freedom' should lead to
an opening out towards others and a concern for 'general freedom'.
Far from leading to isolation, man's freedom should unite him with
other men, and because the existence of others has a positive effect

on him, they enable him to transcend himself: 'Thus the positive interpersonal relation is a reciprocal provocation, a mutual fertilisation.' This is exactly how Simone de Beauvoir sees the ideal interaction of individuals. Indeed Mounier seems to have taken Sartre's early view which, as we have seen, was modified with time, and ignored Simone de Beauvoir's treatment of the theme of *autrui,* which was very similar to his own. Moreover the ideal society which Mounier envisages is based on a series of acts that fit in closely with her view of human relationships. These are the dispossession of the self (which Mounier sees as a Christian act), seeing oneself from the point of view of others while at the same time refusing to lose oneself in others, taking upon oneself responsibility for others and identifying with their destiny, showing generosity towards them, and forever expressing one's devotion to them in 'a perpetual renewal'. It is perhaps a more generous, more binding view of man's relationship with man than hers which reserves more importance to the fulfilment of the self, but it is not so very different. And Mounier is careful to stress, as she does, that this society must be a unit which is at the same time a 'universe of persons': the people who make it up must not be forgotten and submerged in the totality. Otherwise such a society would be a 'totalitarian' society in which 'persons are less than pawns'.[36]

In Simone de Beauvoir's version of existentialism we also have something akin to the Calvinist ethic. Calvinism sees grace as being given, not earned; but the elect are morally required to justify their salvation by revealing it to the world through the constant renewal of the active pursuit of their vocation – *per vocationem.* Guilt and shame are the stigmata of inactivity. When Simone de Beauvoir began to realise that during the first two years of her relationship with Sartre she had become parasitical upon him and his ideas, amusing herself but not working towards any goal, she saw this as an unpardonable abdication from a duty. It was a moral, almost a religious problem; just as the girls in *Quand prime le spirituel* had needed a replacement for their lost faith, 'the notion of salvation had lingered on in my mind after belief in God had vanished'. It was her belief now that every individual was responsible for finding his own salvation. Once she started writing seriously, she was able to regard this as fulfilling her responsibility. Both she and Sartre (perhaps in redemption of their past sins of moral indifference) saw the pursuit of their vocation as 'seeking some kind of salvation'.[37] They felt a compelling personal duty to reveal to others, through their vocation of writing, the insights which they possessed, this being one form of action.

But for Simone de Beauvoir, of course, God is not a necessary hypothesis in order for man to live a life which conforms to this ethic. Morality is not contained in a set of absolute values imposed from outside, which man is free to accept or reject. The values are constructed entirely by and for himself and if he lives according to these it is because he wishes to be right not in God's eyes but in his own. This dependence on oneself alone is important, she believes, in terms of motivation: if God exists as a perfect being, as existence fully realised, this limits our freedom because we cannot then see it as contributing to the world and therefore feel it is pointless to continue our own struggle to exist fully by exercising it. Again, she rejects the Christian idea of God being necessary to man's yearning for transcendence. Man of his own accord transcends himself and his situation by setting his own goals, and these are firmly based in this world and not in some spiritual ideal. After all, she asks, how do we *know* God's will, when every type of society claims its own version of God? At least man knows his own will.

However, this formal rejection of the metaphysical does not lead to materialism; on the contrary, the spiritual element is always in evidence. The very concept of man's freedom, circumscribed as it is, has great spiritual force. The possibility it gives to man of surpassing himself allows him to aim higher and higher: 'Man...is a movement that is always going further yet.'[38] Simone de Beauvoir's existentialism may not be a religion, but it is a stern ethical system. She sees clearly that man needs to believe in something, and this something is the possibility of transcendence through using his freedom for action, and of the efficacy of this action.

The optimism of this philosophy is evident, in spite of the austerity of the morality it proposes and the difficulties inherent in such a demanding conception of man's role. The important thing is first to accept the essential ambiguity of the human condition and 'its twin elements of misery and splendour' – something she had only realised with the war. Man is a sovereign subject and at the same time a mere object, an individual but placed in a collectivity. He is conscious of his solitude and his bond with the world, of the truth of life and of death, of his freedom and his servitude. All these paradoxes of existence must be faced and not ignored as has so often been the case with religions and philosophies other than existentialism. It is difficult, of course, not to be affected by the pessimism inherent in such a view of man, and Simone de Beauvoir talks of 'the abortive aspect of the human adventure' which Sartre stresses in particular in *L'être et le néant* – the impasse, the tragedy, the despair. In her own work, in contrast, it is the positive, constructive, optimistic side of his philosophy, well hidden and often ignored, which she attempts to explore. She clearly goes much further than Sartre in the confidence she has in man.[39] Success and triumph over adverse circumstances are not excluded from her view of existence. On the contrary the message is one of hope. Even death has a positive role: it is part of the human condition and without it life would be meaningless, as Fosca discovers. For Sartre, death is not positive but negative. It is a final absurdity, of no importance in itself. Simone de Beauvoir has always been obsessed with death and described it as 'the major peril of loneliness and separation'. But the other side of the picture, the optimistic side, is death seen as 'the key to all communication' and 'a common link between the individual and mankind'. It is death which gives life its meaning and without it there would be no 'projects' or values. This is one of her arguments in *Pyrrhus et Cinéas*. The commitment and action which man must undertake to justify his life would lose their import of repeated indefinitely and he would sink into indifference. Their value depends on there being a notion of past and future; not even death cuts man off from this future, because his actions can be seen as transcending his death. The fact that there is in her view no other life than the earthly one makes this life all the more valuable, and prevents man from succumbing to the temptation of indifference and inaction. In a sense she derives from her atheism the motive for action which a Christian might infer, in spite of what she seems to believe to the contrary, from the notion of eternity.[40]

There is hope, too, in the warmth of human relationships, in 'a common link between the individual and mankind'. Those people who realise this seem to her to be filled with hope, and their fear banished: Hélène in *Le sang des autres*, suddenly aware of the warmth of humanity in the world, now sees it as a place where she is no longer useless; Clarice in *Les bouches inutiles*, the play whose *leitmotiv* is the word 'ensemble',[41] loses all fear, even of death. Simone de Beauvoir defends existentialism against the criticism of being a philosophy of despair. The only disturbing thing about it is that it makes constant demands on man: 'Thus the separation between conscious beings is a metaphysical fact, but man can overcome it; everywhere he can unite with other men. Existentialists do not deny the reality of love, friendship, fraternity. Far from it: in their view it is only in human relationships that each individual can find the basis of his being and its fulfilment. But they do not consider these feelings as given; they must be achieved.' This relationship is not with 'Man' or 'humanity', it is with 'all men'. She makes it clear that it is possible to establish a concrete relationship not with all humanity in a vague way but only with those people who exist for us. They exist – either as allies or as enemies – if links have been consciously created with them, 'if I have chosen to treat them as fellow human beings' (*prochains*, or 'neighbours' in the biblical sense). It is impossible for her to accept that each man should not be treated as an individual, as an end in himself, but as a means for furthering some cause. Here she is totally at odds with Marxism which she, like Mounier, sees as treating men like pawns, and much closer to the Christian idea of *le prochain* as defined by the parable of the Good Samaritan, told by Christ in answer to the question, 'Who is my neighbour?' For her, as for Christ, a man is more important than the idea of man in general.[42]

We have seen that when she came out of isolation at the beginning of the war, her previous attitude of *non-engagement* was equated with *anti-humanisme*. Thus it follows that *engagement* for her is essentially humanitarian and manifests itself in a sympathy for and understanding of the difficulties of her fellow human beings, a solidarity with them in their immediate struggles, rather than in specific political action. Conversely, her philosophy is almost entirely political in content, in the same way as that of Plato or Aristotle can be called political. It is about how we should live, and about our relationship with others in the context of the society in which we find ourselves. As time went on Simone de Beauvoir reached the third stage in her developing concept of freedom when the interrelationship of the individual with society came to the fore and the political implications of her philosophy became predominant. Man's freedom, she now believed, was real and concrete only if it was *engagée*, committed to the goal of bringing about changes in the world. In fact she had begun to realise, as Sartre puts it, that all moral issues are political issues.[43] Ethics cannot be separated from politics.

3

Where ethics and politics meet

Before looking at the practical consequences of Simone de Beauvoir's political *engagement* it is necessary to analyse her theorising about politics, especially what she has to say about particular political systems, attitudes and behaviour. These are for the most part set out in a series of articles written for *Les Temps Modernes* and published between 1945 and 1955. They will be considered in conjunction with her changing political attitudes before and since: the earlier ones, belonging to her 'moral' period, need to be seen in the light of her subsequent criticism of them.

The articles do not amount to a coherent theory of politics or even to a full statement of her own political beliefs; at no time has she attempted anything as comprehensive as that. Sartre was different: 'philosophically and politically the initiative has always come from him...Sartre is ideologically creative, I am not; this bent forced him into making political choices and going much more profoundly into the reasons for them than I was interested in doing.' It is clear that Simone de Beauvoir had no wish to elaborate a political theory and such a project did not interest her any more than the elaboration of a philosophical system: 'Such an ambition was foreign to me.'[1] By contrast, what Sartre tried to do was to construct an ideology which would both enlighten man about his condition and at the same time suggest forms of practical action. These were now for her as well as for him inevitably political, with the reservation that for Simone de Beauvoir political action was mainly left to other people. Commentators have not always seen this as a *sine qua non*, and the task of marrying existentialist philosophy to the Marxist politics of revolution proved a difficult exercise for Sartre's logic. In spite of this, there are certain basic elements in their philosophy, and more particularly in hers, which can only lead to certain political views.

In her mind ethics and politics are one and the same thing: 'A set of principles necessarily includes a political attitude.' She argues in 'Idéalisme moral et réalisme politique' that the one does not exclude the other; on the contrary they are identical. How could it be otherwise, since any action which man undertakes engages him in his entirety? After all, 'Nowadays nearly all men have a political dimension, nearly all of them must face the problem of action.' The truly moral man must refuse to take refuge either in ready-made values and pre-established codes of conduct or, on the other hand, in supposedly objective political realism; instead he must plunge himself into the agonies of making decisions which take into account both 'human reality' and the possibilities for realising his aims. He makes political choices in the full consciousness of their ethical implications. If he chooses to carry out both a moral and a worthwhile activity, 'by his action he participates in the real world, and the world in which he acts is a world endowed with meaning, a human world'.[2] Sartre, too, believed that ethics and politics are the same, that political problems and economic problems always raise moral issues which are closely tied in with them, although he admitted to having thought at first that they were quite separate and that it was a question of having to choose between them. One of the aspects of Maoist thinking which appealed strongly to Sartre was the fact that ethics are not superimposed on politics but that together they form the basis of Maoism.[3]

The two fundamental concepts of Simone de Beauvoir's philosophy, personal freedom and commitment to others, are the basis of all her political attitudes. It is because she believes that the present bourgeois capitalist society denies basic human rights that she sees revolution as being the only answer. Revolution was conceived in rather vaguely Marxist terms in her apolitical period before the war. It was then more specifically connected with the French Communist Party and with the regime in Russia, and it is this relationship which will be studied below in terms of her attempts (and Sartre's) to reconcile these manifestations of Marxism with existentialist philosophy. For the last ten years it has appeared to them as being epitomised rather in the far-left groups in France (in particular the Maoist groups) and in localised attempts elsewhere in the world to replace an entrenched regime by a socialist alternative. She has always been in favour of any move to overthrow the system which she hates with such passion: 'I am absolutely opposed to capitalism. My struggle is to bring it down because I'm totally against the system – especially in France with all the scandals and the monstrous abuses. I am for any action which is likely to shake its foundations.'

This total denunciation of French society is nothing new, for she has professed hatred of it ever since she started writing. Moreover she has always seen the possibility of change lying only in one direction: revolution. Reformism is absolutely out of the question and some of her sharpest criticisms have been reserved for people like Aron and Merleau-Ponty who she considers have betrayed the cause by arguing for 'bourgeois democracy' or for pluralism. To uphold the present parliamentary system and work within it is to choose a regime which is opposed to the working classes; besides, no change was ever achieved through parliamentary channels. This refusal to participate in the system involves a refusal to vote: 'The ballot box is a most inadequate mechanism of change.' It is not clear whether Simone de Beauvoir and Sartre ever voted, but in principle they were both always against voting, and on many occasions she has specifically stated that they did not do so. Sartre explained this in existentialist terms in an editorial published in *Les Temps Modernes* at the time of the 1973 parliamentary elections. He saw universal suffrage as meaning that the individual delegates to a party his own authority ('When I vote, I abdicate my power'), and that this, the citizen's only political act, is no act at all; it is a confession of impotence. Simone de Beauvoir views it in more practical terms: 'It's a matter of total inconsequence whether one votes or not. It amounts to changing one bunch of villains for another.'[4] To both of them it seemed that a 'popular front' government of the Union of the Left (the alliance of communists, socialists and left-wing radicals established in 1974) would hamper the progress of revolution and the impact of the far left, which wants no part in the institutions of government. The Communist Party, for so long the only hope of a socialist revolution in France, appeared to them from 1968 onwards to be reformist, to act as a support for the system and to be in collusion with it, apart from minor attempts to improve wages and conditions. This led them both to advocate 'direct democracy', which means, according to her, that 'grievances should be aired with direct action'; Sartre defined it as the organisation by the people of 'the vast anti-hierarchic movement which fights institutions everywhere'. It is worth noting that in the 1974 presidential elections, Simone de Beauvoir and part of the editorial board of *Les Temps Modernes* were in favour of advising its readers to vote for Mitterrand, while Sartre and another member wanted to advise abstention,[5] so her views and her practices are not quite as clear-cut as she sometimes makes out.

The passionate espousal by Sartre and Simone de Beauvoir of the

cause of socialist revolution and in particular of its manifestations in
Eastern Europe has provoked much criticism. Raymond Aron refers
to Sartre's 'partisan attitudes' and 'left-wing conformism' and to
Simone de Beauvoir's rejection of pluralist thought and her view that
there is only one truth, that Western society is corrupt, and its
corollary that the socialist regimes of Eastern Europe offer the only
example of a just society. Simone de Beauvoir's answer is given in
Les mandarins: you have to choose, and if you choose the U.S.S.R.
rather than the U.S.A., it indicates a *preference*, not an uncritical
acceptance of everything. If you expected perfection, you would
never choose, just as you would never love. In the view of Philip
Thody, also, Sartre treats socialism as privileged, in the sense that
different moral criteria are used for socialism and for bourgeois
capitalism, the benefit of the doubt is always given to East rather
than West, and crimes committed in the name of socialism can be
condoned, unlike those committed in the name of capitalism. This is
only partially true: as Thody himself admits, in unambiguous cases
Sartre and Simone de Beauvoir always opted for a critical stance
against the U.S.S.R., for instance in 1950 over the question of Soviet
labour camps and in 1956 over the suppression of the Hungarian
revolt. She does not include herself when she refers in a recent
interview to those who were blind enough to give their unconditional
support to the U.S.S.R.[6] Where there was doubt they hesitated to
condemn the system which in their view offered the best hope for
mankind; this moral dilemma is reflected in Simone de Beauvoir's
discussions of the problem of ends and means. The decision to
support or criticise is never lightly taken, never automatic.

On the rejection of the present capitalist system of the West, there
was no doubt. Simone de Beauvoir still sees this aspect of politics in
black-and-white terms, in contrast to her relations with individual
people, where she claims to have become much less categorical and
more open-minded: 'In political terms I am still Manichean, because
after all we are talking about a battle where you have either opponents
or allies.' Her hard-line attitudes in the face of 'the enemy', belying
the doubts and indecision which are often concealed behind them,
come out as 'prejudices', 'radical slogans', 'imperious judgments',
'sentences without appeal', 'dogmatism'. Anne-Marie Lasocki is less
critical, and it is with some admiration that she notes that the
positions which Simone de Beauvoir takes up are always absolute.[7]
Jean-Marie Domenach argues that political problems cannot be

solved on this moral plan of absolutes, but her political attitudes, at least in the terms in which they are expressed, have always been extreme. For this reason they have provoked intense hostility from the right, often couched in terms of the crudest abuse.

It could generally be argued that this repudiation of the system is dishonest in various ways. First of all, it is riskless. In the context of an affluent Western society of today, such as France, the verbal violence of the attack is more akin to play-acting than to a real-life situation which might bring death as a result.[8] Revolutionaries can afford such a violent language in these circumstances. In some cases they don't actually want any real changes and preserve what Ernest Gellner describes as a lifeline back to the existing society against the time when they give up their revolt. This cannot be said of Sartre and Simone de Beauvoir, although before the war, during their apolitical period, their attitude was certainly somewhat hypocritical: 'We wanted the defeat of capitalism, but not the accession of a socialist society which, we thought, would have deprived us of our liberty.' Later, however, their attitude changed, and they never gave up the struggle for a society which in their view would be the best for all men, in spite of their conviction that they would hate to live in such a society: 'In other words, you're hoping for the triumph of Communism, knowing that you'd never be able to live in a Communist world.' Anne, in *Les mandarins*, surely speaks here with Simone de Beauvoir's voice. Such altruism is admirable, but the ambivalence which lies behind it might well have weakened her potential for action. Like Gellner's pseudo-revolutionaries, they never really left the society rejected so vehemently. They were assured of a place for themselves within it and so without any real risk were always able to display detachment or opposition. Their bourgeois upbringing sponsored and made possible their vocations which were no less based on the security of privilege.[9]

A second dishonest element in the revolutionary argument arises out of the fact, thrown up by this lack of risk involved, that the regime in which they lived was a tolerant one: 'As is well known, the protestor's impassioned denunciation of iniquities of the current system tacitly supposes the fact that the system tolerates such denunciation without any real sanctions, even economic or social ones, let alone penal ones.' Of course it can equally be argued that such toleration does not mean that any account is taken of the criticism. Herbert Marcuse goes one step further and argues that because

tolerance equally extended to all – to those who advocate aggression
or hatred as to those who work for peace and humanity – simply
fortifies 'the status quo of inequality and discrimination' and therefore of oppression, certain people should *not* be allowed a voice.
In fact, he says, opposition is only tolerated if it does not threaten the
established society. Simone de Beauvoir likewise argues that parliamentary opposition is tolerated precisely because it never allows the
voice of the proletariat to be heard. She attacked Merleau-Ponty for
believing that by working within the framework of Parliament one
can exert influence: 'If you accept a regime which is against the
proletariat. . . on the pretext that it permits opposition. . . you are
doing more than that: you are abandoning the proletariat whose
cause you make out you support. Proletarian opposition, as is well
known, is not recognised by Parliament, which only allows the
privileged the right to quarrel amongst themselves.'[10] She does not
understand that even the role of the intellectual critic of society who
remains outside the party political system is suspect. By mediating
between the system and its contradictions he enables it to make the
necessary adjustments to avoid structural change and thus be sustained. It is this very toleration in Western democracies which
defuses revolutionary impulses.

Thirdly, action does seem to be confined to overthrowing the
present order, without any clear idea of what will replace it, or the
feeling of any need to begin to construct a future society in advance.
During the 1970s Sartre talked vaguely about 'libertarian socialism',
and said that the only thing to do was to support with all one's might
'whatever aspects of a particular political and social situation can
produce a society of free men'. Simone de Beauvoir recognises that
politically negative action is much easier than positive construction,
and cites the example of the common purpose of the Resistance
uniting men of differing views in opposition to an oppressor, whereas
these same men were unable to agree on constructive and more
distant objectives after the war. She even concedes: 'It has often been
observed that revolt alone is pure. Every construction implies the
outrage of dictatorship, of violence.'[11] Hence her refusal to commit
herself to what form a future society might take.

Their faith in the possibility of such a society ever existing is
surprising in view of their recognition that it has never yet been
realised, but not perhaps in view of the philosophical premises on
which this faith is based. The idealistic element in Marxist thinking

is, according to some people, its basic flaw, the belief that revolution will lead to a more just society, that the end of economic alienation will mean the end of all alienation, 'a utopian and Messianic expectation that total fulfilment is available when certain defects in the present social order are removed'. Sartre argued in *L'existentialisme est un humanisme* that 'one need not hope in order to undertake one's work'. Although the intellectual must be without illusion he must still do what he can: 'For instance, if I ask myself "Will the social ideal as such ever become a reality?" I cannot tell, I only know that whatever may be in my power to make it so, I shall do.' During the 1970s both Sartre and Simone de Beauvoir became increasingly disillusioned about what had so far been achieved. Sartre, while declaring his pessimism, still had some hope left that man might achieve the one thing that could save him, libertarian socialism. If you did not work for this and believe it possible you would have to agree 'that man is a piece of shit'. He compares this belief to Pascal's *pari* – 'with the difference that I am wagering on man, not on God'. The two positions are very close in the sense that they both depend on faith, and Sartre concedes that revolutionary optimism cannot be founded on any rational basis. The faith is in human nature, in man's working for his own freedom and that of others, and in the eventual success of this struggle because if one believed this to be doomed to failure there would be no point in fighting.[12] The consequence of Simone de Beauvoir's disillusionment has been to modify considerably her political thinking: she has been forced to question some of her assumptions. When and how will the socialist revolution take place? Will it ever happen? What is her definition of a socialist revolution?[13] Her attempts to answer these questions will be considered below in their chronological place. It is the earlier period, when her faith in revolution was still firm, that concerns us now.

The relationship between existentialism and Marxism has posed many problems which have not really been solved satisfactorily, and in this context it is essential to consider Sartre and Simone de Beauvoir separately. Their approaches are quite different, as one would expect.

Sartre devoted a large amount of his writing during the period of what is so often seen as his flirtation with the Communist Party (from 1953 to 1968, if one discounts his vague thoughts of joining in the 1930s) to analysing the differences between the two philosophies in an attempt to iron them out, and to pointing out the common ground in order to reconcile the two. Some commentators believe that he was successful; many believe that the synthesis of the two was impossible.[14] Sartre's aim was always to construct an all-embracing universal philosophical system which would be a complete explanation of reality. His attempts to make this system appear coherent and integrated were valiant, but he was not always successful in explaining away the inherent contradictions and confusions which increased as his thinking evolved. He was adept at the use of rhetoric to carry his reader along with him when his logic was faulty. Both he and Simone de Beauvoir were guilty of making deductions which not everyone sees as logical. The apparent logic is too often based on the juxtaposition of statements which are *non sequiturs* but which appear to follow one from the other because linked by a 'therefore' or a 'because'. Germaine Brée points out Sartre's use of 'if...then', in which the hypothesis suddenly becomes a fact. This method, akin to that of the Sophists who claimed they could argue convincingly that black was white, must cast doubt on the validity of the arguments. Prompted by a cynical friend of theirs, Pagniez, who claimed as early as 1930 that Sartre's fine theories usually rested on some underlying sophistry, Simone de Beauvoir often looked for these and found them – when she did not agree with his ideas.[15]

The reconciliation of Marxism and existentialism was to prove exceptionally difficult. The problem was essentially that of overcoming the contradictions between a philosophy of subjectivism and individualism, where the solitary working out of one's personal destiny is taken for granted, and a philosophy of the collective salvation of humanity, based on social concepts. Sartre's ethics of *engagement* required him to enter the struggle for the freedom of all men, not just his own; this did not follow from the basic elements in his philosophy but rather from a conviction about what he *ought* to do which was both at odds with this philosophy and a difficult step for him personally. We have seen how Sartre bridged the gap through the character of Goetz; he also attempted to do it theoretically in 'Les communistes et la paix' (1952–4) and in the *Critique de la raison dialectique* (1960). Simone de Beauvoir states that by 1950–2 Sartre had reached the same point as Goetz. Having decided that there was no possibility of personal salvation, 'he was ready to accept a collective discipline without denying his own liberty'. This sounds rather like having his cake and eating it. He was never really able to make the synthesis in the practical terms of his own life. In the *Critique de la raison dialectique* he recognised that in certain situations man does not have freedom of choice – only in a group structure could the situation be changed and freedom recovered, but he still maintained the view that the individual remains a free being, and that once man has been liberated from scarcity and necessity true freedom will flourish in conditions which will then be ideal. It has to be said that if one looks at the writings of Marx in particular, and to a lesser degree Engels and Lenin, Marxism is not as strongly deterministic as has often been made out. The extent to which individuals are determined in their actions by social and economic factors is a matter of degree, and these influences are seen as ceasing with the advent of communism. Historical necessity applies to socio-economic structures and not to individuals, who are relatively free to realise themselves, even though their activities are delimited by factors outside their control. What is true is that during the construction of socialism in the early days, it was necessary to emphasise the more determinist aspects of Marxism, and that since then the aspect of individual autonomy and personal realisation has been deliberately played down in favour of the view of the human individual as existing only in collective terms, for the purposes of state control in the communist states. It was, in fact, with certain manifestations of Marxism, and in particular the French Communist Party, that Sartre was quarrelling. Sartre accused the communist bureaucracy of subordinating men to ideas and of denying all subjectivity. He said that they lacked 'a point of insertion between the individual and the social', but it could be said that Sartre, too, found the reconciliation of the individual and the social difficult, except that the emphasis was the other way round. The communists, for their part, accused Sartre of losing sight of reality in subjectivity, but Sartre insisted on this element that existentialism could bring to Marxism. The objective world of Marxism had abolished individual human endeavour and until this human dimension became part of the Marxist doctrine, existentialism must keep its separate existence. According to Simone de Beauvoir, 'In opposition to the brand of Marxism professed by the Communist Party, he was determined to preserve man's human dimension.'[16]

Simone de Beauvoir, in contrast to Sartre, made no effort to synthesise her philosophical and political beliefs with Marxism. She simply uses the *Temps Modernes* articles to express her own views in certain areas, and in the process points out discrepancies with Marxism, and voices her criticism. It is clear that, once she became conscious of her responsibility towards others, she was able to accept far more easily than Sartre the limitation imposed on individual freedom by the presence of others. For him, collective action was the only way man could overcome his basic state of conflict with others, the only way his *engagement* could be made manifest, and his problem then was to resolve the contradiction between committing himself to the collective struggle and preserving individual autonomy. For her, the difficulty of human relationships can be solved on the individual level and therefore submission to the group is quite un-necessary for her personal salvation – happily, for the communal approach is totally alien to her and she would have found it far more difficult than Sartre to accept. Similarly she refuses the constraints that are implicit in any sort of dogma that attempts to impose its version of the truth on the individual. She has an aversion to any-thing rigid and doctrinal that does not allow of individual decision-making and to anything theoretical and abstract that is not firmly rooted in reality.[17] These strongly held views made it impossible for her to accept Marxism in its entirety and account for most of her criticism of it in her theoretical writings on politics.

It is now time to turn to these writings themselves, to see where the political implications of her philosophy lead her. They are not strictly political, as has already been stated, but are for the most part an analysis of the political behaviour of others in terms of what is and what ought to be. The criterion is always ethical, based on the principles of freedom and concern for others. She insists on her belief that freedom is a basic human right and necessity, and on the need not to forget the individual, the human dimension, in the course of any political action that has to be taken.

When she considers freedom in the political context, one of her major quarrels with Marxism comes to the fore. In her view, if you are fighting for socialism you are fighting for freedom, and when threats to freedom come from within Marxism they are unacceptable. As an existentialist, she believes that man is free to accept or reject the situation in which he finds himself, therefore she cannot accept historical determinism. Thus the disappearance of the proletariat as a class, which is imperative, is so in moral terms only, not because it is dictated by an inevitable historical process; it depends on those who are oppressed realising this and doing something about it. They are free to submit or revolt: their future cannot be imposed from outside by, for instance, the Communist Party. The proletariat, like the bourgeoisie, can want the revolution (and it can seek it through any party it chooses) or it can do nothing and choose the path of quietism. If this is betrayal, then it must be free to betray. She neatly turns the tables on the Marxist argument by claiming that, instead of existentialists having difficulty in reconciling their philosophy with Marxist determinism, it is Marxism that experiences this problem since it implies man's freedom of action by talking in moral terms, and then tries to reconcile this with a view of his action as a purely mechanical process, determined in advance. In view of the ever-present moral standpoint taken by Marxists, going right back to Lenin himself who clearly saw political action as moral action, she cannot accept that they should refuse the notion of choice which is, after all, the manifestation of morality in action. She states that the only difference between a doctrine of dialectical necessity and a doctrine that allows some part to be played by contingency is a moral, not a political or tactical one. The argument used by Marxists, that freedom would make any concerted action impossible, reminds Simone de Beauvoir of a similar one used by certain Christians: that it is too dangerous for man to be left to his own devices, that it is better for him to have his morality imposed from outside and that to act freely is to accept the imposed course of action. Just as the Christian can be guilty of *mauvaise foi* by accepting ready-made rules, thus avoiding responsibility, so Marxism allows men to avoid the risks and the anguish involved in making their own choices by accepting the reassuring inevitability of historical materialism. The Marxist, like the Christian, must accept what he is told, without question, something Simone de Beauvoir could not do. She recognises that it is inevitable that an authoritarian party should wish to stop people from thinking for themselves. Thought is dangerous. It leads to doubt, to questioning and ultimately to opposition.[18]

In one sense, however, she sees Marxists as believing in subjectivity as much as existentialists do. For them, revolutionary impetus can only come from those who experience a subjective impulse of revolt that is rooted in their own situation, and here Simone de Beauvoir is in agreement with them. It is for this reason that the bourgeois intellectual can never be truly revolutionary, because he can only support from outside in an abstract way. For the Marxist, this makes him suspect. For Simone de Beauvoir it is a matter of deep regret that the objectives of the proletariat can never fully be those of the intellectual who comes from the middle classes because they do not arise from middle class experience and needs. The notion that although one can act in the interests of others, one cannot act *for* them has already been discussed in the context of her ethics. In 'Idéalisme moral et réalisme politique', she develops the question of the necessity for the working classes to conquer their own freedom, and her argument here is worth analysing because of the extraordinary emphasis put on the moral aspect of political activity. She claims that the fight is not for bread but for freedom, that is, not for material necessities but for moral ones. The conservative elite often wants to retain the exercise of freedom for itself while satisfying the workers with adequate material conditions; but immediate improvement of their material conditions is less important to the working classes than their freedom. Their demands, she says, are not material but political, because their claims are not for themselves alone but are made together with others for the rights of all men to live fully, and moreover they are made for the future as well as the present: 'To take up a political position is to struggle free from one's individuality, to transcend oneself in a movement towards others, and to transcend the present in a movement towards the future.' In other words, political action represents the living out of her own philosophy. But the important thing is that the working classes are fighting for power to improve their own condition *themselves*, and this participation is more important than the result. Therefore the proletarian revolution itself is absolutely necessary. It is not enough to have the reforms for which they are fighting given to them, they must achieve them for themselves. The good of man can never come from outside. The same argument is reiterated in *Pour une morale de l'ambiguïté*, where she argues that the slave must fight for his own freedom: 'the oppressed can fulfil his freedom as a man only in revolt. . .it is only in social and political struggle that his transcendence passes beyond to the infinite'.[19] Although only those who are victims of oppression are totally involved in this struggle, she says that bourgeois and intellectuals can contribute by using their own freedom in a positive way; in any case all men are morally obliged to be concerned even if they don't take an active part.

Denial of freedom is regrettable within a party whose ultimate aim is the freedom of all men. It is unforgivable when it turns into oppression in the hands of those who actively pursue this policy for their own ends. In *Pour une morale de l'ambiguïté*, Simone de

Beauvoir details certain forms this oppression can take, some of the reasons for it, and the arguments used in its justification by those who are guilty of it. First of all she looks briefly at the political implications of the attitudes present in various types of character which she categorises in a sort of 'hierarchy' of men. At the lowest end of the scale is the sub-man who rejects all participation and whose political action is always negative. He is dangerous, however, because so easily swayed by others. The serious man tends to be a slave to one unquestioned aim, and the political implication is that he will sacrifice others to his aim and in his pursuit of it can become a fanatic and a tyrant. If he fails, he can become a nihilist, who wishes to destroy the world and to drag all others down with him; she cites nazism as an example of this. The adventurer is more authentically moral than any of these because he enjoys action for action's sake and positively throws himself into his ventures. However on the way he does not hesitate to sacrifice others if he needs to in order to achieve his own interests, for which privilege and status are often necessary, so even he can descend into tyranny. Moreover he cannot be authentically free because one cannot achieve anything for oneself without consideration for others: that, after all, is what gives life its meaning. The passionate man, too, can become a fanatic. He is so dependent on his dominant passion that it alone exists for him, and everything else is discarded, including other men. He is not free himself and he does not recognise the right of others to freedom.[20]

All these types are potentially capable of tyranny to achieve their own ends. For Simone de Beauvoir the world is divided into two sets of people, those who exercise their own freedom and transcend themselves, and those who are prevented from doing so. If other men can open up our future for us, they can also refuse us that future. They then use all sorts of arguments ('ruses' as she calls them) to justify their refusal, which amounts in fact to oppression of one sort or another. They claim that certain situations – the distribution of wealth, slavery – are quite natural and that one should not revolt against nature. According to her, these situations can only lead to conflict, and it is a conflict that concerns all men. If the slave is deluded by being led to believe that his state is natural, he should be enlightened so that he may fight for his freedom. One of the ruses of the oppressor (and this is the paternalistic approach) is to argue that the slave is happy as he is, and that if given his freedom he would be lost. Simone de Beauvoir says that he must be given it, but at the same time taught to use it. Similarly, the elite often argues against universal suffrage by claiming that the masses are too incompetent to use it properly. Again she attacks this argument because one cannot make choices on behalf of other people, thus limiting their freedom; however unenlightened they are, they must choose for themselves.

Another argument used by oppressors is that in the name of freedom they are sometimes deprived of their own – the freedom to possess slaves for instance, or to exploit the working classes. Her central theme reappears here, that is, that no one can be free without willing the freedom of others: 'I am oppressed if I am thrown into prison, but not if I am kept from throwing my neighbour into prison'.[21] The oppressor defends himself in terms of universal values, claiming that he is defending civilisation – that is, the institutions and values that he wishes to see maintained. Or, instead of defending the past, he can make claims for the future by invoking the possible achievements of capitalism which, according to him, is the regime that is most capable of developing and using the riches of this earth. Such utilitarian arguments carry no weight with Simone de Beauvoir. Her question is always the same: using for what? The only criterion is that any action should be of use to man – and that means to all men. This point will be discussed at greater length in a moment, for it is a problem for revolutionaries and capitalist exploiters alike.

Political action, then, has one aim, freedom for ourselves and for all men. But in the pursuit of freedom it is of the utmost importance not to lose sight of the individual, who must not be thoughtlessly sacrificed to society as a whole. Individual freedom cannot be envisaged in terms of collective situations only. She refutes the notion that only the community exists. If you deny the existence of individuals, you are denying the existence of the community itself: 'The essence of the community lies in the individuals of whom it is composed...the community is a collection of individuals, none of whom is more real than another.' And again: 'Society exists only by means of the existence of particular individuals.'[22] Concern that the individual should not be submerged in a collective was not unique to Simone de Beauvoir. Simone Weil and Emmanuel Mounier had already in the 1930s, as well as since, expressed very similar views of society. While rejecting Marxism totally, instead of only partially as she did, they both fought the established capitalist bourgeois order: 'the established disorder'. Mounier called it, because in it social injustice reigned. Simone Weil, critical of all political parties and of the bureaucratic machine wherever it was to be found, was convinced that the revolution had to come from the individual. In true socialism, society must be subordinated to the individual – in contrast to the situation in the U.S.S.R. where any individual member of society may legitimately be sacrificed to the collective interest. Mounier saw it rather differently. He wished to set in motion a 'personalist and communal' revolution; the ideal society thus created would achieve a perfect balance between private life and community life, and the personal and the collective could co-exist, neither being subordinated to the other. Individual autonomy would be preserved but only in the context of collective responsibility.

The refusal to recognise the importance of the individual, the missing human element which means so much to Simone de Beauvoir, constitutes a further major criticism of Marxism. Such a stance does not allow for freedom of thought or action; neither does it allow for all those other things that make it possible for life to be fully lived by every man. For instance, 'A collectivist conception of man does not concede a valid existence to such sentiments as love, tenderness, and friendship.' The pursuit of long-term aims for the greater good of society as a whole often means that men have to be sacrificed to some abstract future objective. Indeed Marxism has this in common with fascism, that they can both persuade men to sacrifice their lives in the interests of a common cause. Marxists in general and the French Communist Party in particular are guilty in her eyes of something quite unacceptable when they treat men as objects: 'Communists treat human beings like pawns on a chessboard, the game must be won at all costs; the pawns themselves are unimportant.' In her eyes human effort and human lives are not simply instruments, means to an end. Man is also an end in himself: 'to treat man as a means to an end is to do him violence'.[23]

The discussion of the problem of ends and means has preoccupied Simone de Beauvoir and she has returned to it several times. In her view they cannot be treated separately but go hand in hand; you cannot, for instance, be fighting for humanity, brotherhood, friendship, if in the course of the struggle you deny these very things. You cannot be working for the future (and have only ends in view) without recognising that it is made up of a series of presents (the means of reaching that future). To say that the end justifies the means is just as bad as to allow the means to become an end in itself.

However, the question is not a simple one. According to Jean Blomart, 'all means are bad'; you cannot use only moral means, preserving your purity and peace of mind, but must be prepared to dirty your hands, because certain choices will have to be made which will hurt someone, certain sacrifices will have to be made. Sometimes the decision has to be taken between conflicting causes or between different lives. Sometimes it is a question of whether to act at all. Violence and sacrifice are often necessary but they are not justified *a priori* by the end, and the man of moral integrity will always question before taking such action. Are his own motives suspect? Will the action be successful? If so, will the good that can be realised by it, when weighed against the sacrifice, further the cause sufficiently to be justified? It is clear that although theoretically she recognises the need for violence, she personally abhors it, whatever the end. Most violence, she asserts when discussing Stalinist methods, can be avoided, especially since no individual action can have more than a slight accelerating or retarding effect on the revolution, never a crucial influence. In reaching his decision, which is often extremely difficult because the problems are so complex, he should have one criterion only: what is the benefit in human terms of the abstract goal he has in mind? 'Servir l'homme' should be his precept. If he follows it, he will not indulge in vain and useless actions, and if he is absolutely honest in his assessment of whether the cause of man will be served by his action, then all means are good. Revolutionary politics should never lose sight of this, the original aim.[24]

Simone de Beauvoir rarely writes about politicians in the conventional sense. When she defines political realism in 'Idéalisme moral et réalisme politique', she says she is referring to the behaviour of anyone who takes a moral – and therefore political – stance: 'We shall not here be talking about professional politicians for whom politics is simply a personal career and whose activity is devoid of principles and objectives, but about the genuinely political man whose aim is to build the world of the future.' Interestingly enough, this sort of political being is defined by her as a realist. Political realism is seen by her as being very important. Although any coherent policy defining future aims is idealistic in the sense that its objectives are not yet realised, yet these must always be realistic, that is, within the realm of the possible. For her it is 'obvious' that 'a valid policy is above all a policy which is successful'. Thence the notion that the truly moral man must be a realist: 'That is to say that genuine morality must be realistic; through it man fulfils himself by fulfilling the aims which he has chosen.' But politicians do not usually bother too much about ethics. Perhaps, she says, this is because a concern for ethics is often not in the interests of action, or because it is easier to act without bothering to question the rights and wrongs of the action, which is then redefined as political necessity. It is the role of the opposition to bring ethics into politics. Ethics must on no account be neglected: in arriving at decisions about the difficult and complex problems that politicians face all the time, with the gamble and the risks involved, it is essential that no action should be taken without careful thought about all that is involved: 'And that is why political choice is an ethical choice.' It should be a positive decision and not a question of chance.[25]

One of Simone de Beauvoir's *Temps Modernes* articles deals with a very specific contemporary problem, the *épuration*.[26] This article is 'Œil pour œil', in which she discusses the question of punishment, and in particular the death penalty, in purely metaphysical terms. Julienne-Caffié has pointed out the *malaise* of left-wing intellectuals when faced with the issue of the death penalty. Simone de Beauvoir feels obliged to make a distinction: it is acceptable in the political area, but not in the context of civil law. Criminals who offend against the values of the present regime have been created by that regime and are its victims, but collaborators had offended against values which everyone was concerned to defend. She sees the punishment of these offenders (to whom she usually refers as *bourreaux*) as satisfying a need for revenge, and indeed it is in these terms that the whole problem is put. She makes it clear that she does not see the need to punish as a practical need (to prevent their offending again, or to act as an example that would stop others behaving in the same way) but as a metaphysical need. First of all, the thirst for revenge is as important and as strong as the need for bread, arising out of the hatred of the victim for his torturer. Secondly, the oppressor must be made to understand what he has done. This is achieved through the reversal of roles: having been in a position of pure freedom himself while his victim was treated as an object, he must now experience the humiliation of the victim and be made to understand in a concrete way that the latter has equal rights to freedom. This way, the reciprocity between two human beings is re-established and justice is done.

She concedes that perfect revenge is difficult to attain. Ideally, the victim himself should administer the punishment, though this style of private revenge (even more so if it is carried out by someone other than the victim) is dangerous because it can degenerate into tyranny and because mistakes can be made, and therefore it is not a practical proposition. Even so, it was a common occurrence during the *épuration*. On the other hand official administration of punishment carried out by the courts is also a failure: it is so distant from the original crime that it becomes a rite, in which the original purpose of the punishment is lost, as hatred and contempt fade. Moreover, in such circumstances, one often begins to feel pity for the accused, even to understand his behaviour, and in these cases it is difficult to refuse human sympathy and to punish in cold blood. But to understand is not to excuse. There are certain crimes for which no indulgence is possible: 'when a man deliberately and relentlessly degrades other men by turning them into objects, it is a public offence for which nothing can make amends'. However unsatisfactory the mode of revenge such men must pay for their crimes, because they were free to choose between good and evil and must therefore take responsibility for what they have done.[27]

The purely ethical stance taken in 'Œil pour œil', the emphasis on the moral aspect of the problem instead of placing it in historical reality, is something which Simone de Beauvoir later deplored. She says that in her justification of the *épuration* she never used the strongest argument, that these people should be punished by death, not to prove that man is free, but to stop them from starting all over again: 'there were certain men who could have no place in the world we were trying to build'.[28] Indeed she is strongly critical of this lack of realism in all her theoretical writing of the 1940s. Their moralising, she says, is deplorable – if understandable in view of the postwar situation – but she is appalled by their idealism, which is in complete contrast, she claims, to what she really felt at the time. Their distance from social reality, the abstract arguments about moral values and the meaning of life – all this is hollow. What really matters, she later asserts, and she knew it perfectly well at the time, is real men of flesh and blood, their work, their needs, their hunger, their will to live. Why, she wonders, did she write 'liberté concrète' when what she meant was 'pain'? At the time of writing these articles, in the 1940s, there had clearly been some development since the occasion when she had told Simone Weil as a student that what mattered was not bread but giving life a meaning. In them the importance of material needs was no longer in question, but she was writing about them in metaphysical terms: the fight for bread was a manifestation of liberty, not just the means to satisfy hunger.[29] By 1963, when she made this criticism of the articles, she had no doubt in her own mind that the revolution was first and foremost about improving man's material situation.[30] Her later writing is more rooted in reality and depends less on abstract and metaphysical arguments, giving what she thinks of as its due place to economic factors. The last of the *Temps Modernes* articles to be discussed here, 'La pensée de droite, aujourd'hui', demonstrates this later rejection of abstract idealism.

  Les Temps Modernes planned an issue in which the theme of 'the left' was to be treated. Simone de Beauvoir decided that her contribution would approach the problem obliquely by analysing the ideas of certain right-wing writers. It is their turn now to be accused of producing a system of values and concepts which they claim as universal but which are far removed from reality. This is a deliberate attempt to disguise what she calls 'the practical truths', that is, the fact that their real concern is to defend and perpetuate the interests (largely economic) of a particular social class, a privileged elite – 'the defence of privileges by the privileged'.[31] It is to be noted that in this essay the words 'droite' and 'bourgeoisie' are interchangeable, and what she is attacking is not so much the political right as the attitudes and ideology of a certain class.

  She believes the bourgeoisie has evolved from being absolutely sure of its future before the first world war, through growing self-doubt, to near panic in the mid-fifties. It was now clear that its disappearance was inevitable, and this explains the fear that is displayed by all the authors she studies. This fear of change, which would threaten the privileged position that the bourgeois wishes at all costs to preserve, centres largely on communism because it appears to him as the greatest threat. The various ideologies of the right are purely negative and are defined in relation to communism, which means that instead of a constructive programme they can only offer 'counter-propaganda' and 'Their thought is primarily and essentially counter-thought.' In their attacks on communism, she says, they see no need to present a scientific criticism or evaluation, and they ignore the material and economic arguments. Instead they talk in psychological terms of envy, inferiority complexes, religious instincts, the search for power, opinion and feeling, in an attempt to cut Marxism off from any basis in reality. They do not wish to recognise that it is all about the material world and not about the absolutes that concern *them* so much, removed from reality as they are by their life-style and their idealism. What preoccupies them more than anything is the erection of a system which they believe to be universal, based on eternal truths and values, and valid for all humanity. But in their vocabulary, 'man' means 'bourgeois', and when they claim that they hold the key to civilisation and values they have no universal aim in view, only the defence of their own privileges as an elite. If man the possessor of civilisation is equated with the bourgeois elite, this conveniently dismisses the masses to a negative existence, having no human substance. The elite is distinguished by its capacity to seize the truth instinctively, this superiority being given as part of its essence, and so inaccessible to those who would wish to learn it. Moreover, this culture is presented in mystic terms, difficult to understand, and it is never defined in terms of reality or defended in terms of logic. Aestheticism works on a similar principle of exclusion: the masses and art are mutually exclusive because only what is rare is precious. It is important for the privileged few that the masses should be refused access: 'there is no wealth without poverty, there are no masters without slaves'. Only the elite should have the possibility of authentic realisation of self – if everyone had this right 'it would be a levelling down, uniformity, socialism'.[32] Hierarchy is important and must be preserved because it favours those who are already privileged. Human nature is given and, as with other species, it is pluralistic; inequality is not unjust because it is natural. This will not change, because there is no progress. History is seen by some of them as consisting of alternating elites, by others as a chance succession of civilisations. This argument does not allow man any say in the future and leads to quietism and passivity, she claims, and that, of course, favours those who wish to preserve the *status quo*. If all you want to do is to retain your place in the hierarchy, then action is superfluous, so those on the right pursue the negative policy of defence. Her conclusion is that all bourgeois thought is empty and arid, refusing change and refusing the future: counter-thought.

It is clear that these articles from *Les Temps Modernes* are only political in the broadest sense of the word: Simone de Beauvoir was not concerned with elaborating political theories. They are really an extension of her philosophical writing in that in them she details some of the political stances that are in her view implied by her ethical stances. She shows no interest in party political activity, no understanding of the functions of the state or the necessities of government and day-to-day politics.[33] Her concern is with the values and attitudes that not merely do, or should, lie behind political activity but actually give rise to it, and her criticisms and proposals are intended less for those who are active in politics than for those who, like herself, talk and write about them. Here we can find no blue-print for action, no constructive suggestions, no outline of policies – but then, if you don't wish to work within the existing system, these might appear superfluous. She is, however, very much concerned with analysing and discrediting certain political and social attitudes, and in this she epitomises Sartre's view of the classical intellectual as 'un grand dénonciateur', whose job is to condemn French society.[34] The next chapter will look at the way Simone de Beauvoir visualised the role of that intellectual, and the critical action to which, theoretically, his *engagement* should lead him.

4

Possibilities for action:

I The theory

If most French intellectuals immediately after the second world war felt the necessity for practical commitment rather than the pursuit of pure literature or pure philosophy, it is to the 1930s that we must look for the origins of this type of commitment. The moral and intellectual ferment of the thirties followed a period of cultural stagnation in which most of the leading thinkers and writers had been well established for some time. It was with a sense that things were beginning to change that Julien Benda wrote his celebrated defence of the traditional role of the writer, *La trahison des clercs*, in 1927. He asserted that the intellectual must cultivate complete detachment from the day-to-day affairs of the world and must remain enclosed in his ivory tower. Extolling the past achievements of the classical intellectual, he railed against the new notion that the intellectual should descend to the market place and participate in politics: this step must be avoided at all costs and could only compromise the intellectual's prestige.[1] Such sentiments could be of little help in the moral crisis facing the intellectuals between the wars, and were adopted by very few. Most realised that they were living in a period of great change and became convinced that they could and should influence the evolution that was taking place.

In economic terms the period saw the rapid decline of the nineteenth-century version of the capitalist system, which was the first step towards the mixed economy France knows today. State intervention led to important social changes: financial support for the unemployed, for instance, and with the Popular Front the establishment of the system of collective bargaining and the imposition by the state of minimum wages and conditions of work. At the same time there came the realisation that the economic problems triggered off by the Wall Street crash in 1929, which were common to all the developed countries of the world, could not be solved independently by France alone, but only by a cooperative international effort. In Zeldin's view it was this last realisation, unacceptable to some, that led to 'the fierce reassertion of French values [which] was the swansong of nationalism'. So there were two reactions to the changes: a resistance to them leading to an attempt to limit their effects, and a widespread debate initiated by a growing number of vociferous and active intellectuals. The latter had now begun to participate in politics, but they were divided among themselves and already they were consuming their energies in peripheral verbal activity while the technocrats were establishing themselves in those areas where real power was wielded – the civil service and industrial management. It was on the whole the forces of resistance that won the day.

The economic crisis was accompanied by a political crisis that was to last until the collapse of the French political system in 1940. The regime of the Third Republic was seen as morally decadent as well as being impotent in political terms, but the remedies proposed varied from one extreme to the other. It must be remembered that there were two acute threats to social and political stability in Europe, namely communism and fascism. The fascist threat, increasing every year with events in Germany, Italy, Spain and even France itself, was the more obvious. Bolshevism was considered by some to be equally dangerous and fear of it often tempered efforts to counter fascism. In the moral and intellectual confusion people began to question accepted values and examine their consciences, and many intellectuals decided that they must take sides. Isolation was no longer a possibility in this 'total crisis of civilisation' (the phrase is Mounier's), and involvement often meant choosing one of the two dominant ideologies. Some opted for the far right, often closely allied to fascism: believing that the crisis was inherent in any democratic Republic, they wished to establish a strong, authoritarian government in the fascist style. Those on the right included some who saw the association of church and state as the way of reviving spiritual values. For others, and these were in the majority, bourgeois civilisation was the culprit and they wished to overthrow the social order. Many of these either joined or were sympathisers of the Communist Party, although they often became quickly disillusioned by the constraints of supporting such a party. Their attempt at internal social and political renewal was reinforced by a growing fear of fascism which finally awakened the consciences of even those intellectuals like Sartre and Simone de Beauvoir who did not immediately translate this into action.

Having become alerted to the dangers that threatened all of

Europe, the intellectuals sought to warn others of those dangers either through their writing or in more practical activity. Paradoxically it was their considerable disillusionment with professional politicians, who in their view had failed to come to grips with the current situation, that helped to politicise the intellectuals. Most of them took every opportunity of escaping from their former passivity and consequent isolation. They felt that individual concerns must be subordinated to collective responsibility for solving a crisis that was too serious to ignore. Their new-found activity gave rise to a multitude of new small groups, parties and youth movements; more traditional was their attempt to wield influence as writers through the medium of reviews and journals, and this continued through and after the war. John Flower points out the significance of their various titles in this quest for renewal: *Ordre Nouveau, Nouvel Age, Clarté, Réaction, Combat, L'Homme Nouveau, Esprit*.[2]

The traumatic effect of the war convinced those who had previously been reluctant that they must reassess their role, and it was the years immediately following the liberation of Paris that witnessed the greatest political involvement of intellectuals. The crisis of civilisation was now even more in evidence. Politically and intellectually, the Third Republic was totally discredited by the collapse of France, the occupation and the collaboration, all of them demoralising experiences. But if this left a vacuum it made much easier the task of those who, angered by events and determined that such things must never be allowed to happen again, believed that they must recreate a new France from the ruins. There was a certain idealism in the conviction that they could indeed realise these aspirations for a political, social and moral renewal that would transform French society, but at that time everything seemed possible – it had to, if only so that they might regain their self-esteem.

The war had politicised the intellectuals in another way also. The experience, vicarious for some, of solidarity, responsibility and mutual dependence, which came from working in the Resistance or for the Free French, led them to believe that to abandon isolation for a collective effort was not only possible but indeed necessary. Even those who did not wish to mix politics and literature in their own writing felt that they must take a stand and declare their commitment publicly, and this was true of a relatively wide range of writers from the far left, through the left-wing Catholics and the moderate left, to the moderate 'liberal' right. François Mauriac speaks for many of them in this defence of his intervention in politics: 'Our generation has paid dearly for the knowledge that we are all engaged, that we are all embarked in the same tragic adventure, all in solidarity, all responsible, and that of all the partisan positions the refusal to take a side is without a doubt the only one that can find no justification, neither before God nor before men.'[3]

This is quite remarkably close in every way to the viewpoint of Simone de Beauvoir, although it was certainly a common one at the time. The idea that this was a lesson learnt at great cost explains what Victor Brombert calls the 'obsessive proportions of guilt and responsibility...a new *mal de siècle*', observable in many writers. A member of the American audience that heard Camus give a talk entitled 'The human crisis' tells of the effect his words had on them: 'We were all of us responsible for the war...all of us in the huge hall were convinced, I think, of our common culpability.' Simone de Beauvoir's characters experience guilt (as she did) at not having done anything to prevent the Spanish war or Hitler's annexation of Austria because of their lack of commitment at the time. Once *engagés*, they still have an irrational sense of guilt at being powerless to help others who are suffering while they themselves are unscathed, or even at the inaction of their fellow countrymen in the face of certain events – as did Simone de Beauvoir by association over Algeria.[4] Moreover, the assertion that one must mark one's *engagement* by 'taking a side' is not only implicit in Simone de Beauvoir's philosophical notion that man must make conscious choices, however difficult and risky they may be, but is also explicit in her discussion of the necessity for making specifically political choices: 'If conscientious people hesitate for so long before taking a political decision, it is not because political problems are difficult: it is because they are insoluble. And yet abstention is just as impossible, because that too is action.' Just as abstention is not possible in the business of consciously shaping one's own life, so 'Not to take part in politics is simply another way of taking part.'[5]

Apparently experiencing the liberation in the same way and yet significantly different from Simone de Beauvoir and the other intellectuals was the figure of Albert Camus. Camus, born in 1913 in Algeria, was the grandson of settlers. His childhood was spent in poverty, and he suffered all his life from tuberculosis contracted while he was at school, but after graduating from Algiers University he was able to scrape a living during the 1930s in publishing and journalism, and running different progressive theatre groups. He was already writing the books that were to make him famous by the end of the war: *L'étranger*, *Le mythe de Sisyphe*, *Caligula*, and later the best-seller *La peste*. Trapped in France in 1942 while convalescing when the Vichy zone came under German occupation, he eventually made his way to Paris. There he helped at considerable risk to produce the underground paper *Combat*, and then edited it for three years when it began to appear as a daily paper after the liberation of Paris. He became an *habitué* of the Saint-Germain-des-Prés circle of Sartre and Simone de Beauvoir, but always refused to be labelled an 'existentialist'.

He was exceptional among those caring intellectuals who emerged from the war determined to further the moral and intellectual renewal with positive proposals for a better society, for he took the solitary line of refusing to make a *political* choice. While rejecting certain options out of hand, he found it impossible to commit himself totally to one side or the other when there were conflicting interests. The result was that he found himself constantly advocating the moderation of the middle road: he would take idealistic, sometimes naïve, ethical positions and avoid dirtying his hands (his enemies would say) with practical solutions. Seeing both sides of a problem can be totally emasculating, as he was to discover at the time of the Algerian war, and it led him eventually to a position of virtual dis-engagement in Sartrian terms. The break with Sartre and Simone de Beauvoir came with the publication of *L'homme révolté* in 1951, although it had been brewing for some time. Following a hostile review in *Les Temps Modernes* by Francis Jeanson, there was a public quarrel in the form of a letter from Camus to Sartre and a reply from the latter. In *L'homme révolté* Camus was rejecting the Marxist notion of revolution at the very moment when Sartre was coming to terms with communism, but it was Camus's idealistic attitude to which they particularly objected: he had no right to take up this moralistic stance while remaining distanced from the real world of political conflict. Moreover, since he refused to place himself unequivocally in the Soviet camp, Simone de Beauvoir branded him 'anti-communist'. She and Sartre accepted in principle the Marxist definition of collective revolutionary action, in spite of its short-comings. But it was precisely these short-comings, the inhuman elements seen so clearly and rejected as we have noted by Simone de Beauvoir, that prevented Camus from opting for Marxism. His fundamental criticism of Marxism (and of the revolutionary ideal in general) was that it sacrifices real people living today to future generations in a world as yet unrealised. All means – cruelty, terror, inhumanity, murder – are defended as being in the service of a just cause. Although Camus did admit that violence was sometimes necessary, he could not accept this institutionalised violence that reduced men to objects for political ends. Again we see the similarity with Simone de Beauvoir. His compassion centred on the individual: he could think of the workers not as a class, but as separate persons, with a right to a full life. When he joined the Communist Party in 1935 for a brief period he wrote: 'I have a strong desire to help reduce the sum of unhappiness and of bitterness which empoisons mankind.' If he saw examples of human suffering, of oppression, of injustice, it did not lead him to look for collective action or to take up an ideological position, but to take modest practical action within his means on behalf of a particular individual or group of individuals. Again and again he intervened to ask for clemency towards individuals condemned to death, for fair trials or release from prison for those out of favour with a regime. Sometimes these were public protests, but more often they were private efforts through letters and interviews using his fame and influence to obtain what he wanted. As we shall see, this became one of Simone de Beauvoir's preferred methods of action, and yet because of the very nature of such interventions she was ignorant of them. If he was condemned by her it was partly because of his rejection *in principle* of collective action which she herself refused *in practice*.[6] The public dispute with Camus had not been resolved when he was killed in a car accident in 1960. For Simone de Beauvoir the break was not merely personal but was of major significance. She referred to the appearance of the first part of Sartre's 'Les communistes et la paix' and his 'Réponse à Camus' in consecutive issues of *Les Temps Modernes* in these terms: 'These two pieces of writing had the same meaning: the postwar period was over.'

The cold war now divided the intellectuals into two camps but the situation immediately after the liberation had been quite different. In the atmosphere of exuberant optimism about the new and different society that was to be created and the intoxicating sense of working together in a common cause, the intellectuals believed absolutely in the effectiveness of the part they could play in bringing it about. Thus they considered in these circumstances that they could not stand aside from political commitment. First they had to atone for their past sins of abstention. The sense of guilt at their previous isolation and inactivity led many intellectuals into the Communist Party. Similarly, H. Stuart Hughes believes that Sartre's espousal of Marxism answered 'a need to take upon himself the sins of the bourgeoisie'. In the case of Simone de Beauvoir, it seemed that her philosophy must lead her inevitably, from a sense of responsibility towards her fellow men and commitment to action on their behalf, to some kind of participation in politics.[7]

It can be argued that responsibility and commitment do not of necessity lead to political action. Raymond Aron questions the inevitability of this process for existentialists: 'political action is not the only form of action, revolution is not the only form of political action'. Perhaps not – but after the war political involvement appeared to a large number of intellectuals to be morally required of them. If politics are seen as an essential part of that society to which all men belong, then it is difficult to consider political activity as a separate area. The definition of the political can then be widened to include what normally comes within the social sphere – and indeed John Mander judges that the separation of politics from all other human activities is 'a heresy peculiar to our age; it is not the traditional view'. Furthermore, although the call to revolution is admittedly the most extreme form that commitment can take, and although commitment is perfectly possible at the other extreme for those on the right, in practice it tends to be limited to moderate or left-wing intellectuals. As Adereth puts it, 'interest in the social problems usually springs from the wish to change the present system', and the main aim of the right is to preserve the *status quo*.[8] Sartre and Simone de Beauvoir go towards an extreme in argument. Sartre virtually eliminated the possibility of an intellectual being other than on the left; Simone de Beauvoir has declared that feminists are by definition on the left. Intellectuals and feminists are genuine only if they create a critique of bourgeois society and this must lead to radical action.[9] Certainly in the particular period with which we are concerned the circumstances were bound to turn large numbers of people leftwards, as was shown by the first postwar elections. The reaction was against right-wing, anti-democratic collaborators with fascism, and the Resistance, still a powerful force with great moral prestige after the war, was dominated by those who wished to change radically the prewar regime.

How, then, did the intellectual who was *engagé* see his role and what possibilities for action did he believe were open to him? Intellectuals have always been accorded the greatest respect in France, a country where an appreciation of ideas, art and literature is accepted as a normal part of education, and where intellectuals have traditionally been involved in the specific controversies of their day as well as investigating in more general terms man's beliefs about society and the universe. This high status makes the role of the intellectuals potentially a powerful one, and explains why those who see themselves as *engagés* expect that by pronouncing on the moral and political issues of the day they can influence public opinion and change the course of events. Their concern with 'the truth of men's beliefs and the morality of their actions' leads them to question current values: 'In expressing this concern, [the intellectual] is likely to be critical of the beliefs, institutions, and actions of the men of his society, attacking either the content of their ideas and values or the inevitable failure to act according to them.' This corresponds to Sartre's description of the intellectual as the great informer and critic who denounces injustice: because he knows full well the contradictions in himself of the universal and the particular, he can expose the contradictions between universal political truths and particular political actions, thereby being in a position to condemn certain of these actions. The task of the revolutionary intellectual is critical analysis. He should write denouncing 'with rigorous objectivity' French society, combating false interpretations, and he should analyse the current situation in France. Raymond Aron comments, rather deprecatingly, that 'the tendency to criticise the established order is, so to speak, the occupational disease of the intellectuals'. But why not? Such people are more likely than most to be critically aware and to have constantly in mind a moral ideal of which that order falls short. He complains that they 'judge their country and its institutions by comparing present realities with theoretical ideals rather than with other realities'; but it is the view of critical intellectuals that their task is to bring their country nearer to these ideals, rather than to sit back because it is an improvement on the France of yesterday or some other country of today. For Sartre and Simone de Beauvoir this critical role is vital. The intellectual should not himself become professionally involved in politics, and Sartre is careful to distinguish between the task of the intellectual and that of the

politician: 'But the intellectual is not a politician...it is not his job
to get down to working out the precise, concrete details.'[10] He gives
the example of the Algerian war. It was for the intellectual to condemn it as a colonialist war, to incite the troops not to fight, to say
that the French should get out, but not to define the terms on which
the F.L.N. should negotiate with de Gaulle. So he must not act like
a politician and – even more important – he must not become a
politician. He is morally obliged to remain independent of the
regime, even if he supports it, because he still has a critical role to
play. When Malraux accepted a post in de Gaulle's government in
1958, they came to the conclusion that an intellectual should never
do this: 'Even if he supports the government, he should remain in
the ranks of those who oppose and criticise, in other words, he should
judge policies, not execute them...his role must not become confused with that of the rulers.'[11]

André Malraux (1907–76), novelist, art historian and politician,
was a rather special case. A strong communist sympathiser until the
Nazi–Soviet pact of 1939, he had been involved in the Chinese
revolutionary struggle in the 1920s (about which he wrote his most
famous novel, *La condition humaine*), the Spanish civil war in the
1930s, and the French Resistance during the second world war.
He then revealed himself as having become virulently anti-communist and a devoted supporter of de Gaulle, in whose government
he briefly participated in 1945. He then produced his two comprehensive works of art history (*Les voix du silence* and *Le musée
imaginaire de la sculpture mondiale*), and when de Gaulle returned
to power in 1958 became Minister of State for cultural affairs, an
office he retained until de Gaulle resigned as President in 1969.
It is easy to see why he was viewed as something of a traitor by
Sartre and Simone de Beauvoir.

If the intellectual should not take part in government, should he
then join that political party whose declared aim was to overthrow
the regime? The answer for both of them was a reluctant no.
The saga of Sartre's hot-and-cold relationship with the Communist
Party is beyond the scope of this study, but it is important to look
both at his view and at hers of what should be the committed
intellectual's attitude to the party and at the reasons why they felt
that it was impossible for them to become members. The attitude of
the P.C.F., the French Communist Party, towards intellectuals is, of
course, an important factor.

According to Lenin, the intellectual had a positive role to play in the revolution, for it was the revolutionary theory he provided from without that would make the workers politically conscious. H. Stuart Hughes writes of the cultural convention by which French intellectuals assume it is their responsibility to create universal value systems for others. Sartre fits into this tradition and certainly he and his circle saw themselves for many years as the conscience of the working classes, the voice of the people, with a duty to speak out publicly when others were silent.[12] The P.C.F. has always made use of intellectuals. But the intellectual must come to the party in a 'spirit of discipline, total devotion to the cause of the working class' and must not expect to pronounce on its doctrine. So while the P.C.F. has used its tame intellectuals in various ways, those intellectuals have to submit at all times to the discipline of a party whose dictatorial approach allows of no dialogue or debate, and certainly of no criticism. They must simply accept the party line in a spirit of absolute faith.[13]

Sartre defined *engagement* after the war as being 'what a left-wing intellectual could do if he did not join a party'. Although this is a somewhat narrow definition, it is certainly the way he saw his own role. It might be possible for others to be justified in joining the party, but it was impossible for him with his philosophy of freedom: 'The Communist Party and freedom just don't go together.' He knew that if he joined the party he would have to repudiate some of his previous writing, and that his future work would be subject to censorship: 'The politics of Stalinist Communism is incompatible in France with the honest practice of the literary craft.' The Communist Party was guilty of 'a utilitarianism which degraded literature to the status of propaganda', and he was quite unwilling to admit 'that we should serve it with our pens'. He was not, of course, alone in this. Most committed writers wish to be free to write what they will without having demands made on them by an outside body like a political party or a church. The degree to which they accept constraints varies. Some accept directives, some positively attempt to promote the ideology of the group to which they belong, some (like Sartre and Simone de Beauvoir in their literary works) see the artistic considerations as being overriding, even if their political sympathies are always obvious. All would agree that if propaganda is superimposed instead of emerging from the work, then the result is not a work of literature.[14]

Sartre could never have agreed to accept party discipline: he insisted that he must not be prevented from searching out the truth and arriving at a personal standpoint by thinking things through for himself. The wish to preserve his independence of thought was a logical consequence of his philosophy and of his psychological make-up but it also stemmed from his view that it was essential in terms of the critical role of the intellectual. Sartre characterises the intellectual in his relationship with the party as being 'faithful but critical'. He must not hesitate to criticise and speak the truth if the party does not adhere to certain principles, if the revolution goes off-course, and the only way to be able to do this is to remain outside the party, just as Malraux should have remained outside the government. On the other hand, differences of opinion should not lead the intellectual to withdraw his support in general or to stop defending those views and aims which he and the party had in common. He had no doubt that the intellectual must work *with* a party, but not necessarily *within* one. Once he had made his unsuccessful attempts to form independent groups (Socialisme et Liberté, and the Rassemblement Démocratique Révolutionnaire)[15] he began to envisage his political *engagement* 'as solidarity with a movement that is already in existence' – and until after 1968 that meant, inevitably, the P.C.F. This, says a somewhat disillusioned Sartre, is because 'it isn't up to intellectuals to form groups'.[16] In the course of the 1970s he worked instead with different Maoist groups, but always retained the role of the sympathetic critic, remaining outside them while giving them support.

The question whether or not to join the Communist Party was never publicly debated by Simone de Beauvoir. It is not that she was not conscious of the difficulties of making such a decision – she reflects these very accurately in *Les mandarins* – but she did not argue the case either in abstract terms or in personal terms. She vacillated, like Sartre, between rejecting any attempt to bridge the gap with the communists (usually when he was trying to do that very thing), and (influenced by some book she had read or some chance encounter) wondering whether they should not, after all, join: 'At other times...I would wonder if we shouldn't have jettisoned our scruples as intellectuals and fought in the ranks of the Communist Party.' Her criticism of certain Marxist attitudes towards freedom and the individual have already been discussed, but there were other reasons for her being personally incapable of taking such a step. The first was her strong consciousness of being inescapably middle class, whatever her sympathies. She felt that the bourgeois intellectual was simply not in the same situation as those actually involved in the struggle. However much he might feel his destiny to be linked to that of the working classes and their suffering, he can only support from the sidelines, and can never fully enter the world of the Communist Party and the proletariat. He may join the party, but this will not make him one of them because he has not joined from any objective necessity (hunger, for instance) but out of free choice. In *Le sang des autres*, Jean Blomart goes and joins the workers on the factory floor but he can never become one himself – 'you can't rid yourself of the past'.[17] This may simply be a rationalisation of her own inability to throw off her bourgeois *persona* and join in practical action, but clearly she felt she would have been out of place; unable to overcome this barrier, she found herself cut off from the very people who had her sympathy and support.

Another reason for her not joining the Communist Party, or indeed any party, is her refusal to accept any ideology in its totality, because that would limit her personal freedom. Although she felt very close to the *gauchistes* in the action they carried out in France, she has never been able to accept that everyone must think the same way on every issue: 'I regret that the non-Communist left should have grown as monolithic as the Party itself. A left-winger must necessarily admire China without the least reservation, take Nigeria's side against Biafra and the Palestinians' against Israel. I will not bow to these conditions.' She finds all political dogmatism repugnant and dangerous in its claim to have found absolute answers to all problems and to have a monopoly of values.[18] This attitude has not changed with time.

Simone de Beauvoir asserts that, having been rejected and thereby neutralised by the communists, Sartre found a way out through literature: 'Sartre extended his notion of commitment still further and discovered a *praxis* in writing'. The characteristic involvement of intellectuals in politics is through their writings, especially so in France, where great weight is lent to their pronouncements in that area, and Jean-François Revel goes so far as to argue that this is the only way in which they can be effective: 'I consider that as writers they are capable of influencing politics by the pen and by their thought, but certainly not by direct action. I say this quite explicitly because intellectuals of the left have too often regarded themselves as a political party'.

It seems reasonable, then, to assume that for people like Sartre and Simone de Beauvoir for whom so many avenues were barred, either from their own choice or by others, writing would be the prime means of political action for the intellectual who is *engagé*. This was always to remain their view, for although Sartre attempted to manifest his *engagement* through political action of various sorts, he recently justified purely literary 'action' as being a valid alternative: 'Indeed I do not think that politicisation in the strict sense of the word is necessary for *engagement*; it is the most complete form of *engagement*. But *engagement* is first and foremost a critique of the situation or its acceptance – it doesn't matter which – through the medium of a literary work.'[19] Indeed since it was agreed generally that the most obvious and sure way to influence the political scene was by the pen, the question can be asked of Simone de Beauvoir whether the fact that there was an obvious literary way in which to take political action deterred her as much as anything from really bothering to pursue the other routes, except theoretically?

The answer may perhaps be found in her definition of committed literature and the role of the writer who is *engagé*. Unfortunately, Simone de Beauvoir has never at any time presented in a coherent form her views on this matter, the way Sartre did in *Qu'est-ce que la littérature?* The one occasion when one might have expected her to define her views in more general terms was in a debate organised in 1964 by *Clarté*, under the title 'Que peut la littérature?'[20] The main question asked of the contributers, all of whom were considered by the presenter, Yves Buin, to want to change the world, was how this could be done and with what degree of efficiency. When it came to Simone de Beauvoir's turn to speak she specifically stated that she was only going to concern herself with what literature meant to her, both as a writer and as a reader. She did not define committed literature herself, commenting that she agreed with the views of Semprun, a previous speaker. He had made two main points: if a writer is *engagé* it is in his writing that his commitment manifests itself – and clearly this is how she sees her own major action; and committed literature should always be able to question everything with no attempt being made to suppress this important cultural debate. Simone de Beauvoir herself made only one statement about the committed writer in the course of her contribution to the debate.

This fits in with what Adereth says about committed literature, claiming that it is 'the application of commitment to the special field of literature. Its one and only requirement is that the writer should take part in the struggles of the age.' As long as 'take part in' is taken in the sense of being aware of these struggles and not remaining in the ivory tower, this is how Simone de Beauvoir sees it: 'an individual involved in his times' is the only one capable of interesting his readers, because of the breadth and richness of his contacts with the contemporary world. The writer should attempt to understand the society and the times in which he lives and in which he should be firmly rooted. She is very critical of the *nouveau roman* for not being *engagé* in this sense, and or Nathalie Sarraute in particular for her statement that when she sits down to write she leaves 'politics, current events, the world, outside the door', implying a return to the ivory tower of old.[21]

If we want to know what Simone de Beauvoir thinks can be achieved by *other* committed writers (and we must remember that what is prescribed as theoretically possible for others must be distinguished from what she herself wishes to do or does) then we must as usual go to Sartre for a coherent answer. As so often, she left it to him to fill out her ideas and to present the theory. It is reasonable to assume that she agrees with most of what he said, since she usually points out the differences in their view in the autobiography. It is therefore important to look in considerable detail at what Sartre's views were on this subject.

For Sartre, literature was certainly the main form of political action, although he saw the limits as to what could be achieved and although his ideas changed considerably with time. He refused to make the distinction between literature that is *engagé* and literature that is a pure art form: 'Art for art's sake is as *engagé* as political writing; it has a social significance.' The only difference is between writers who cling to their belief that their own writing is free from commitment and those who realise, as he did in 1945, that 'all writing is political'. It is a social act and therefore by implication political because in every book the writer's view of society can be seen even if it is not made explicit. In *Qu'est-ce que la littérature?* he seems to believe absolutely in the powers of literature and the sacred role of the writer. The only theme of the committed writer, he says, is freedom. A writer constructs a work in total freedom and the readers to whom it is addressed are free people, thus 'in its own way

[it] manifests the totality of the human condition as a free product of a creative activity'. But the writer must also have a sense of social responsibility and for Sartre this means more than that his works should reflect the society of his time: 'We must take up a position *in our literature*, because literature is in essence a taking of position.' He states, for instance, that 'we must militate, in our writings, in favour of the freedom of the person *and* the socialist revolution'. However, he insists that: 'In committed literature, *commitment* must not under any circumstances cause *literature* to be forgotten.' If the ideology is superimposed, it becomes valueless. The political and the aesthetic must be combined so that literature does not degenerate into 'pure propaganda' or 'pure entertainment'. Convinced that 'To speak is to act', Sartre believed that literature can give society its only chance: 'The "committed" writer knows that words are action. He knows that to reveal is to change and that one can reveal only by planning to change.' Sartre's continuing conviction about the absolute importance of the written word is demonstrated by his virulent attack in 1964 on a journalist who had challenged the effectiveness of commitment that was purely verbal, like that of Simone de Beauvoir. Sartre defended her hotly saying that the writer must act only with the means at his disposal – the written word. The social act of revelation and change is achieved by the following process: the writer communicates with his readers and engages their responsibility by telling them the truth ('to reveal the world' is the phrase he uses); unable to claim ignorance, they begin to reflect and their conscience begins to work; they themselves then become *engagés* and seek to change and improve society.[22]

At first, Sartre felt that certain things had to be said by him and that this would justify his existence: 'he... was really seeking "salvation" in literature'. By 1954 he had passed, he says, from 'literature held sacred to action which nevertheless remains that of an intellectual'. *Les mots*, first published in 1964, but ten years in the writing, shows how Sartre's conception of the writer as High Priest with a literary duty, and of words as having some magic power, had become tinged with scepticism. The glorious mission of the writer to expose certain truths which were apparent only to him had become a simple task to be done. Betwen 1954 and 1964 he began to realise that other sorts of action, to which he had turned, also presented difficulties and that 'we are not saved by politics any more than by literature'. Without rejecting the books he had written, he felt that with time he had gained a sense of reality that had been missing from his earlier work, and this made him question the role of the writer. He concluded that the writer's task was 'to place his pen at the service of the oppressed', but more than anything it was simply 'not to ignore the reality and the fundamental problems that exist'.[23] The actual result of this evolution, it seems, was a new attitude and awareness in the writer himself, rather than any great change in the sort of writing he produced.

One question which always troubled Sartre and about which he remained somewhat ambivalent is that of the public whom the committed revolutionary writer is addressing. On the one hand he claimed that 'The strength of a writer lies in his direct action upon the public', criticising the surrealists, whose revolutionary statements were purely theoretical because they had no readers among the working classes. At the same time he writes of his own problems in finding a working-class readership because of the domination of the Communist Party. In the postwar period he saw a possible readership and support for his efforts towards a socialist Europe among non-communist workers, the petit-bourgeois and elementary-school teachers – a pious hope, as Thody points out. He soon realised this, and was well aware of the incongruity of being read not by the exploited, for whom he was working, but by the exploiters, the hated bourgeoisie, whom he was attacking but who avidly read all his books. In 1964 he felt that the writer's task in non-revolutionary societies was to 'pose problems in the most radical and intransigent manner', thus preparing for the time when everyone will read. This does *not* mean a 'popular' literature that will aim at the lowest levels, because he believed that the public, too, must make an effort in order to understand the writer. That this is possible is proved, he claimed, by the vastly changed readership that resulted from the publication of his books in paperback. So it is worthwhile for the writer to direct his efforts at 'the meeting between writer and public'.[24]

In the 1970s there was a change in Sartre's ideas brought about by the events of May 1968 but not immediately obvious. He felt the need to redefine his conception of the intellectual and, in theory at least, his relationship with his public. He describes the intellectual of before 1968 as being either the 'chien de garde' ('watchdog')[25] of the bourgeoisie, transmitting bourgeois culture, or the 'classical' intellectual who signed petitions, joined protest organisations, but remained essentially in a privileged position, supported by the bourgeoisie, as a teacher or a writer. This is how Sartre saw himself up to 1968. After that date, the classical intellectual could remain an elitist, allowed to continue protesting and professing revolutionary ideas because he spoke the bourgeois language; or on the other hand he could, like Sartre, have no further dialogue with the bourgeoisie, and give up his privileged position by allowing his ideas and his role to be called into question. Sartre at this point suggested that the intellectual might perhaps renounce his privileges and go to work in a factory, disappearing into the mass of ordinary people. He later denied that he had said all intellectuals must go into the factories. He had merely meant that they must find some other way of getting over the contradictions inherent in their situation than signing petitions and writing articles for other intellectuals. He himself, being too old to work in a factory (!), had become fully *engagé* by supporting *La Cause du Peuple* and other papers, so that the working people could communicate with each other and express their anger in their own language and in their own press: this is 'to let the people speak for themselves'. Sartre recognised that even then his position was not without contradictions: although he had joined those who fight the bourgeois dictatorship and rejected the elitist aspects of his work, the other side of him was still a classical intellectual, addressing the bourgeoisie in its own language: 'I still write books for the bourgeoisie and yet I feel a sense of fellowship with the working classes who wish to destroy it.' This is because he was not willing to give up writing his great work on Flaubert. That side of his work was important enough for him to say that he desperately wanted to find a bridge between this sort of writing and the masses – something he never succeeded in doing.[26]

Sartre was concerned to define the role of the writer in general as well as to debate the ways in which he himself would best exemplify that role. Simone de Beauvoir tells us only what she has attempted to do in her own writing and what literature means to her personally. Necessarily a survey of her views is very much of a construct of fragments since as a matter of principle she avoided any formal or complete explanation of her own position.

Her definition of the intellectual gives a clue to her main preoccupation: 'I am an intellectual, I take words and the truth to be of value'. In this statement she indicates her love of writing and her conviction of the importance and value of literature, and also her concern with transmitting through her work what she believes is 'the truth'. Unlike Camus who was always troubled, if we are to take note of his journals, as to how to recognise the truth, she seems to have no doubt about what constitutes it. There are certain words that reappear frequently when Simone de Beauvoir explains what she has tried to do through her writing: 'make people see', 'bear witness', 'reveal', 'demystification', 'communicate'. At first she wished to record her own experience in order to capture it for ever: 'I was called upon to open my eyes to the manifold glories of life, and I must write in order to snatch that vision from obliteration by time'. This was in 1929, at a time when she was throwing herself wholeheartedly into experiencing life to the full. Creating the world anew in an imaginary form 'was a way of justifying the world'. To be able to do this the writer must take nothing for granted but must look at reality with a fresh eye: 'only then can one both perceive it, and make others do so'. There is, then, another element. The writer is not only someone who sees the world clearly, he is also a social and political witness, whose task is 'to testify', to transmit his experience of it to the reader by re-creating it in words. Yves Buin describes this as the 'mediating quality' of literature, which is the only possible one between the universe that it reveals to us and ourselves.[27]

Although she says, 'Any literary work involves a portrayal of the world', it often appears that Simone de Beauvoir is primarily concerned with transmitting herself to the reader. She confesses that one of her early reasons for wanting to become a writer was that she simply enjoyed communication. In the 1930s she still felt the same way: 'I wanted to communicate the element of originality in my own experience'. Sometimes the reader does not even enter into it: 'I want to write: I want to put down phrases on paper, to take elements from my life and turn them into words.' For her own satisfaction she wished to 'fix', to 'preserve' moments of her life – though she confesses that once she had written her autobiography everything that had now been committed to paper disappeared from her mind so that her past life is now petrified for ever in the written version. She wanted to 'realize myself in books' and she tells of the feeling of excitement which comes from writing: 'by creating a book I am creating myself in the imaginary dimension'. In spite of the fact that there were other aspects to her idea of what it was to be a

writer, this is one that has never altered. On the final page of
Tout compte fait she sums up her achievements as a writer: 'I wanted
to make myself exist for others by conveying, as directly as I could,
the taste of my own life; I have more or less succeeded.' Of course
this was not purely selfish. She now claims that what she wanted to
do above all in her work was 'parler', to speak in the ear of the
reader and to pass on as much of her own experience as possible
'so that it might be of help to others'.[28]

The important thing is the resulting empathy with the reader,
and this is what distinguishes literature from information. With
literature, the reader enters the world of the author and identifies
with him instead of remaining in his own world. Putting herself in
the position of the reader, she describes the process thus: 'Another's
truth becomes mine without ceasing to be another's.' This concentration of the writer on himself is in fact merely a way in which he
can communicate with others: 'the writer attempts to set up communication with others by means of the uniqueness of his personal
experience'. Literature expresses universal truths from an individual
viewpoint, and so long as this viewpoint is recognised as being only
partial and not the whole truth, then it can enrich those to whom it
is communicated. Subjective experience is transposed to another
level, the individual is 'universalised'. The reality which an author
communicates is *his* view of reality at a certain place and a certain
time – 'en situation', in the existentialist phrase. Thus literature
becomes for both writer and reader a way of escaping the prison of
one's individual existence in this world which is the same for all of
us and yet different for all of us. Because this unity and this
singularity interact, communication is possible. Literature can allow
us 'to communicate through that which separates us one from
another...if it is genuine literature, it is a way of transcending
separation by affirming it'. It allows men to understand each other
by a reciprocal action: 'It ought to make us crystal clear one to
another.' Writing is one of the few tasks undertaken by man that
preserve his humanity instead of becoming an end in themselves:
'I believe that the task of literature – and this is something which
makes it irreplaceable – is to preserve from technocrats and bureau-
crats all that is human in man. It can do this in so far as through it
he reveals himself to other individuals who are at one and the same
time bound up with each other and entirely separate.'[29] The individualistic mode of reception (the emphasis being on the single

reader) corresponds to the individualism of the whole theory. For Simone de Beauvoir the relationship between the writer and the reader is essentially a one-to-one relationship, or rather it is many one-to-one relationships. It is nothing like Sartre's attempt at the meeting between writer and public, which is a one-to-many relationship. The result is to make literature the epitome of the communication of man with *l'autre*. The theory is totally consistent with Simone de Beauvoir's philosophy and demonstrates why for her the problem of 'the other' disappeared from view once she became a writer. She did not need the experience of mass political action in order to solve the problem; on the contrary, for her it could only be solved on an individual basis, which nevertheless she sees as political. For she recategorises this part played by literature in the relationship of man with man, from an ethical into a political role. Quoting Camus writing at the end of the war, she accepts his definition at that time of politics: ' "Politics is no longer dissociated from individuals...it is man's direct address to other men." We were writers, and that was our job, to address ourselves to other men.'

Literature, then, has a political role to play. Or has it? When questioned in an interview with Madeleine Chapsal in 1960, she seems to deny this absolutely. In answer to the question, 'Do you consider yourself to be engaged in a political battle?' she replies, 'A writer never engages in political work as a writer.' However, after the initial apparently categorical denial, she goes on: 'but when I wrote "La pensée de droite" and *La longue marche*, my purpose was to refute certain errors and express certain ideas of a political nature'. These are works in which she attempts to 'put the record straight' by setting out the truth as she sees it, and in this sense she defines action through literature in exactly the same way as Sartre. It is by this process that she hopes to change the world. All she has to do is to start the process by telling the truth and the rest will follow: 'to name is to unmask, and to unmask is to change'. That is what writing is all about: 'For me it is an activity which is carried out by men for men; its aim is to unmask the world and *this unmasking is itself an action*.' She left it to Sartre to explain the process by which this action takes place.[30] Whether or not she categorises this attempt to change the world as political action, if she has this end in view she can certainly be called *un écrivain engagé*. Oddly enough she wished to do precisely this even as far back as 1929, long before she considered herself *engagée*: 'to combat error, to find the truth, to tell it and expound it to the world, perhaps to help to change the world'. The attempt became more political from the end of the war onwards. She relates the launching of *Les Temps Modernes* and specifies what its founders, of whom she was one, wished to do: 'we hoped to influence our contemporaries by our choice of texts and by the orientation of our articles'.[31]

If the writer is to exert influence, it will certainly not be by writing propaganda for literature must not be purely informative, nor must the writer moralise or be too didactic. He is not forbidden, at the other extreme, to produce something that is totally 'gratuitous'; there is not really a conflict between aesthetics and commitment, because the writer is at liberty to write something that has no utility, no practical purpose, to write about something beautiful ('pure entertainment'?), so long as he is aware that there is ugliness, unhappiness in the world as well. She also came to dislike writing that was obviously didactic, including some of her own, like *Les bouches inutiles* and *Le sang des autres*. If the message is spelt out too clearly, if it can be reduced to maxims and concepts, then it is a failure. Political problems and social questions should not be presented in abstract terms, but in a fictional framework which is nevertheless clearly 'anchored to the real world' and situated in a specific period and in a certain set of circumstances. Here she is saying the same as Sartre. At the same time she does not go as far as Sartre in that she does not believe the author's own position should be spelt out. The writer should present the problems inherent in the human condition, ask those questions which worry him personally and which will strike a chord in the reader's own experience. But he should not come to any conclusions or provide 'correct' answers to the problems raised, particularly in a novel. Ambiguity is essential. The aim of literature is 'to make manifest the equivocal, separate, contradictory truths that no one moment represents in their totality'. This is what she was doing in *Les mandarins*. Even before she succeeded in doing this herself, she had felt that reality was far too ambiguous to be totally contained in anything one might say about it, to be reduced to the clarity and precision of words. Indeed what literature should do ideally is to indicate this ambiguity, to suggest that other things lie beyond the reality of which we are conscious: 'a writer's business is not to transcribe the thoughts and feelings which constantly pass through his mind so much as to point out those horizons which we never reach and scarcely perceive, but which nevertheless are there'.[32]

If Simone de Beauvoir hoped to achieve some improvement in the world through her writing, it can also be said that what she personally derived from it sometimes appears to have exceeded what she hoped to transmit. She had always wanted to write, but until 1939 she felt a basic difference of attitude between herself and Sartre: he lived for writing, whereas to her it was an activity secondary to that of experiencing the richness of a full life. That life included writing, but she did not have the same compulsion to express herself as she had felt before meeting Sartre, when her life had been empty. She still considered literature as a sort of salvation, justifying not only the world but also one's own life: 'Literature, I thought, was a way of preserving one's own existence.' Then with the war and the experience of unhappiness, writing became necessary to her once again: 'literature had become as essential to me as the very air I breathed'. She felt more than ever the moral need for writing: 'It also guaranteed my moral autonomy; in the solitude of risks taken, of decisions to be made, I made my freedom much more real...For me, my books were a real fulfillment.' So was no other fulfilment necessary to her? Here, writing seems to be not a substitute for action, but a truly existentialist action in itself: we are in the moral world of choices, risks and free acts, and of salvation *per vocationem* – through the vocation of writing. Writing became a passion, almost a mania: 'a day when I do not write tastes of ashes'. For her this creative work was 'adventure...youth and liberty'. Even as late as 1971–2 she was describing 'the exalting feeling that writing still gives me at times', which was still important to her, although she could now sometimes do without it. By 1962, she says, the idea of mission, of salvation, had gone; she had stopped believing it justified her existence, 'but without it I should feel mortally unjustified'. It always seems to have continued giving her personal satisfaction and great comfort at times of unhappiness, 'the same comfort that prayer gives to the believer'.[33]

In spite of her personal gain, she did hope to have some influence through her books. Her readership, however, was the same as Sartre's: middle class. Towards the end of *La force de l'âge*, which takes the reader up to 1944, she justifies this, though with some regret, by arguing that for the writer to be read by a working-class public the bourgeoisie must be entertained, like it or not. He must first sell a large number of books to them in order for his work to appear later in cheap editions which the working class can afford. With Sartre, she sees the paperback as one way of reaching the sort of people she most wished to communicate with. She would like to live for posterity through her writings, but her main concern is not to be ignored but to be read by her contemporaries: 'It is my relationship with them – cooperation, struggle, dialogue – that has meant most to me throughout my life.' It doesn't seem to matter much from which class they come: at any rate she is not troubled by this to the same extent as Sartre. By the time she wrote *Tout compte fait* in the early 1970s, she had come to recognise that she had little hope of reaching a wide range of readers: 'But I reach only a limited audience...So I no longer see writing as a privileged means of communication.'[34] She asserts that she had realised this already in 1962,[35] so May '68 was not for her the great turning-point that it was for Sartre. From this time onwards she was no longer sure of the role of the writer, but still felt she must go on writing and she never attempted to redefine her role as Sartre did. At the very end of her autobiography she is still optimistic about what can be achieved by revealing the truth. She hates misfortune, she says, and when she comes across it she is so appalled and indignant that she feels the need to communicate her reactions: 'To fight unhappiness one must first expose it, which means that one must dispel the mystifications behind which it is hidden so that people do not have to think about it. It is because I reject lies and running away that I am accused of pessimism; but this rejection implies hope – the hope that the truth may be of use. And this is a more optimistic attitude than the choice of indifference, ignorance or shame.'[36]

Looking back over the action envisaged by Simone de Beauvoir for the intellectual who is *engagé*, the possibilities seem distinctly limited. He cannot work through and therefore have experience of the system, for he must not belong to the government or to a political party, and he has the negative task of undermining and ultimately destroying that system by abstaining from recognising it by any form of participation. The normal channels of political influence and activity are closed to him, because they imply support of the system and in any case would involve him in compromises and reformism. Moreover the fact that the intellectual's task is to reveal and to criticise, not to make constructive suggestions or political programmes – the responsibility of professional politicians – puts the whole exercise on to a moral plane. Simone de Beauvoir's own attitude is exemplified by two recent comments made by Sartre. The first appears in *On a raison de se révolter*, in a reference to *Les Temps Modernes* which, he asserts, was not militant in the early years, except that 'everything is political, that is to say everything calls into question the whole of society and must inevitably lead to contestation'. The other is in *Situations X*, where he talks of 'a political man' and says that by this he is referring to man as a political animal 'in the sense that every man is a political man'.[37] Political issues are therefore seen as ethical issues which concern all men, and policies or political actions are judged by their compatibility with moral values. The problem with this is that it can lead to an oversimplification of issues which are seen as being clear-cut moral choices. The practice of politics can never ignore the complexities and contradictions that are nearly always inherent in concrete situations, whereas those who take a moralistic standpoint see these situations as a set of values, not as a set of practical possibilities. It is therefore open to question how much can positively be achieved by such an attitude, and whether the sort of action prescribed by Simone de Beauvoir, circumscribed as it is by so many limitations, could ever have the hoped-for result of changing society.

The possibilities for action that according to Simone de Beauvoir are open to those intellectuals who consider themselves *engagés* were, of course, just as open to herself as to anyone else. The next chapter will look at the practical actions to which her own commitment led her.

5

Possibilities for action:

II The practice

'There's only one matter on which she completely staggers me, and that's politics. She doesn't care a damn about it. Well, it's not exactly that she doesn't care, but she won't have anything to do with the sordid manœuvres of politics' ('la cuisine politique'). This comment about Simone de Beauvoir, made by Sartre in July 1965, goes right to the heart of the matter. Unlike him, she has never expected to be active politically; her abstention should not be considered a failure to do something she felt she ought to be doing, but a deliberate choice. Through Anne, in *Les mandarins*, she spells out her own attitude quite clearly: 'I never for a moment dreamed of taking an active part in politics. In that domain, theories can interest me deeply and I harbour a few strong feelings, but practical politics aren't for me.' Anne, she claims, is not apolitical. Like her creator she feels that she is not qualified to take an active, 'technical' part in politics. If Simone de Beauvoir deliberately excludes practical politics, yet she has no hesitation in thinking of herself as *engagée*, and so inaction and *engagement* are not incompatible. As recently as 1974, she confirmed this in an interview: 'Since [the war] I have never ceased to be involved. But I've never been militant.'[1] It must not be assumed that she undertook no political activity at all. It is simply that it was limited and variable in intensity, taking different forms at different times. In formal terms, the difference between Sartre and Simone de Beauvoir can be expressed as follows: for Sartre, public political action is necessary for *engagement* but not in itself sufficient. There cannot be commitment without public political action, but on the other hand commitment is much more than that, for it is above all that private and personal activity that ideally gives rise to the existential experience. For Simone de Beauvoir, public political action is neither sufficient nor necessary – though she was ambivalent about the latter point. The private side of commitment is elevated to such a degree that she is only exceptionally dragged un-willingly into the public arena, by Sartre for instance, or because circumstances make it impossible for her to avoid it and still feel morally justified. This chapter will detail her actions such as they were, taking 1941 as a starting point.

Sartre returned from prisoner-of-war camp having derived from his experience of close contact with other human beings an intensified moral awareness. He claims that this new sensitivity, when translated into the practical action of resistance, was the turning-point for him: 'That was definitely the beginning of *engagement* for me.' The importance of action as a manifestation of commitment was in this instance conceded by Simone de Beauvoir after an initial hesitation. Sartre wished to break their isolation by uniting with others in organising some sort of resistance, but she thought he was nursing illusions and remained sceptical. In spite of this he persisted and looked for political contacts, forming a small group which he called 'Socialisme et Liberté'. Its immediate purpose was to collect and disseminate information, and its long-term aim was to hammer out a postwar socialist doctrine. Its members, who included Simone de Beauvoir and Merleau-Ponty, met in hotel rooms or in studies in the Ecole Normale, where they typed out news-sheets. Sartre attempted to make contact with other groups so that they would snowball into a popular movement, a hope he later realised was naïve. Apart from the communist groups, which were backed by an organisation strong enough to keep them going, they all remained isolated and most, like Socialisme et Liberté, soon disintegrated. Sartre eventually decided the risks were too high and disbanded the group after a few months. Simone de Beauvoir's excuse for their rather minimal Resistance activity is that it was impossible for such groups to flourish or be effective in the occupied zone, but the problem also lay in their composition: they were made up of middle-class intellectuals 'without any experience of underground action – or indeed of action in any form'. Sartre's first attempt at political action, then, was shared with Simone de Beauvoir, for she took an active part in the group. This is the only time she ever admits to enjoying it: she loved the sense of fraternity and danger and threw herself heart and soul into it. It possessed two other characteristic aspects which she does not mention: it was a literary activity – of a sort – and it took place behind the scenes. It was to be her last authentically political activity for some years for although acutely aware of her new-found responsibility towards other people, she nevertheless concedes that she felt herself 'wholly incapable of action'.[2]

In 1943 the communists asked Sartre to join the C.N.E.[3] and she was delighted at the move: 'I was very glad we had emerged from our isolation'. Once she had published *L'invitée*, she was eligible to go to the meetings, but did not do so. There were two reasons for this, both of which are used as excuses for inaction on many future occasions. One was that she did not like the official, routine atmosphere of the meetings, and the other was that there was no need for her participation as well as that of Sartre: 'I was so completely in harmony with Sartre's views that my presence would simply have duplicated his, to no useful purpose. To go also struck me as both inopportune and ostentatious.' It was not until the mid-fifties that this pattern began to be broken, and then from time to time only, so it is worth looking at it more closely.

As far as we can tell, any political action by either or both of them originated with Sartre. She specifically states this in *Tout compte fait*, looking back over her life: 'It was Sartre, after he had come back from his camp, who took the necessary steps.'[4] Often she acted as a brake on these initiatives,[5] but he nearly always convinced her in the end that he was right, though not always that she should follow in his footsteps. She says that in those early days during the war she and Sartre were agreed that they had to fight capitalism, imperialism and colonialism in their writings *and if possible by their actions*. However she immediately cuts her commitment off from practicalities: 'I was intellectually committed in this struggle, but on the practical plane I was not very active.' Later, when Sartre was searching in the early fifties for practical solutions to man's situation, she was not interested, 'and at the same time I did not desire to play even the smallest political role'. Why was this? Her explanation is that the sheer boredom of congresses, committees, meetings, manifestos, discussions, was hard to bear.[6] There are possibly other reasons, which will be considered later in the light of what she actually did. Whatever they were, she had the perfect excuse for inaction in Sartre. He had thrown himself into politics as soon as it became possible at the end of the war and was engaged in action in a far more radical way than she was. Although they always discussed his attitudes, and she claims to have influenced them on occasion, it was he who carried out a kind of joint action on behalf of both: 'In this realm, I must talk about him in order to talk about us.' Even during the Algerian crisis, when she felt totally involved and later wished she had done more, she looked at the possibilities open to her – talking at meetings, writing articles – and concluded: 'I would only have been saying the same things as Sartre less well than he was saying them. I would have felt ridiculous following him like a shadow.' Sartre apparently agreed with her, on the grounds that their names were so closely linked that they were almost thought of as only one person.[7]

The activities that Simone de Beauvoir avoided were part of the public face of *engagement*, and tended to involve large gatherings of people. It was the more intimate, private tasks behind the scenes that appealed to her, particularly if they happened to be literary and involved a small group of friends working as a team. She therefore entered with enthusiasm into the launching and subsequent running of *Les Temps Modernes*. From 1943 she and Sartre had planned together with Merleau-Ponty this major expression of their commitment. Maurice Merleau-Ponty (1908–61) had been at the E.N.S. while they were there, and their lives had crossed once again during the war when Merleau-Ponty joined in Socialisme et Liberté. His doctoral thesis, *La phénoménologie de la perception* (1945), was an existentialist work and it was he who first made the connection between Marxism and existentialism. Sartre was considerably influenced by *Humanisme et terreur* (1947) in which Merleau-Ponty set out his position regarding the communists. Through it he convinced Sartre that a choice could be made between the U.S.A. and the U.S.S.R., and that the aims of the latter corresponded to their own wishes for a just and classless society. At this period he was closer to communism than Sartre and Simone de Beauvoir, but from 1950 their positions became reversed, the change first making itself felt when Merleau-Ponty refused to take sides over the question of the Korean war. This was the turning-point in their relationship. By 1953 he had withdrawn from politics and become immersed in his philosophical interests. The differences with Sartre came to a head when Merleau-Ponty published *Les aventures de la dialectique* in 1955, in which he criticised the political stance which Sartre had taken in 'Les communistes et la paix'. It provoked a reply from Simone de Beauvoir in *Les Temps Modernes* ('Merleau-Ponty et le pseudo-sartrisme'). The quarrel was patched up in a common opposition to de Gaulle in 1958.

Sartre and Simone de Beauvoir saw their work for *Les Temps Modernes* as a political activity that was the practical manifestation of their theoretical *engagement*: political in the sense that it would always define its position with regard to political and social events, but without aligning itself with a party. It was literary, but like all literature it had a social purpose. A review offers the possibility of immediate reaction to – and therefore influence on – events in the form of denunciation, support or response of some other type, which books cannot offer: 'in a review, it is possible to catch the news on the wing'. Much later, Sartre was still convinced that to be on the editorial staff of a paper was to have political power. The aim of the review, as expressed by Sartre, conformed absolutely to Simone de Beauvoir's notion of the purpose of literature: 'We would be hunters of meaning, we would speak the truth about the world and about our own lives.' In a sense this puts the review in the direct tradition of the French press for revealing scandals, although scandals were here seen not as transitory or peripheral phenomena but as fundamental to current society. The editorial of the first issue set out its aims, which were to be achieved by the usual 'truth-telling' and 'unmasking' method: 'In short, we intend to work together to produce certain changes in the society in which we all live.' Simone de Beauvoir emphasises that it was to be firmly located in the contemporary world. The name *Les Temps Modernes* (Modern Times) was intended to be indicative: 'The title was to convey our positive commitment to the present.' They believed that although some good reviews were being published, like *Esprit*, either they were inadequate to express the essence of the times, or they could be faulted on some other count. Mounier's review had similarities with *Les Temps Modernes*: it relied on subscriptions from friends so as not to be dependent on bourgeois financial backing with the consequent constraints on its policy, it was committed to the struggle against oppression, and it made independent judgments on the vital issues of the day. Presumably the *Temps Modernes* team felt that what was lacking was a similar journal which would not have *Esprit*'s commitment to spiritual renewal. Camus's paper *Combat* was not political enough, according to Sartre; it was too concerned with moral questions. Nevertheless the purpose of *Les Temps Modernes* was philosophical as well as political: 'we place ourselves firmly on the side of those who wish to change both the social condition of man and his conception of himself'.[8]

In September 1944 the editorial board was formed and included Aron, Merleau-Ponty, Simone de Beauvoir and Sartre. The first number appeared in October 1945. Its initial success happened to coincide with the unintentional 'existentialist offensive', as Simone de Beauvoir describes the appearance of two volumes of *Les chemins de la liberté*, the first issues of *Les Temps Modernes*, the production of *Les bouches inutiles*, and Sartre's lecture, 'L'existentialisme est un humanisme', all within a few weeks. Existentialism was suddenly fashionable and Sartre's notoriety can only have helped *Les Temps Modernes* to get off to a good start. Its success continued, and Simone de Beauvoir was delighted with her editorial task of selecting articles, as well as writing for the review herself. Once a week the editorial staff would see would-be contributors, or people bringing suggestions or even simply asking for advice, and once a week there was a conference to report on manuscripts and decide on publication or rejection. The personal aspect of this side of the work was mirrored in a sense by the public side of things in the articles she herself wrote: 'our polemics had the intimacy, the urgency and the warmth of family quarrels'. The choice of articles, as has already been stated, was aimed at pointing its readers in the direction of the political position taken by *Les Temps Modernes*, that is, a position firmly on the side of a kind of democracy which would alter the social and economic structures of France: 'In short, Marxism *faute de mieux*', Sartre called it. Although the review was not militant in its early years, it was committed to fighting with and for the proletariat against capitalism without giving its unconditional support to any party.[9]

Simone de Beauvoir has not herself written any *Temps Modernes* editorials but since she has been on the editorial board from its inception, she must be considered to share responsibility for the policy adopted. It is therefore instructive to look at the position taken on some of the major issues since the war. She asserts that they always kept an open mind, enabling themselves to remain detached and to judge in complete freedom each question as it arose, and attributes this ability to their philosophical training.[10] However, the claim to impartiality must be seen as operating within the general framework of a predominantly socialist view of the world. Two features are very noticeable and varied little with the political evolution of the review. The first is its absolutely consistent anti-colonialist stance, first demonstrated in an outspoken attack on French government policy towards Indo-China in an editorial signed '*Temps Modernes*' in December 1946. The review never faltered in its demand for independence to be given to all colonies and in its unconditional support for those who had been colonised against the colonisers. Its denunciation of the wars in Indo-China and later Vietnam, as well as Algeria, was unremitting. The second feature, sympathy with Marxism whether relations with the P.C.F. were currently good or bad, never precluded its being severely critical both of the Communist Party and of the U.S.S.R. when this was warranted by the situation. The first important example of this was its publication of information on the Soviet labour camps (November 1949–January 1950) followed by an editorial by Sartre and Merleau-Ponty denouncing them on the grounds that the Soviet system was not working as it should. Two other episodes stand out: the denunciation of the Soviet intervention in Hungary in 1956 with a triple issue (November 1956–January 1957) on Hungary, and a similar attack on the U.S.S.R. for its invasion of Czechoslovakia in 1968 (after which Sartre and Simone de Beauvoir never visited the Soviet Union again).

When there is a public issue considered of vital importance it has been usual for some years now for it to be the occasion of an editorial article signed *'Temps Modernes'* – for example the colonels' *coup d'état* in Greece in 1967, the repression in Chile following the overthrow of the Marxist government in 1973, the Arab–Israeli conflict in the same year. This collective responsibility for the political line taken implies a consensus of opinion on the editorial board, but it is noticeable that over the years there have been many changes of personnel which have largely corresponded to the evolution of the position adopted by its nucleus, and in particular by Sartre. Of the original team, Aron and another member left very early, in 1946, because of the attitude taken towards de Gaulle. Between 1945 and 1950 Sartre allowed Merleau-Ponty the greatest possible freedom in defining the political line and it was he who wrote the editorials. Merleau-Ponty was in Sartre's view 'much better orientated than I in the ambiguous world of politics'.[11] The Korean war in 1950, raising doubts in Merleau-Ponty's mind about communist intentions, was the start of a period of hesitation for *Les Temps Modernes* and there was a noticeable lack of definite policy for a couple of years.[12] Merleau-Ponty was withdrawing from politics just as Sartre was beginning to take the view that they were all-important. Convinced that he must now play an active political role, Sartre was coming to terms with communism. He was confirmed in his stance by the communist sympathisers Lanzmann and Péju who joined the review in 1952. Sartre had by now taken the political leadership from Merleau-Ponty who finally left the board in 1953, preceded by Etiemble in 1952, also because of disagreement about the political line. Between 1952, the year when Sartre started publishing 'Les communistes et la paix', and 1956, the review was both highly politicised and most closely aligned to the communists. Simone de Beauvoir had now been persuaded by Lanzmann, and by the hope of de-Stalinisation following Stalin's death in 1953, that this was the right direction to take, although she still had reservations. In 1956, the *rapprochement* came to an abrupt end with the Hungarian uprising. Criticism of the Communist Party now became outspoken and the emphasis was on the cause of de-Stalinisation, while at the same time there were attacks on Gaullism and the government policy in Algeria. After 1963 when it seemed to have been achieved, relations with the U.S.S.R. were more relaxed in an atmosphere of general *détente*. The Russian invasion of Czechoslovakia and the French student uprising of May 1968 ushered in the next phase of the review's policy. Attempts at reconciliation with the communists were now abandoned as was *entente* with Russia. *Les Temps Modernes* now sympathised with the various groups of the far left, and in particular with the Maoists. As a result of this *gauchiste* line adopted under the influence of Sartre and Gorz after the May events, two members of the board resigned in 1970, leaving what Simone de Beauvoir calls 'a reduced but homogeneous team'. Sartre described this remaining group in 1975 as having in common a whole past as well as similar thought processes and ways of expressing themselves. They were also set in their ways and the policy of the review was not likely to change as long as they were there: 'Their ideas have been elaborated over a long period of time. Their options are clearly defined, and they are not eager to change them.'[13]

The part played by Simone de Beauvoir has diminished with the years, but not significantly. As well as her work behind the scenes she took part in a series of broadcasts organised in 1947 by *Les Temps Modernes*. These radio programmes took the form of discussions amongst the group, and the subject was always political. They were soon banned, after a particularly vicious attack on de Gaulle, in which he was compared to Hitler. Simone de Beauvoir did not herself write articles for *Les Temps Modernes* after 1955, although some of her work has appeared there before publication in book form. She continued and still continues to select manuscripts

for publication and to attend the fortnightly meetings at which the
political line is decided and future numbers planned. This last
activity particularly pleases her: 'We are all friends, so the work
merges with the pleasure of conversation.' Since December 1973
she has been in charge of editing a feminist section of the review
called 'Le sexisme ordinaire'; women's liberation is a subject which
is dear to her heart. According to Sartre, her interest in and dedication to the review has not waned: 'She directs the magazine
scrupulously and firmly.' This has been her only long-term action,
carried out faithfully over the years. Sartre, on the contrary, had to
be dragged to the meetings in later years, but he explained his
reluctance in these terms: 'I would say that if I have been less
interested in it for some time now, it is because the magazine has its
own life. There are no more major decisions to be made, unless we
should decide to wind it up.' He felt that this was unlikely as it was
still, he claimed, a good review. In spite of its elitist character, he did
not wish to alter it, to make it into a kind of *Cause du Peuple*, for
instance. When Gorz suggested that one way to communicate with
the working classes might have been through *Les Temps Modernes*,
by aiming it not at an intellectual public but at the masses, publishing the sort of thing that appears in pamphlets and news-sheets
distributed in the factories, Sartre replied that he did not at the time
wish to abandon the sort of theoretical research which that type of
review necessitated and which was of no interest to the masses.
He was never very satisfied with the political items that appeared in
publications like *J'accuse* because the problem there is to find a way
of being understood by the working-class reader while still studying
a problem in depth or analysing an idea in all its aspects. 'In my
opinion the new style of intellectual must give everything to the
people today' – he did not know how, although he was sure it
was possible. It still remained a very elitist attitude. It also has to be
said that it was his blindness that forced him to give up completing
his work on Flaubert, not the knowledge that it could never be
appreciated by the very people he had always wished to reach.

Following the death of Sartre, the editorial board considered the
possibility of ceasing publication of *Les Temps Modernes*, since for
all of them it was essentially Sartre's review, but it was decided to
continue producing it after all. Simone de Beauvoir felt particularly
strongly that its continued existence was important, and this was
supported by many of its readers who wrote expressing their opposi-

tion to any suggestion of closure. No new editor has been named. The cover now bears the statement 'Fondateur: Jean-Paul Sartre', instead of 'Directeur: Jean-Paul Sartre'.[14]

In 1945 the communists began to sense the dangers of the suddenly flourishing existentialist philosophy and started their attacks on Sartre. For nearly six years he took no part in any of their activities and put his efforts entirely into *Les Temps Modernes* and his writing, through which he endeavoured to find a way across the gap that separated them. There was one attempt on his part at non-literary political activity during this period, and it was a failure. This strange episode deserves some attention as the only attempt for many years to group together the non-communist left into what was expected to become a powerful and possibly large-scale movement, the Rassemblement Démocratique Révolutionnaire. Simone de Beauvoir took no part; she did not have anything to do with its journal and as far as we know never became a member.[15] When it was first mooted she tried to dissuade Sartre on the grounds that he would be wasting his time and so she clearly had no faith in the outcome. However, from her account of the movement in *Les mandarins*, it is clear that she was very much involved in all the background discussions and shared the excitement, the hopes and the disappointments with Sartre. The conclusions they drew about the relationship of non-communist intellectuals of the left with the Communist Party stood for her as well as Sartre.

The R.D.R. was founded early in 1948 by a group of intellectuals including Altman, Rosenthal and David Rousset. Altman, a year later, claimed that it was started by 'certain activists of the left and far left, trade-unionists, journalists from working class newspapers, members of Parliament who were hostile to the reactionary policies of their own parties'. They invited Sartre to join them and in spite of Simone de Beauvoir's reservations, he did so: 'He told me he could scarcely preach commitment and then avoid it when he was offered the chance.'[16] The communists had rejected his support and there was no means of political involvement open to him just at the very time when he had decided that he must find a synthesis between his ideological position and action. Here was the political vehicle he needed.

The committee published an appeal for support in the press in February, and in March there was a press conference two days before the first general meeting. It was decided to start a paper since Altman, although a founder-member, would not make his paper, *Franc-Tireur*, into the organ of the movement. *La Gauche R.D.R.* was launched in May and appeared fortnightly at first but monthly from May onwards. According to Simone de Beauvoir the first issue 'was not particularly scintillating', largely because of lack of money. The aims of the R.D.R. were set out in the various numbers of the paper and later in *Entretiens sur la politique,* by Sartre, Rousset and Rosenthal, as well as at public meetings. They were, briefly: to work for peace by refusing to opt for the U.S.S.R. or the U.S.A., but for a neutral Europe; this Europe would mean international cooperation on a truly socialist basis; everything possible was to be done to help the workers towards direct participation in management; independence must be given to all overseas territories. The main recurrent theme is that of freedom, which is the watchword of all the articles on the front page of the first edition of *La Gauche*, summed up by Sartre's editorial: 'The primary aim of the Rassemblement Démocratique Révolutionnaire is to relate revolutionary demands to the concept of liberty.' For Sartre the R.D.R. meant principally '(1) Middle classes and proletariat...(2) Europe...(3) Political and economic liberty...'

The R.D.R. considered itself to be 'astride two classes' (the bourgeoisie and the proletariat), rejecting both Gaullism and Stalinist communism.[17] It was a 'rassemblement', not a new party, and it wished to draw support from all the parties on the left. It appeared to be fairly successful for a time, drawing large crowds to its public meetings, but the membership was probably only about 2,000 in mid-1948 and this had more than halved by the end of the year.[18] Gradually internal dissension began to grow as David Rousset and others moved towards the right and particularly towards a pro-American position. Rousset toured the U.S.A., returned to organise a *journée* in April 1949 which was American biassed and supported – Sartre refused to attend, following for once Simone de Beauvoir's advice – and took steps to procure funds from the U.S.A. There was more and more disagreement and Sartre finally resigned amid considerable publicity in October 1949. The movement soon folded up.

The reasons for its failure are multiple. In its attempt to be non-party and thus to reach a wide public, it achieved precisely the opposite and aroused the hostility of all the parties on the left. The communist campaign against it was violent, the S.F.I.O. (Section Française de l'Internationale Ouvrière, the French Socialist Party) decided to expel those who became members of the R.D.R., and other small socialist groups disagreed with its policies. According to Burnier 65% of its active members were not from other political organisations. Exclusiveness and ostracism have always been a feature of the French political system with its large number of parties, and this was especially true of that period. The large parties that are to be found in England and the U.S.A. are really themselves coalitions, albeit cohesive ones; in France with its relatively small parties the problem of self-definition was dominant. The R.D.R. also lacked funds, as Rousset had said, and its organisation was weak and very poorly structured. Internal dissension, as we have seen, was tearing it apart from within: the clash of personalities and viewpoints was particularly destructive in such a tiny organisation. The policy of the organisation, based on 'positive neutralism' (a contradiction in terms?), seemed to its leaders to be able to appeal to the widest possible audience, but the public was too diffuse and the message too vague, although Simone de Beauvoir calls it 'a definite policy'. The political conditions of the period were against it, as is shown by the lack of success of the 'neutral' candidates in the 1951 elections which followed not long afterwards. In fact, although it took time for Sartre to realise this, the international situation did not allow of neutralism: the movement was destroyed by the very cold war against which it was making a stand. According to Julienne-Caffié, Sartre was expecting too much in hoping to reconcile humanist culture with the necessity for action, and moreover the R.D.R. was ten years ahead of its time, both in anticipating the thaw in the cold war and in seeing the need for a non-communist movement on the left. Indeed Sartre has said that if the *gauchiste* groups had existed after the war, they would have provided an answer to his problems: 'If there had been a left-wing movement after the war, I would have joined it immediately.' For Sartre the failure of the R.D.R. was a hard lesson in realism and he had his own terse explanation: 'Splitting up of the R.D.R. Hard blow. Fresh and definitive approach to realism. One cannot *create* a movement.' Rousset had wanted to create a mass movement, Sartre a small but influential one. Sartre began to realise that he had been idealistic in believing that a relatively small group could have any effect. In fact what the R.D.R. had needed, according to him, was the vast organisation of the Communist Party in order to get sufficient support, but it was not possible to do anything similar to the Communist Party because two such organisations could not exist side by side.[19]

Sartre had understood that there was no possibility of creating a middle group in France; both he and Simone de Beauvoir saw the international situation in the same terms: 'It was now certain beyond doubt that there could be no third course between adherence to one of the two blocs.'[20] At the same time it was impossible to choose between them. The consequence was that Sartre 'had by now practically given up all political activity', and they both felt completely exiled: 'All political action had become impossible for us and even our writing was going to trickle away into the sand.' Simone de Beauvoir, writing *Les mandarins*, was as convinced as Sartre in 1951 that it would be acceptable neither to the right nor to the left. Yet it was this very realisation of what she calls 'the paradoxical quality of our situation'[21] that led to a change of attitude in Sartre and made him accept that he was powerless to change the world either by his own efforts or together with people who were as incapable as he was. He now felt that the only valid course of political action was for him to become aligned with the communists, and this is what he began to do between 1950 and 1952.

Les mandarins was not published until 1954, by which time a truce had already been declared between the Communist Party and Sartre and Simone de Beauvoir. Instead of being attacked by the right and by the left as she had feared, the book was welcomed by all; she was correct in believing that what she was writing about would find an echo in a large number of people. Putting into practice her definition of the writer as someone immersed in the times in which he lives, she describes in the novel her own very specialised milieu, that of the French intellectuals in the period stretching from 1944 to the early fifties.[22] These years were at first full of joy and hope. The real-life group, adjusting to normal life after the war and the Resistance, endeavouring to come out of their ivory tower and to construct a brave new world based on socialist and humanist principles, had great expectations about what could be achieved. At first they seemed to be succeeding. People of very different persuasions were working together: Aron with the *Temps Modernes* team, Sartre writing with Mauriac in *Le Figaro*, Sartre and Simone de Beauvoir contributing to Camus's *Combat*. Gradually it all disintegrated. By 1949 their hopes had been dashed to the ground as they found all avenues to action closed to them: 'the ground was littered with smashed illusions'. This failure, according to Simone de Beauvoir, enabled her to distance herself from her recent experience sufficiently to write about it and 'redeem that failure with words'. Not just her own experience but that of a whole circle which was disintegrating and whose shared hopes had been snuffed out: 'To talk about myself I had to talk about *us*, in the sense in which we used that word in 1944.'[23] The only way in which this ambiguous, contradictory, multiple-faceted, constantly changing, true situation could appropriately be communicated was in a novel. It is generally agreed that *Les mandarins* has no equal as a chronicle of what these postwar years meant to a particular coterie of people, observed and evoked by Simone de Beauvoir with sympathy and exactitude.[24]

The political, ethical and literary debates of these left-wing intellectuals, filled with hopes and beset by doubts, are faithfully recorded by Simone de Beauvoir. It is not a *roman à clef*, she insists; the characters cannot be identified as specific people and there is, for instance, something of Sartre in both Henri and Dubreuilh, and something of herself in Henri and Anne. But their aspirations, their attempts at action and their endless debates were all familiar to those who lived in that circle and mirrored it exactly. H. Stuart Hughes rather cynically states that 'her unremitting conversational exercises went on within a circle which was both personally and intellectually self-contained while believing that what it had to say was 'of supreme importance for the rest of humanity'.[25] Perhaps for a time they did believe they could change the world, but the debates that went on were largely personal in the sense that they felt morally obliged to do the right thing, if only they could be sure what that was, for their own peace of mind.

The left-wing intellectuals in *Les mandarins* are dramatically faced with the problem of how to reconcile a literary activity with the type of *engagement* that the war has taught them is necessary. How can they go on writing when political action is what is required of them? Henri, while not wishing to write propaganda, feels that he cannot write pure literature any longer. He tells Dubreuilh: 'You preached action, and action made me fed up with literature.' Dubreuilh disagrees. Henri, however he might feel about the need to act, has Simone de Beauvoir's dislike of politics (as has Anne): 'committees, conferences, congresses, meetings, talk, and still more talk. And it means endless manœuvring, patching up of differences, accepting crippling compromises, lost time, infuriating concessions, sombre boredom'. In fact, exactly what Sartre called 'la cuisine politique'. However, he has a way of acting, and that is through his paper, *L'Espoir*. The purpose of journalism is to influence public opinion, which (like Sartre in *Les Temps Modernes*) he tries to do without submitting to any one person or party, or defining any political programme: 'Obviously *L'Espoir* would eventually be forced to take a political stand – but would do it entirely independently.' Neither does he wish to dictate opinions to his readers, just 'teach them to judge for themselves'. There are disadvantages to this and in particular, as Dubreuilh points out, his wide public depends on his committing himself to no particular line, saying nothing that would embarrass anyone, and avoiding all the real problems. He wants Henri to remove this weakness by representing a political movement, his 'S.R.L.' (the equivalent of the R.D.R.). Henri eventually agrees – something that Sartre never did. Dubreuilh has thrown himself heart and soul into 'real' political action, the creation of the S.R.L. He describes his Resistance activity as 'négatif' and now his action will be positive: 'Today, it's a question of building, and that's much more interesting.' Unfortunately, the requirements of party politics involve him in over-simplifying issues and also fill his time so that he can no longer write. Whatever advice he might have given Henri, he has no time for such gratuitous activities when his new interest is absorbing, exciting, exhausting. Simone de Beauvoir explains that Sartre was never as frantic in his enthusiasm for any group as she made Dubreuilh, and that he never considered giving up writing.[26]

The major debates in *Les mandarins* centre round the problems of the intellectual who wishes to work for 'real' socialism while refusing to accept the dogmas of the Communist Party in terms of the national context, and the infallibility of the U.S.S.R. in the general framework of international socialism. With regard to making the choice between the U.S.A. and the U.S.S.R., the latter is usually given the benefit of the doubt (as in reality with Sartre and Simone de Beauvoir, in spite of their attempts at a neutral stand). In an argument between Scriassine and Dubreuilh we learn Dubreuilh's attitude: he considers that it would be fatal for France to be colonised by the U.S.A. (the implication being that this might well happen). But when Scriassine argues that it would be better than being taken over by the U.S.S.R., Dubreuilh merely asserts that Russia has no intention of annexing any country. The attitude is stated less equivocally in a discussion that Scriassine and his American friend have with Henri, when the latter says that if he had to choose between America and the U.S.S.R. he would choose the latter. But in fact the views of Henri and Dubreuilh on this matter reflect the ambivalence of the position of Sartre and Simone de Beauvoir. Towards the end of the book Henri is tempted to have nothing to do with the communists on the grounds that he only half believes in the cause for which he would be giving up his freedom: the U.S.S.R. is 'moche' ('lousy') compared with what it could be. Dubreuilh argues passionately that you cannot expect perfection. The real thing is never as immaculate as the pure idea, and so 'acceptance is always a matter of choice, love always a matter of preference'. You cannot expect perfection, but must work for it. This is the public position that Sartre took up in the early fifties.[27]

The whole question of unconditional support for the U.S.S.R. arises earlier in the novel, over the question of the Soviet labour camps and whether to break the news of their existence in *L'Espoir*. At first Henri hesitates to be convinced of the truth of the story because it would destroy the only hope there is for socialism – the U.S.S.R. But he decides, once convinced, to publish the truth, which is what he promised to his readers: 'It has to be brought out into the open. . . If not, I'll be an accessory to the crime.' In a discussion with Anne, who sees silence as playing the game of the communists and as abnegating his duty as an intellectual to tell the truth, Dubreuilh argues that by speaking out he would be helping the enemies of the U.S.S.R., that is all those who wish to preserve the world as it is. Anne (Simone de Beauvoir?) is much less indulgent towards the U.S.S.R. than he is: 'But what reason have you for thinking that the Russian cause is today still identified with the cause of humanity?' Dubreuilh believes that to publish would be to give ammunition to the right and alienate the party for ever but Henri's view is that if *L'Espoir* broke the news first it would give credibility to their attitude towards Russia of qualified support and that the whole point of remaining outside the Communist Party was to be able to speak out when necessary: 'I'm not a Communist precisely because I want to be free to say what the Communists don't want to say and can't say.' He publishes, and that is the start of a long estrangement between the two men. The reaction bears out Henri's sense that whatever he does appears to be wrong: 'You say a word against the Communist Party, and you're playing into the hands of the reactionaries! You criticise Washington, and you're a Communist.'[28]

The problem of whether or not to join the Communist Party preoccupies both men, and it can never be answered satisfactorily. This, together with the wider issue of whether to become fully aligned with either the U.S.A. or the U.S.S.R., is the impasse which dominates the book, and a large part of Sartre's and even Simone de Beauvoir's life. There are various points at which the fictional characters consider joining the party, for instance at the time of Hiroshima, when Dubreuilh believes it is vital to work for the unity of the left, but their reservations are too strong. For Henri, the greatest weakness of the party is to treat other people as if they were things instead of free, thinking individuals;[29] but at times he wonders whether, in view of all those in the world who are unable to discuss, judge, decide freely for themselves, the intellectual should not give up his individualism and 'submerge his will in the general will'. Anne sets out the impasse as she sees it for Dubreuilh: if he had to join the party because there was no other way, it would mean submitting to rules and regulations instead of making choices as he thought best, writing to order rather than with sincerity, and suppressing his own ideas about what is best for humanity. When he is closest to joining, he believes he could manage to keep his mouth shut if he had to, but Anne cannot see this happening, because to stop writing would be the equivalent of suicide for him. On the other hand to remain inactive and powerless to construct the future would be equally impossible: 'for Robert that would be living death'.

When Dubreuilh throws himself into the task of creating his own movement, the S.R.L., Anne for a time believes that he has found the answer, a happy balance between writing and action. It soon becomes obvious that the communists will only tolerate the existence of the S.R.L. as long as it remains small, works in the shadow of the Communist Party showing no signs of independence, and has no paper behind it. A movement with its own paper is dangerous. The attitude of the party is that any movement on the left apart from itself must be considered an enemy, even if the aim is to work with the party itself for unity on the left. And so the impasse is reached: 'He could neither give up his programme nor

maintain it against communist opposition, and there were no inter-
mediate solutions.' The S.R.L. folds up.[30]

It is really not at all surprising that the Communist Party should
have seen a movement like the S.R.L. (or the R.D.R.) as a threat.
If a *rassemblement* of individuals with similar aims is to be politically
effective, it must manifest that 'volonté collective' ('general will') of
which Henri is so fearful, and take on the characteristics of a
political party.[31] The communists knew this, but Sartre did not
seem to recognise that the wish to negate organised political parties
by creating such a movement was bound to be a failure. If individuality must be kept intact and not compromised in the general will
then an influential movement could not come out of it; if the movement was to be successful, individual freedom could not be preserved, except to a limited extent. Simone de Beauvoir's refusal of
participation in the R.D.R. may mean that her natural dislike of
such collective action enabled her to see this more clearly than Sartre,
and certainly her early feeling that Sartre was being too optimistic
about the possibilities indicates that this was so.

Besides the failure of the S.R.L. in terms of its relations with the
French Communist Party the situation was similar at the international level. Scriassine has always said that the French intellectuals
were caught between the U.S.A. and the U.S.S.R., and that there
is no middle way. Even Dubreuilh has wondered at times whether
his dream of a socialist Europe isn't utopian. Now he realises that
the S.R.L. never had any chance of success in promoting a neutral
Europe, because the world was already divided into the two blocs:
'we were trapped'. Dubreuilh's reaction to this failure on both fronts
is exactly the same as that of Sartre: 'I don't want to work with
the Communists or against them. What's left?' The only solution is
to give up politics: 'Politics and I – that's all over. I'm crawling
back into my hole.' He has begun to see the intellectual as having no
longer any role to play, and for the moment, the sort of literature in
which he had believed has no value. He will give up writing.[32]
However, the novel ends with new plans for future activity, and
clearly the renunciation will only be temporary.

Les mandarins is the perfect example of the sort of novel Simone
de Beauvoir had decided to write when she became critical of the
didactic and theoretical ('idealistic') style of some of her earlier
work. It has both feet planted in the real world of the postwar era
and its problems. The reality which it re-creates is ambiguous and

she does not suggest that there is any obviously right or wrong answer to the problems over which her characters hesitate. She believes that this makes for better literature, and few would contest the view that *Les mandarins* is one of her best books, combining all aspects of her work: romantic fiction, autobiography, political testimony, and existentialist philosophy.[33]

There was another type of literary work in which Simone de Beauvoir endeavoured to 'bear witness' during the period up to 1955. This took the form of accounts written as the result of travelling to other countries, in which she details her personal reactions and tells the reader what she believes to be the facts. The two works in which she does this are *L'Amérique au jour le jour* and *La longue marche*. Even earlier, at the beginning of 1945, she had made her first postwar journey outside France, to Spain and Portugal, later recounted in fictional form in *Les mandarins*. On her return she wrote an article for *Combat-Magazine* on Madrid under her own name, and two on Portugal for *Combat* upnder a pseudonym so as not to compromise her brother-in-law, who worked at the French Institute in Lisbon and who had arranged her lecture tour. She says that she had grateful letters from private individuals and protests from official sources, but it seems odd that she should expect to have much effect using a pseudonym, when she believed that the value of such criticism depended largely on the fame of the author.

Simone de Beauvoir spent several months in America at the beginning of 1947. *L'Amérique au jour le jour*, published the following year, is a chronological account of her stay there, with digressions on general questions as they arise, but showing the evolution of her views as her journey progressed. It is deliberately subjective. Her intention was 'to relate...how America revealed itself to a single conscience day by day: my conscience'. Nevertheless it also claims to be factual: 'A faithful testimony'. The result is a lively, readable, striking picture of the U.S.A., but one that is incomplete. This arises from the fact that for the most part she mixed only with marginal groups: writers, artists, coloured intellectuals, French nationals. She was still able, in spite of these limited contacts, to throw light on certain aspects of American society for her readers. Two of these are of particular interest: the condition of life of the coloured population, and the commitment of American intellectuals.

She sees the situation of the American negro in terms of the oppressed and the oppressor.[34] The idealistic side of every American is seen in the theoretical stress put on absolute equality and the principles of freedom, but this credo is belied by the flagrant denial of these rights to the black population. This is justified by the whites on grounds of the mentality of the negroes, their intellectual and physical inferiority, and their lack of culture. Simone de Beauvoir refutes each of these arguments, and finds in them the common factor that they are all arguments used by other oppressors (French colonists, for example) about every other subjugated race. She puts the attitude of the whites down to fear: the black community spells danger, and must be kept in its place, segregated, so that any relationship with it is distant. The guilt felt by the whites at the discrepancy between their democratic ideals and their treatment of negroes explains their use of arguments that will rationalise this. The resultant anger, protests and hatred among the blacks is something that Simone de Beauvoir experiences directed at herself when she is made to feel out of place in a bar in New Orleans frequented by blacks. There she is considered an enemy and she feels guilty, merely because she is white: 'we were enemies through no fault of our own, yet responsible in spite of ourselves by the colour of our skins and all it implied'.[35]

Her observations on American intellectuals of that period are particularly interesting in view of the sharp contrast they present with the French committed intellectual of the postwar era. Simone de Beauvoir is astounded by the way all American students and intellectuals abstain from political and social matters apart from a few writers (most of whom are non-academic and have never seen the inside of a university). The *literati* and the philosophers, she asserts, do not consider they have any human or political responsibilities. The indifference to political events displayed by people in all walks of life appals her, and on occasion she has to wait to join French expatriates before she can discuss the news of the day. She sees this passivity as having several causes. Sometimes it is fear at being branded as 'Reds' and having their careers ruined which prevents them from speaking out, even when they are outraged by events. Often (and here the problem is conceived in existentialist terms) it is the result of the American aversion to making choices which might imply, as choices do, weighty responsibilities: 'they could not even imagine a situation in which they might be required to acknowledge the existence of evil'.[36]

They have not understood that by refusing to take the risk they are refusing the only means of fighting evil. For the most part, though, it is because they have a feeling of utter impotence in the face of the vast machine that is America, and cannot imagine being able to influence the course of history. This defeatism leads to a vicious circle: 'Nobody can do anything, for everyone thinks he can do nothing; fatalism triumphs as soon as you believe that.' There are those, however, who speak out, following what she calls 'a tradition of self-criticism in America', in a spirit of love for their country. She expresses the hope that this will not be stamped out in the growing phenomenon of McCarthyism.[37]

Burnier quotes Jean Touchard's comments that Simone de Beauvoir is harder on America than Claude Roy, who was a communist, in his nearly contemporaneous book, *Clés pour l'Amérique*.[38] She certainly denounces the incomplete realisation of the democratic ideal as well as the various manifestations of capitalism, and her critical comments drew violent reactions from American critics. But what is surprising is the way she seems able to divorce her fierce criticism and loathing of the abstract notion of the U.S.A. from her love of the real America which she experienced, its natural scenery, its man-made towns, and the warmth of the American people in general as well as the individuals she met. It is this enthusiasm and delight that bring America alive and remain in the mind after reading the book.[39]

One of Simone de Beauvoir's intentions in writing *L'Amérique au jour le jour* was to open people's eyes to what was wrong with the U.S.A. by passing on her own experiences. The aim of *La longue marche*, written as a consequence of her visit to China in 1955, was also to relate the facts by means of an impartial account, but from exactly the opposite starting point. It was an attempt to dissipate Western hostility towards China and to present a reply to the anti-Chinese propaganda to which her readers were used and which they accepted through ignorance. It was to be a work of 'demystification' with a political aim. In order to present China in perspective, highlighting the transformation under communism by comparison with the past, she undertook a massive programme of research. The result is a book that is weighed down with long studies of the peasantry, the family, the industrialisation programme, the revolt against elitist culture. Her own knowledge was not sufficiently specialised in all these fields to make these sections very successful, in spite of her efforts to fill the gaps. She herself recognised already in 1963 that it was partly out of date; she also saw later that it was largely 'a re-hash', and it is one of her works that she would now happily discard. As an impartial account, it shows signs of an effort on her part to present a fair picture. Some of it is devoted quite specifically to contradicting the accounts presented by previous travellers to China who were hostile to the Revolution. On the other hand she objects strongly to the automatic admiration of those visitors who were prejudiced in its favour. The latter are blind to the inadequacies of what has already been achieved and the problems that still exist. China, she says, must not be judged on what it is now: 'In this country which is ceaselessly on the move, the present derives its meaning from the past it has left in its wake, from the future it is ushering in.' She appears to be somewhat naïve herself on occasions, accepting without question the explanation given her. Later she was less happy with the propaganda coming out of China, and she has now become more critical, while retaining her sympathy.[40]

It was in 1955 that Simone de Beauvoir undertook the first of a series of what was for her a new type of activity. She joined Sartre in some of his work by attending certain congresses – partly, one suspects, because they involved travelling abroad. The first was the Congress of the World Peace Movement at Helsinki. Sartre had been active in the movement for some time; this time she decided to go with him: 'my political evolution had led me to a point where I wanted to take part in that event', she says. It was a moving experience, especially the fact that, with the end of the cold war, they were now able to travel in Eastern Europe: 'the realms of socialism were now part of our world'. The Congress sessions bored her with their interminable speeches, but she notes the effort made by everyone to be conciliatory. In July 1963 she and Sartre were invited to Leningrad to the Congress of the C.O.M.E.S., the Communauté Européenne des Ecrivains, an organisation for encouraging contacts and exchanges of views between European writers from the two blocs. The cultural situation had begun to deteriorate in the U.S.S.R. and the Congress started with Soviet writers attacking the 'decadent' literature of the West. On the whole, she confesses, there was no exchange because neither side listened to the other. Afterwards the French delegation was invited to spend the day with Kruschev, who harangued them about Soviet literature, apparently because he had been forewarned by Thorez about 'these dangerous anti-communists'. They attended another C.O.M.E.S. meeting in Rome in October 1965. The third example of her participation was the Russell Tribunal protesting against the war in Vietnam. This was held in 1967 in two parts, in Stockholm and then in Copenhagen. When Sartre and Simone de Beauvoir originally agreed to be on the Tribunal they did so on the understanding that it would be held in Paris and that they need not attend all the sessions. In the event, it turned into a much more extended exercise, with Sartre chairman of the executive committee. The organisation was chaotic, but eventually it took place, and although it involved far more than they had anticipated, Sartre and Simone de Beauvoir became fully committed to carrying it through: 'we had become deeply involved and we were ready to devote ourselves to it unreservedly'.[41] The war in Vietnam was now at the forefront of her thoughts and she was revolted by the official American attitude towards the people of that country, so it was not surprising that she should feel it important to do something. Yet apart from appearing on Swedish television with Sartre and others at the end of the Tribunal, she does not seem to have taken an active part, other than attending the lengthy and exhausting meetings assiduously; indeed she never seems to have spoken at any of these congresses. Sartre conceded later (1975) that the Tribunal had had very little effect other than to allow people to judge for themselves what was going on.

Running parallel to her interest in these conferences, there was a further concern that occupied Simone de Beauvoir's attention ever-increasingly for more than five years, and which elicited from her more political action than she had ever been prepared to take before: the war in Algeria.

In 1955, at the World Peace Movement Congress in Helsinki, the Algerian delegation had met with the French to reveal to them the situation in Algeria, where the insurrection had spread throughout the country, and had asked the French to negotiate. The French delegation was divided about the question, and nothing came of it. Sartre was silent since his own knowledge was too limited. Francis Jeanson had already written criticising French colonialism in Algeria in *Les Temps Modernes* in 1950, and in 1955, together with his wife, had produced a book that supported the revolution (*L'Algérie hors la loi*). In 1956 he helped to shelter militants of the Front de Libération Nationale (F.L.N., the Algerian terrorist organisation fighting for independence) and soon became responsible for the funds of the F.L.N. in France. Jeanson claims that when Sartre and Simone de Beauvoir learned of his clandestine activities in 1957 they were not willing to help, partly because Sartre disapproved initially of the violence of the Algerian rebels.[42] Simone de Beauvoir, on the other hand, says that it was because they felt that although in Algeria one had to choose between the alternatives of the F.L.N. or fascism, it was different in France: 'we still believed that it was possible to work for their independence by legal means'. Presumably this was because they felt that this was preferable to violence. When writing of their attitude, she asserts that in 1956 they were among the handful of people in France who were accused of being anti-French because they refused to become indignant about F.L.N. methods. At this time, the communists were not willing to support the rebels, and when Sartre attempted to get the World Peace Movement to condemn the war, the Soviet delegate argued that it was not a war of aggression by the French. Sartre was already writing articles and going to meetings, but as usual she left it to him, unwilling to accompany him like a shadow. When writing about it in the winter of 1961 she felt that she would now have thrown herself into this sort of activity: 'Today, however little it might affect the outcome, I could only throw all my weight into the struggle. In those days, I still wanted to feel that an effort would not be in vain before I was willing to make it.' They still did not wish to do anything that seemed to be a denial of their own country, putting themselves into the category of traitors. She confesses that this argument was an excuse and that behind it lay 'something inside me – timidity, vestiges of mistaken beliefs', which prevented her taking that step.

Gradually she began to play a part. In January 1958 she testified as a character witness for a former pupil accused of a bombing, and helped to have her death sentence commuted. In May and June, she and Sartre took part in anti-Gaullist demonstrations. By this time they were working with the communists in a 'Comité de résistance contre le fascisme'. She reproached herself for her inactivity, made the usual excuses, and decided that she would do more on their return from a visit to Italy. She then helped to organise further demonstrations in the autumn, but her local branch of the committee was badly organised and very vague. One of the communists there pointed out the similarity of the real-life situation to *Les mandarins*: ' "It's exactly the same situation, the same problem: with us or against us. . ." I answered: "Yes, and the same solution: we're *obliged* to work with you." ' She involved herself more: 'I'm still being "militant": writing posters, lectures, articles', she wrote in her diary. The inverted commas show that she did not consider this to be real action. In the meantime, she and Sartre were coming round to Jeanson's point of view and began to see the political as well as moral justification for his action. By the time he created his movement, Jeune Résistance, in September 1958, she really believed that clandestine action was the only way for anyone who needed to express anti-colonialist convictions – but she herself was incapable of it: 'I admired those who took part in such action. But to do so demanded total commitment, and it would have been cheating to pretend that I was capable of such a thing. I am not a woman of action; my reason for living is writing; to sacrifice that I would have had to believe myself indispensable in some other field. Such was not by any means the case.' This seems an extraordinary statement for someone who had proposed, in theory, an existentialist philosophy of action. Action was always left to others, while she was absolved from doing what she did not want to do by the conviction that it would have been useless anyway.

Probably Simone de Beauvoir's most important undertaking during the whole of the Algerian crisis was her effort on behalf of Djamila Boupacha. The aspect of the war that had most appalled her, right from the time of the first rumours about it, was the use of torture by the French army against Algerians. As more and more proof came to light about what was going on, the situation seemed more and more horrifying. It is not surprising that this was a cause for which she was willing to act. Gisèle Halimi, a barrister who often defended Algerians on trial, contacted her, asking her to write an article demanding an enquiry into the tortures to which Djamila Boupacha, the Algerian girl accused of terrorism, had been subjected. Simone de Beauvoir wrote an article in *Le Monde*, after which she helped to form and became President of a 'Comité pour Djamila Boupacha', which launched a press campaign. She then lent her name to Gisèle Halimi's book on the case, and wrote a foreword for it. In this she pointed out that there was widespread torture two years after Malraux had declared that it had been stopped, implying that de Gaulle was simply unable to control the army. She appealed to readers to take political action. Since they no longer had the excuse of ignorance they must now refuse to countenance torture and also, by a logical consequence, the very war in whose name it was carried out.[48]

From 1955 to 1960 *Les Temps Modernes* had published many articles against the Algerian war, but without apparently envisaging any very precise way of combating it. There were three types of article: appeals for negotiation, statements from witnesses about Algeria, and analyses of the situation. Once Jeanson's network was blown in February 1960, Sartre and others began to support him publicly, and the review came out clearly in favour of the F.L.N. and its violent tactics, on the grounds that reasonable argument had up till then proved powerless to affect the situation. At first there were violent attacks from all quarters, and Jeanson and his allies were completely isolated. Eventually there was evidence of growing support for their viewpoint, culminating in the *Manifeste des 121*, published in September 1960, just before the trial of certain members of Jeanson's ring. This was a declaration affirming the right to refuse compulsory military service in the Algerian war, and was signed by almost all the *Temps Modernes* staff, including Simone de Beauvoir, but also by many others in the world of literature, theatre, cinema, and the arts in general. Only a small number of people would commit illegalities as a result, she felt, but 'we thought that this piece of avant-garde action might create serious repercussions'. In all, 124 other intellectuals added their names later, but interest faded as the autumn went on. Sartre and Simone de Beauvoir put the anti-war viewpoint during tours abroad, for instance in Brazil. Throughout 1961 more demonstrations and manifestos followed: Simone de Beauvoir talked to students at Antony and later lectured in Belgium. Sartre, together with the communists, founded the 'Ligue pour le rassemblement anti-fasciste', and Simone de Beauvoir demonstrated with them. All these activities were fairly riskless in themselves. Repressive measures had been taken against certain signatories of the *Manifeste des 121*, and while Sartre and Simone de Beauvoir were in Brazil, the French Embassy spread rumours that they would be arrested on their return. This did not happen, although they attempted to provoke it partly because they felt that all signatories should receive the same treatment and partly to gain publicity for their cause. It is said that it was de Gaulle who intervened, declaring: 'One doesn't arrest Voltaire.' The fact is that they were now establishment figures, like it or not. There was really little chance that they would be hounded, either on this or on later occasions when they attempted to goad the authorities into treating them like ordinary people.[44] Their stand on Algeria certainly earned them the attention of the O.A.S., the secret army fighting to keep Algeria French, and there were plastic bomb attacks made on Sartre's home. These could have had serious consequences, but in the event only property was damaged. Such attacks were, of course, made on many journalists, politicians, writers and academics of the left.

After their initial, lengthy hesitancy with regard to the Algerian problem, they had committed themselves totally to the cause of the F.L.N. This was understandable in view of the fact that by this time France was polarised into two camps, the partisans of *Algérie française* who supported the settlers in their wish to see Algeria remain part of France, and those who argued for independence and for whom the only legitimate rulers of Algeria were the indigenous Moslems. For this reason Sartre and Simone de Beauvoir condemned out of hand the position taken by Camus who refused to take sides and eventually retreated into silence, at which point their estrangement from him became complete. What they ignored totally or forgot was that Camus had championed the cause of the Algerian Moslems as long ago as the 1930s, proposing specific reforms to end the injustice of colonialism as it was practised there. It was because of his insistence on continuing this support for Moslem nationalists that the Communist Party expelled him after a volte-face in party policy. He had called for more reforms in 1944–5 through *Combat*, and in 1955–6 he had been one of a group of people including F.L.N. members who saw the crisis looming and made largely unpublicised efforts to limit it by means of a civilian truce before it went too far, risking his life at the hands of right-wing *pieds-noirs*. But Camus, whose main aim was to avoid violence and who on humanist grounds believed that no one section of the community should be sacrificed in this struggle, was soon also defending the rights of the French Algerians, themselves in danger now. In Simone de Beauvoir's view this meant that 'the humanist in him had given way to the *pied noir*', a very unfair criticism in view of what we now know of him but understandable in view of her state of mind at the time. Integration with France was the solution he favoured as being the only one that could safeguard the rights of all who were involved. Unfortunately the reformist campaign was ineffective in preventing the violence from escalating and by the time Simone de Beauvoir and Sartre began to concern themselves with the problem it was clear that such a compromise solution had become impossible. However, much as she condemned Camus's theoretical position, his action resembled hers in a way that is not generally known. He made personal efforts to help individuals and on several occasions intervened on behalf of Moslems who had been imprisoned even, according to friends, approaching de Gaulle more than once to ask for pardons.[45]

Eventually peace was concluded with the Evian agreement of March 1963, and a long, dark period in Simone de Beauvoir's life was over, not without marking her. Not only did their initially isolated position on the left lead to what she calls their exile in their own country, but gradually they began to feel that their convictions cut them off from the majority of their fellow countrymen as well as from certain individuals like Camus. With Simone de Beauvoir this turned into an almost physical repulsion, and she could not bring herself to mix with them in the streets: 'I could no longer bear my fellow citizens'. Paris seemed to her to be an occupied city once again, and everyone was guilty of indifference, hypocrisy, or complicity: most of all herself, by association and by the mere fact that she was French. She loved France and it was intolerable for her to be disloyal. The referendum accepting a new constitution in September 1958 had severed her from her country, and by 1961 she could no longer bear to travel in France, where every scene filled her with bitterness and humiliation. In 1961, more and more distressed by the tortures and killings, both in Algeria and even around her in Paris, she had nightmares each night and awoke every morning 'filled with pain and rage'. Powerless to do anything, she sometimes thought that death would be better than this ignominious existence in a world that was horrible: 'the mysterious and untamable force was that of time and circumstance, it was... threatening my past, my life, all that makes me what I am with total destruction'. She had begun to wonder in 1960 whether she would ever be able to love her country again, but at a mass demonstration for the funeral of demonstrators killed at an anti-O.A.S. march in February 1962, she experienced once again warmth and companionship when surrounded by a crowd of her fellow countrymen. Looking back over this period when writing the last few pages of *La force des choses* in 1963, she explains how she had felt compromised and guilty by association with the privileged classes because she was not one of the oppressed herself: 'that is the reason why living through the Algerian war was like experiencing a personal tragedy'. But it was also because at that time she was acutely aware that nothing she could do was of any effect: 'When one lives in an unjust world there is no use hoping by some means to purify oneself of that injustice; the only solution would be to change the whole world, and I don't have that power.' Indeed, for all her sense of guilt and total involvement, what she did was in the end minimal and its effect and influence questionable: she was right to feel pessimistic about action.[46]

Between 1962 and 1968 Simone de Beauvoir stood aside from events in her own country, of which she was not proud. She was interested in a few areas only but 'none of these things affect me directly.'[47] The next important period in her life began in 1968 with the events of May, when student protests about university conditions suddenly escalated, spreading into all sectors of the community. These were significant, not for the part played in them by Sartre and Simone de Beauvoir, but for precisely the opposite reason, their influence on the two of them. In practical terms Sartre did very little and Simone de Beauvoir even less. Like most people they only began to realise what was happening in March, with the student occupation of the administration block at the Nanterre campus. The riots of the night of 6th May seemed to demonstrate that these new erupting forces could not be contained by repression: 'My friends and I hoped that they were going to shake the regime and perhaps even bring it down.' On the 9th Sartre and Simone de Beauvoir signed a manifesto, together with many University staff, supporting the students in their wish to 'escape from an alienated establishment by every possible means'. Sartre spoke on the radio on the 11th, supporting the students' action in attempting to destroy the University system. When the Sorbonne was occupied, Simone de Beauvoir often visited it, wandering around, listening to debates and marvelling: never could she possibly have imagined 'such a party'. On the 20th Sartre was invited to speak to students there; she accompanied him, but took no part. This was the sum of their activities. When the strikes and sit-ins were over and the elections a landslide victory for de Gaulle, she recognised the failure of the revolt: 'the revolution was still-born'. Unlike Simone de

Beauvoir, Cohn-Bendit and the core of the student agitators claimed they had always known the limits of what they could achieve: the revolution would not happen in a day and this was only a beginning. Simone de Beauvoir saw it as 'the crisis...of society as a whole', and drew from the relative success of a determined minority her conclusion that the necessary element for a successful revolution was the creation of 'a vanguard capable of carrying a revolution in the developed capitalist countries through to a successful conclusion'.[48]

The events of May 1968 were originally triggered off by anti-party revolutionary individuals like themselves and the spontaneous chain reaction was precisely the sort of consequence they would have liked their own actions to have produced. But although it might be argued that they had contributed to the possibility of such an occurrence, they had not been responsible. In Sartre's words: 'May 1968 occurred quite apart from me – I didn't even see it coming.' Cohn-Bendit and his group had immediate specific grievances that struck a chord in their fellow students; Sartre and Simone de Beauvoir had a view of the future that was not focussed on immediate improvements but on a general and total reversal of the present situation. On the other hand the effect on them of the events was considerable. It is not unreasonable to claim, as Axel Madsen does, that May '68 'totally radicalised' Sartre and Simone de Beauvoir, and that the fact of the younger generation's doing the things they had written about for years and challenging their very existence as intellectuals led them to 'a decade of radical involvement in French affairs'.[49] If Simone de Beauvoir declares: 'I must confess that I am not one of those intellectuals who were deeply shaken by 1968', she means by this that it did not alter her conception of the role of the intellectual as it did for Sartre, since she had been aware of and had accepted its contradictions for some years. In spite of what she says, the practical result was to draw her into a renewed involvement with what was going on in France and in particular with new left-wing movements that had sprung up. They both kept up their contacts with the *gauchistes* after the events, and offered them space in *Les Temps Modernes* to express their various viewpoints; the offer was refused on the grounds that the review had become an institution. But Sartre had been excited by the revelation that there was a significant left to the left of the Communist Party, and gradually began to see this as a hope for the future. Simone de Beauvoir joined with him in some of his involvement in this area, and one episode in particular stands out for the very untypical action she took.

Various news-sheets had appeared as a result of May '68, a sort of underground press, mostly Maoist. In 1970, the arrest of the editors of one of these, *La Cause du Peuple*, and the confiscation of copies of the paper, resulted in clashes and protests. A young Maoist, Pierre Victor, came and asked Sartre to take over the paper as editor in order to allow it to continue. He agreed. As a protest against the imprisonment of three of their selling force, he and Simone de Beauvoir went into the streets to sell copies. On two occasions they were arrested together with other offenders by the unwilling police, but were not prosecuted and were allowed – indeed asked – to go but refused to leave the police station before the others were released. Simone de Beauvoir's view was that this proved that there was one law for the well known and one for the rest. Together with Michel Leiris, she formed the 'Association des Amis de *La Cause du Peuple*'. Sartre took over other papers in due course – *Tout!* and *La Parole au Peuple* – and gave help to the provincial *Secours Rouge*; she agreed to become the editor of *L'Idiot International* in September 1970, a nominal post to obviate threatened trouble. In spite of this the former editor was arrested. She resigned a few months later because she couldn't support the opinions being put forward in it.

Simone de Beauvoir wrote articles for these various papers. She was particularly pleased to have carried out an enquiry for *J'accuse* into an accident caused by negligence at a factory at Méru, because she herself learned a lot from her visit and because she felt the public ought to be informed about such scandals. She also enjoyed the human contact with the people she interviewed. More surprisingly, she and Sartre lent their names to various articles, not written by them but sent in from various parts of the country, and mostly of little merit.[50] It seems that by this stage she was ready to sacrifice her principles in the cause of revolution, and lend her name to protect the weak. She felt it was very important that the *gauchiste* press should exist, because the bourgeois papers never reported the things that really concerned the workers. For example one of the main purposes was to inform the workers of what was going on in their own class, so perhaps she felt the procedure was justifiable in view of the intended readership. It still seems to be a denial of her idea of what it meant to her to be a writer, perhaps warranted in her own eyes because she sees the help she was able to give to the *gauchiste* press as minor services rendered to the young in *their* struggle. She had many reservations about the Maoists, but she sympathised with them and found entirely admirable their refusal to accept the system. They aroused reactions and awakened public opinion, and they were unconventional in looking to new groups within the proletariat – young people, women, foreigners, provincials. To her it seemed in 1972 that they constituted an *avant-garde* who, if circumstances changed, would have a revolutionary role to play. Although she is still sympathetic she keeps her distance, criticising especially their unquestioning acceptance of a system about which they know virtually nothing.

For various reasons, which will shortly become clear, Simone de Beauvoir played no part in Sartre's next great venture, the launching of a new people's daily in May 1973, *Libération*. It was to be a paper which, unlike *L'Humanité*, had direct contact with the people for whom it was written: they would furnish the news, which would be written up by journalists after volunteers had looked at each story and interviewed the people concerned. There was even a readers' forum – four pages left to readers' own items – a section which soon got out of hand and began to look like the personal columns of *The Times*.[51] It was to be the only 'free' daily not financed by a bank or by advertising, 'free to say anything, to publish anything'. This led it into considerable financial difficulties but it has survived. Behind the idea of journalism by the people, for the people (corresponding to what he had always felt to be the gap, the failure in his own writing), was the ideological aim: 'The paper is intended to help to raise the level of consciousness among revolutionaries, most of whom still lack a theoretical base for their action.' By defining 'revolutionary man', that is, the socialist man of the future, *Libération* would aid this transformation, thus fulfilling Lenin's role for the intellectual.[52] After one year Sartre had to give up editing the paper, and all the other news-sheets he sponsored, because of ill health.

In the meantime, from 1970 onwards, Simone de Beauvoir had become involved in quite a different range of activities which were not strictly political and which were entirely new in another way: they were entered into and carried out quite independently of Sartre. These included all kinds of campaigning for better social conditions in France, over a wide range of areas from prison reform to the treatment of old people, the most important being the emancipation of women. Her writing has virtually come to a halt. She senses that her *œuvre* is behind her now. Apart from the physical difficulty at her age of undertaking a major work requiring research, she does not at present envisage feeling the urge to write anything more than the occasional short piece and indeed she stated in 1978 that she had said all she wanted to say and nothing new would be added.[53]

Apologists for Simone de Beauvoir are eager to point out that she has not always avoided action. André Michel claims without any apparent irony, in the film of her life, that because she took part in demonstrations during the Algerian crisis and appeared as a member of the Russell Tribunal, this proves that 'there is no gap between her thought and her action'.[54] He would be hard put to it to find other examples to add to the list, if action is to be understood in its generally accepted sense. It is clear that Simone de Beauvoir always rejected that degree of public political activity that was the logical corollary of her strong moral disapproval of existing society and her inward sense of the possibility of a radical alternative. Why? Clearly it is largely a matter of temperament: she could never take the plunge into political involvement with power, into the market place of power in action. She finds the political activity open to intellectuals tedious in the extreme, but there is more to it than that. What she does not spell out is the fact that she is an intensely private person, hating public appearances and collective action on any scale. This is quite obvious from her concentration on all activities that are behind the scenes and that involve personal contacts with individuals, even if they are strangers, and working with a small and intimate group of friends as in Socialisme et Liberté and *Les Temps Modernes*. If we remember also that mass action was not necessary for her, as it was for Sartre, in order to solve the problem of man's relationship with other men, then her refusal to be militant becomes totally comprehensible.

This does not mean that she denied the necessity for political action; it is simply that she was happy to leave it to other individuals of whom Sartre was one. When she insists: 'I have not lived through him', one of the implications is that she personally did not feel the need to do all the things she left to him.[55] She even accomplished a sense of action for herself through characters she created, like Jean Blomart in *Le sang des autres*, just as Sartre achieved through Goetz what he could not do personally. A basic problem seems to have been that she was never very sure that any action would lead anywhere. *Tous les hommes sont mortels* epitomises her ambivalence: she may have believed with Armand in the need for human endeavour even if the outcome might not be successful (this, after all, is her thesis in *Pour une morale de l'ambiguïté*), but she takes Fosca's more pessimistic view of the possibility of success. The difficulty of achieving anything for one's fellow men, which is the keynote of Fosca's despair, clearly always affected her personal view of the efficacy of political action; she felt acutely that it was often futile. On more than one occasion her own hesitations, or her attempts to dissuade Sartre, were the result of a refusal to make an effort which she saw as vain.

However much one may look for rational explanations of Simone de Beauvoir's avoidance of action, and in spite of the fact that she has tried to justify it on various grounds in the past, one thing becomes quite clear from comments made more recently in the film about herself. She is now quite explicit about not experiencing any sense of duty that might make her active participation seem imperative. Quite the contrary. Describing the events of May 1968, she first of all justifies not having joined the students on the barricades, although excited and sympathetic towards what they were doing, by saying that it was not her place because she was neither a student nor a teacher. She then goes on to say that in any case she *did not want to*, and 'one must also follow one's own inclinations and desires'. The ultimate excuse is used when she goes back over the Algerian crisis. She says that she supported Jeanson's activities, but 'although I was totally involved I was not very active myself because after all *I am an intellectual*'.[56] It seems that she is now arguing that the committed intellectual's obligations do not extend very far beyond doing what he feels like and giving moral support from the wings to other intellectuals who do not conceive of their duty in such a limited manner.

There is another side to this whole question which is of paramount importance to Simone de Beauvoir. Her inability to sustain practical action is a matter of considerable regret to her when she considers the individual and humanitarian achievements of some people. She is filled with awed admiration for those who have gone out and 'dirtied their hands' working in difficult conditions among the people: Simone Weil, for example, or the nun Renée du Brésil.[57] Simone Weil, she feels sure, would not reciprocate her admiration.

Remembering that in her view *non-engagement* was *antihuman-isme*, so *engagement* is theoretical commitment to improve the lot of humanity, and the translation of commitment into action on a personal and individual basis for particular cases, particular people. This view finds its expression in *Les mandarins*, in Anne's confession of her lack of patience with the slow progress of the revolution. Sartre claimed that it takes a long time for ideas to have any effect or influence. Simone de Beauvoir, like Anne, can't wait: 'And then the future seems so very far off; I find it hard to become interested in men who aren't born yet. I would much rather help those who are alive at this very moment.'[58] The revolution may be inevitable but it is too distant and what matters is the here and now. Social rather than political action is the sustained characteristic of Simone de Beauvoir's *engagement*.

Yet if she has made the great refusal and remained a private rather than a public political person, she has never been faced with emptiness or boredom. Her life has been filled with the immense and self-imposed vocation of writing, a conscious substitute for political action. Underlying this are assumptions about the significance of what she has to say and about the status, power and influence of the writer. Writing is therefore at once a lifelong personal quest and the public solution of the obligations of *engagement*.

6

Engagement as philanthropy

Even before she regarded her relationship with others as creating an obligation to action on her part, Simone de Beauvoir was always distressed by individual examples of exploitation and human suffering. This goes back, in part, to the strong moral code which her mother instilled in her: 'a sense of duty as well as...unselfishness and austerity'. Yet in the restricted social milieu in which she lived the first part of her life she did not come face to face with those who were oppressed by the social system. She therefore tended to subordinate social problems to the general perspectives of metaphysics and ethics, even when she had begun, at the Sorbonne, to suspect that there were wider horizons: 'what was the use of bothering about suffering humanity, if there was no point in its existence?'[1]

In the thirties she began to realise to what extent people could be exploited and destroyed by society. A visit to a factory in Lyon in 1931 provided her first experience of the industrial conditions in which many people worked: darkness, heat, foul air, and above all the unending monotony of mass production. It brought tears to her eyes. Here was a concrete example of the exploitation of which she had known only theoretically (her reading of Marx, she says, had taught her the mechanism behind it) and which she condemned with all her heart. Even so, it was usually newspapers that brought to the attention of Simone de Beauvoir and Sartre cases of hardship and misery, and they were always conscious of the social pressures and deprivations that were partly responsible for the crimes – even the murders – of which they read: the murderers were often victims themselves.[2] One incident in 1934 brought to light a case of social repression (wide-spread, as it turned out) of the sort that has never failed to arouse Simone de Beauvoir's indignation: this was the maltreatment of juvenile delinquents in remand homes. Both the brutality and the arbitrary nature of the remand system were exposed, but the only result was the punishment of a few administrators, not any change in the system. This is precisely the kind of abuse she was to fight against with such vigour later in her life – but not yet.

As with her reaction to the war in Spain, the emotion was genuine, but led to no action.

Simone de Beauvoir's realisation of her morally intimate ties with her fellow men led her to believe that she must commit herself to them in a positive and much closer way than she had previously thought necessary. When she asserted that we must make other men into our neighbours (*prochains*) by the very process of acting like their neighbours, she was indicating our duty, as men living in this human society, towards our fellows. The human warmth of her preoccupation with others, the compassion, the indignation against a society that will allow injustice and oppression – these qualities shine through all her writing. As José Canabis, discussing *La force des choses*, gently comments: 'At the heart of her vision of the world there is a rebellion against injustice, a fellowship in sorrow, and a generous impulse: these act as leaven to raise the rather heavy dough of the whole book.' It is not a question of charity, which she considers patronising and restrictive of other people's freedom, but in the words of Georges Hourdin, the Catholic writer, of 'the fierce passion for social justice which in a communal context is an alternative mode of charity'.[3] Behind all her ideas and theories lies a concern for people as individuals, a philanthropic impulse.

Julien Benda, in *La trahison des clercs*, distinguishes between two types of humanitarianism. There is that which could more properly be called *humanisme* – denoting an abstract, intellectual conception of the human condition in its entirety, 'a pure passion of the intelligence, implying no terrestrial love'. In contrast there is what *he* calls *humanitarisme* – 'the love for human beings existing in the concrete'. He argues that the first is the only justifiable one: if they opt for the second, intellectuals are descending into the realm of the concrete, which is an error. He claims that you can only love *all* men in the abstract because the inequalities that exist between them become immediately apparent in the concrete and make it impossible to love them all equally.[4] This, of course, is in complete contrast to the thesis of Simone de Beauvoir, for whom links can be created only with individuals, not with the whole of humanity. We have seen that she refuses to support any kind of political fanaticism as she defines it, because: 'It is the political fanaticism which empties politics of all human content and imposes the State, not *for* individuals, but *against* them.' It is vital in her view to recognise as important the uniqueness of all individuals. With time she has become preoccupied less with taking up abstract positions than with concrete human problems. Practically all her public political activity which has not been literary has been inspired by distress at the physical suffering of those who were in her view oppressed. Her protests against the wars in Algeria and Vietnam arose from her disgust at the inhuman treatment inflicted on the indigenous population of these countries by their oppressors: the torture and murder of individuals, the wiping out of masses of innocent civilians, the use of unethical weapons like napalm bombs. No longer was the freedom and independence of these peoples of paramount importance as it had appeared to be when she wrote *Pour une morale de l'ambiguïté*. By the late fifties she had gone beyond the idealism and the theory to the reality of human suffering. It is entirely logical, then, that her *engagement* should have begun in time to take a different form, and it became clear in the early seventies that social rather than political action was to be Simone de Beauvoir's contribution to changing the world.

She has actively and unrelentingly campaigned in recent years for improved conditions and for social justice. She has done this on every sort of issue on behalf of innumerable social groups from minority sectors of the community to half of the human race, the common factor being that they are all disadvantaged in one way or another. She is profoundly critical of the Communist Party and most other political groups for their neglect of these areas: they are 'insensitive to many of the human problems which stare us in the face'. She lists these as: the status of women; the 'three million underpaid, over-worked, over-exploited immigrant workers in France'; the homeless; old people; juvenile delinquents; prison conditions; and 'the dreadful conditions in hospital, the awful asylums for the people who are considered to be "mental cases"'. She sums up: 'On all levels the fight is for justice and humanity. That is the essential battle.' The only political groups in her view that make any attempt to fight this battle are the Maoists who 'carry out pertinent actions', including setting up people's tribunals to denounce 'the bosses' when the latter are guilty of such crimes as ignoring the safety of their workers and allowing accidents to happen.[5]

Much of Simone de Beauvoir's work for others, typically, is carried out behind the scenes and without any publicity, for instance meeting and corresponding with individuals from all walks of life who suffer from problems they feel she understands and can help them with, making representations on their behalf or simply giving advice and sympathy – social work, as it were, undertaken at a purely personal, non-institutional level. Occasionally the field of operation is more public. We have seen how she conducted an enquiry for *J'accuse* on the attempt by women injured in a factory accident at Méru to obtain adequate compensation, concluding that the way they had been treated contrasted strongly with the fate of the owner, who escaped very lightly although he was found guilty. She gave her support to some *gauchistes* who had undertaken a sit-in and hunger strike to demonstrate their solidarity with political prisoners complaining about their conditions. She herself took part in a sit-in to protest against the appallingly repressive conditions in a home for unmarried mothers-to-be. These were mostly very young girls, and she felt particularly strongly that they were being unfairly punished by having their education cut short, being treated like delinquents in respect of visits and outings, and receiving no financial help in bringing up their babies when they left the home.

One mode of public action that Simone de Beauvoir has adopted more and more during the 1970s is the promotion of, or support for, appeals on behalf of the victims of state persecution and protests against governments who are guilty of it. It is quite understandable that she should lend her name in such a way, as with time her physical presence has become increasingly difficult. These nearly always have to do with individual cases where human rights have been ignored: appeals against the death sentence on Basque nationalists, protests against the detention of political prisoners by the Indian government, against the arrest or disappearance of Venezuelans and Guatemalans, appeals to the Soviet authorities at different times to allow certain Jews to emigrate, protest at the treatment of Padilla, the Cuban poet, by the Cuban authorities. It is noteworthy that governments towards whom she might be expected to be sympathetic do not escape the protests when they transgress the criteria of human rights. She sometimes goes so far as to write articles on such matters, as when she wrote in *Le Monde* denouncing Syria's violation of the Geneva Convention in its treatment of prisoners after the Arab–Israeli conflict in 1973. On a more strictly practical level, she has donated manuscripts to be auctioned to provide financial help for people who have been victimised. When asked in 1978 whether she believed in the efficacy of signing protests she replied that even if many have been of no use, occasionally they have helped and if that is so then one must always make the attempt: 'In any case, one cannot *not* sign.'[6]

The public face of Simone de Beauvoir's human concern is as usual conspicuous more in her writing than in any more practical activity. What is particularly striking in her work is the resolute honesty, even aggressiveness, with which she exposes the injustices she identifies. There is no hypocrisy, no glossing over the facts. She is so outraged by social injustice that she has no hesitation in disconcerting and shocking her readers out of their complacency. Not for her the conspiracy of silence that surrounds so many issues, the habit of sweeping under the carpet some of the worst problems of human existence on the grounds that they don't have to be faced personally because they can be dealt with by some anonymous social service or are sanctified by convention. Her writing abounds with examples of 'revealing the truth', but there are two works that are *par excellence* essays in demystification for a social purpose: *Le deuxième sexe*, and *La vieillesse* which she calls 'le symétrique' ('the counterpart') of the first.[7] In these works Simone de Beauvoir attempts to expose the myths and prejudices surrounding two categories of persons, women and old people. The method is that of presenting with meticulous care the evidence accumulated from immensely detailed research; by describing the reality in this way, she hoped to improve the situation. Her mission was all the more pressing because she was involved by her own experience of being a woman and of growing old in a society that treats these two groups unjustly or with indifference. Society, she felt, had created a role within itself for women, and persisted in ignoring the very existence of old people. She wished to look at how both groups experienced their own social existence. The two causes were taken up for the same reason. She says of *Le deuxième sexe*: 'Wanting to talk about myself, I became aware that to do so I should first have to describe the condition of women in general.' As so often with her, general theses arise out of personal experience. Again, when she came to write *La vieillesse*, it was for the same reason: 'I needed to understand a state that is my own, and to understand it in its implication for mankind as a whole. I am a woman, and I wished to throw light upon the woman's lot; I was on the threshold of old age, and I wished to know the bounds and the nature of the aged state.'[8] *La vieillesse* was written more than twenty years after *Le deuxième sexe*, but since the latter cannot be examined and assessed without reference to Simone de Beauvoir's present involvement in the feminist movement, it is appropriate to take the second of these two essays first.

In spite of the view of death in Simone de Beauvoir's philosophy as giving a meaning to life, she has been terrified by the idea of death since her sudden realisation as a child of what it meant to be mortal. Later, and increasingly as time went on, there was an attendant worry: the horror of growing old. As early as twenty-six years old she was struck by the fact that it was already happening to her: 'I was getting old.' Old age raised its ugly head again when her affair with Nelson Algren finally ended in 1951. She said to herself: 'Well, that's that.' It was more than just her happiness with him that had ended: ' "I'll never sleep again warmed by another's body." Never: what a knell!...suddenly, at one blow, a whole piece of myself was being engulfed before my eyes.' At the same time she was conscious that her body was gradually, insidiously deteriorating from year to year. The following year she and Claude Lanzmann decided to live together. His youth and his very presence in her life helped her to control her attacks of depression and despair, 'freed me from my age'. But by the end of 1958 their relationship had begun to change and their ways parted, although they were always to remain friends. She has explained in interviews that she believes everyone, whatever their situation, comes at some time to a crisis point in terms of growing old, and that it can happen at any age. It is the moment at which you suddenly realise that you are no longer what you were and that you must give something up. The crisis is 'not old age itself, but the onset of old age'. For her it came in 1958 when she was fifty, and she confessed five years later in *La force des choses* that she had not yet got over the shock of discovering she had passed this point of no return.[9]

In 1970, when she wrote *La vieillesse*, she was able to see the situation more calmly. Looking around at herself and her friends who were all getting older, she wondered how to treat the problem of old age. She tried a short story (*L'âge de discrétion*) but was not happy with the result and decided to write a quite straightforward study of the subject. Demystification was to be the method, 'doing away with cant and humbug' and breaking the conspiracy of silence which surrounded society's treatment of the old. She would force her readers to look at the reality of the place accorded by society to old people – for it is a social and cultural as well as a biological problem. At the same time she would make sure that the voice of these *human beings* was heard, by looking also at old age from the inside, in terms of how individuals realise and learn to accommodate themselves to physical decrepitude and the treatment meted out to them. The situation would therefore be seen from two points of view, from without and from within. Her method was a favourite one, already used by her for *Le deuxième sexe*: in an attempt to produce an exhaustive survey she assembled a dossier of evidence from every field – science, medicine, psychology, history, anthropology, art, sociology. She justifies this by stating that it was necessary because of the existence of so many interconnected facets to the problem of old age. A vast work of research was needed before she could attempt the subject: 'when I began to look into the problem of old age, I was empty-handed'. By the time she had finished she had an accumulation of detailed evidence that enabled her to tackle the subject in its totality, in the form of a comparative study 'through space and time'.[10]

Right at the beginning, Simone de Beauvoir makes a bid for an attentive and sympathetic hearing of her case by reminding her readers that old age is inevitable. We should therefore face this fact instead of ignoring it, and concern ourselves with the condition of old age since one day it will be our own. The first part of the essay, 'Old age seen from without', consists of a study of the biological deterioration experienced in old age, a comparative survey of old age in primitive societies and then through different periods of history. Already her thesis is evident. Across the world and through the centuries it is apparent that the real problem is that of the class struggle, at whose door so many of the problems of old age may be laid: 'Both today and throughout history, the class-struggle governs the manner in which old age takes hold of man.' She returns to this point later: 'Far more than the conflict between the generations, it was the class struggle that gave the notion of old age its ambivalence.' This aspect becomes of major importance when she arrives at a consideration of contemporary society, where class origins are dominant in deciding what sort of old age people will have. She asserts that everyone knows that 'the condition of old people today is scandalous', and she wonders why it is that society closes its eyes to this fact. This may prevent its peace of mind being disturbed, but it seems extraordinary, when we all know that this fate awaits each and every person, and that old people are therefore in a quite different category from the handicapped or the delinquent. Although their condition is imposed on them by the ruling classes, everyone is party to the crime. She surveys the financial provision for retired people and concludes that in most countries it is insufficient, and that this follows on the many disadvantages of becoming old (even before retirement) in a working world where young people have all the opportunities because of the emphasis on competence and productivity. The result of all this is dire poverty for most people in their old age, appalling housing conditions or the humiliation and misery of life in old people's homes, a sense of being useless and unwanted, loneliness and boredom. In this situation it is, paradoxically, the women who come out best, partly because 'they have less far to fall', and partly because they still have their 'feminine' activities in the home. But among the poor of our society there are few who have resources or sufficient interest to keep them mentally alive and help them to adapt to their new life.

One thing of which Simone de Beauvoir became conscious once she started writing her book was that old people are powerless to alter their condition. They do not exist as a separate category, like women, for instance, who are women all their lives. Moreover discrimination against the old is hidden (not obvious to all as in the case of women) because they apparently have equal rights with everyone else and also because some of them are in positions of power. But those who enjoy power and respect are very few compared with the mass, who can achieve nothing for their cause because they cannot exert economic pressure. Their greatest disadvantage is that there can be no movement of unity amongst them because they are dispersed throughout the country and 'they do not know one another and as usual they carry out no joint action'.

In the second part of her book, 'The being-in-the-world', Simone de Beauvoir looks at the situation from within, in terms of the personal anguish, often hidden, of old people themselves. This is a compassionate study of how they react to their own ageing. Unable to think of themselves as old, they are shocked that other people should see them in this way; unable to accept the accelerating changes brought by the progress of history, they see time in a new dimension as the years rush by; this does not prevent the boredom that arises from the lack of 'projects' and ends-in-view, or the resultant *nausée*; despair sets in with every setback in the progress towards a better future and a new tomorrow which they might never see. Then there is death: first of all the sensation of being 'a survivor' as friends die and part of one's own life disappears with them, and then the fear of death itself. The worst thing about death is the difficulty of conceiving of it as a reality, but in some ways its approach is made easier by the vagueness with which we envisage it and, paradoxically, by the difficulties of old age. Indeed she claims that old age, not death, is the opposite of life, and reiterates her optimistic view of death: 'Old age is life's parody, whereas death transforms life into a destiny: in a way it preserves it by giving it the absolute dimension.'

In the course of this second half, Simone de Beauvoir takes as her example of people's experience of growing old, of their worries and the way they overcome them, outstanding people, mostly intellectuals, literary men, politicians and other famous men. Only in the practical study of contemporary society at the end of the first half does she look at examples from the working classes. It seems rather strange that she should have chosen to use those who have all the advantages – fame, intellectual resources and interest, a wide acquaintance, and usually money as well – to illustrate the difficulties of growing old and the possibilities for overcoming them. Again, in her conclusion she poses the question of how to prevent old age being a parody of one's earlier life, and concludes that the best thing is to work for a variety of individual or communal good causes, or do political, social or intellectual work. Unfortunately, as she concedes, this is possible only for a minority of people. First, it is a fact that physical and mental decline comes earlier to those who have been exploited all their lives, and who are reduced to penury in old age. Second, the manual worker cannot kill time in his retirement because there has never been anything in his life apart from his work. This is 'the crime of our society': if its 'old-age policy' is scandalous, even more scandalous is the systematic destruction of men in earlier life, so that the misery of old age is prefabricated. For her, such a society is a failure in personal, human terms: 'Old age exposes the failure of our entire civilisation. It is the whole man that must be re-made, it is the whole relationship between man and man that must be recast if we wish the old person's state to be acceptable.' In this context all remedies that are proposed for old people are derisory. What is the point of a more generous policy, higher pensions, better housing and health care, greater leisure, if the damage has been done already? She doesn't mean, she says, that one should not try to improve their present condition, but very little can be achieved that way: 'It is the whole system that is at issue and our claim cannot be otherwise than radical – change of life itself.'[11]

If Simone de Beauvoir offers a depressing view of the treatment of old people, it is because she believes that the social class to which they belong has always been a crucial element in deciding society's attitude towards them. She sees that historically it could be claimed that the old have often enjoyed honour and respect, although their position deteriorated considerably with the disappearance of the patriarchal family unit in the nineteenth century. She argues that for the poor there has never been an honourable place. Until the nineteenth century they are rarely mentioned in any writings because only the privileged classes produced writers and they wrote only about their own kind. Since then, the true condition of old people from the exploited classes has become apparent in all its awfulness.

Axel Madsen calls *La vieillesse* a 'fierce indictment of society's indifference and cruelty towards old people'.[12] Simone de Beauvoir certainly forces the reader to question his own attitudes and to put himself in the place of old people. The book gains, too, from the development of her own views about 'la réalité matérielle', that is, the importance of the material circumstances upon which the human condition is so dependent. Unfortunately, although she hotly defends it against the criticism of being dominated by second-hand material, it is largely a compilation of evidence and her insistence on looking in detail at every conceivable aspect of growing old tries the reader's patience without always adding to his understanding of the problem.

What sort of impact can such a work have? Simone de Beauvoir relates that just before the book was published, in January 1970, a report appeared on the social problems of old people, and was given immediate publicity in the press. This proved, in her view, that she had caught the right moment: 'All at once the question was very much in the news. My book appeared just when the public was ready to receive it.'[13] So that the book and the cause would have the maximum publicity, she gave two interviews on Radio Luxemburg. But apart from the fact that she received many letters from individual old people who had read the book or heard her talk, the effect seems to have been very limited. She might well disagree, since for her personal contact with her readers was of paramount importance, and argue that if a few individuals have been supported by her sympathy and understanding of their problem, she has done some good. However much a work like this may enlighten its readers about a scandalous situation, it is difficult to see how that situation could be improved in any way by it. Her dismissal of the effectiveness of social reform (raising pensions, for instance, or improving care of old people) is akin to her rejection of political reformism. It is, as so often with her, all or nothing – and that must mean nothing, since we must wait for society itself to be transformed, and *La vieillesse* was certainly not likely to trigger the necessary revolutionary process.

We must now go back twenty-one years to Simone de Beauvoir's earlier study of the oppression of a group – this time it was women – in *Le deuxième sexe*. If it seemed to her that *La vieillesse* appeared at the appropriate moment, it is quite clear that *Le deuxième sexe* was a book written out of its time. Not until about 1970 did the first effects of the American feminist movement begin to show themselves in France by which time her own views on the struggle of women had been modified. It is of interest, therefore, to look at her reasons for writing such a book so long before militant feminism became widespread and respectable.

In earlier feminism[14] many of the arguments later adopted by Simone de Beauvoir are to be found, but although the book's potted history of feminism refers to most of those who have in the past advanced the feminist cause, she does not always pick out those elements in their thinking that they have in common with her. For instance, both Mary Wollstonecraft in the eighteenth century and John Stuart Mill in the nineteenth had put the case for woman's right to be educated so that she could fulfil her potential, and to be treated as an equal rather than a subordinate being. Mill claimed that no one could know what was innately feminine and so it could not be assumed that woman was, for instance, submissive by nature. He argued in the House of Commons for women's suffrage, and at the turn of the century the Suffragettes began their militant action to the same end. Simone de Beauvoir had little in common with the majority of these women who were instrumental in achieving the vote and some measure of legal equality for their sex, for they were mostly reactionary. One of the exceptions was Sylvia Pankhurst, whose fight for female suffrage was part of a wider concern that was pacifist, socialist and agnostic. In the 1920s the American anthropologist Margaret Mead, to whom Simone de Beauvoir makes no reference until *La vieillesse*, began publishing the results of her research among tribal societies. In *Sex and temperament* she concluded that while there are *biological* differences between the sexes, *temperamental* differences are between one person and another, irrespective of sex. In 1936 Mounier, nearer home, produced a special edition of *Esprit* on women, entitled 'La femme aussi est une personne',[15] in which the fate of women was compared to that of the proletariat, unable to achieve any real existence as autonomous persons. But at that time, Simone de Beauvoir had hardly considered the problem, for in her eyes, men and women were equal since they were all human beings. She insists that she began to worry about living like a parasite through Sartre not because of feminist principles but because 'to accept a secondary status in life, that of a merely ancillary being', was contrary to her own philosophy: 'it was qua individual that I attempted to resolve it. The idea of feminism or the sex war made no sense whatever to me.' She had no theories about women's rights and it was as a human being, rather than as a woman, that she was concerned to achieve reciprocity with Sartre. She never thought of her feminine condition because she never felt disadvantaged or oppressed because of being a woman, and in fact she claims: 'far from suffering from my femininity, I have, on the contrary, from the age of twenty onwards, accumulated the advantages of both sexes'. It seemed to her that to be treated as an equal by men, all that was necessary was to *be* equal (that is, as intelligent as they), and indeed Sartre never thought of her as anything else. For this reason, she felt able to tackle the subject objectively, without being emotionally involved, and was convinced that her female sex had never been of any importance – until Sartre suggested that she should study the question more closely, considering that she had not been brought up in the same way as a boy. The result was a revelation: 'It is both strange and stimulating to discover suddenly, after forty, an aspect of the world that has been staring you in the face all the time which somehow you have never noticed.'[16]

The ethical basis of *Le deuxième sexe* is existentialism. Just as Simone de Beauvoir refuses to accept the idea of human nature, so she insists that there is no such thing as feminine nature: 'One is not born, but rather becomes, a woman.' Individuals are born human beings, not women or men, and they all have the same right to freedom and the same duty to use it – to create and be true to themselves, to become autonomous subjects by what they accomplish through action, to establish reciprocal relations with other human beings in which both parties are equal. She does not deny that there are physical differences between the sexes ('Have I ever written that women were the same as men?', she protests in *La force de l'âge*), but the fact that men and women are made differently does not lead automatically to the struggle of the sexes, or to the relegation of women to a secondary, subordinate role. It is the exaggeration and extension of these physical differences by social and cultural conditioning that determine their situation in a male-dominated world: 'what distinguishes my thesis from the traditional one is that, as far as I am concerned, femininity is neither a natural nor an innate entity, but rather a condition brought about by society, on the basis of certain psychological characteristics'. These biological facts are important, but they do not mean that for woman there is only 'a fixed and inevitable destiny', preventing her from achieving the *dépassement* which is necessary for her self-realisation. It is society that decides whether the effect of these differences between the sexes will become significant or remain irrelevant, and it has done that right through the course of history, in all corners of the world, by treating her as an object and giving her a fixed place and role. This is largely due, she believes, to the notion of woman as property, belonging first to her father and subsequently to her husband. Her subservience originated with the principle of private property and the importance of its possession and conservation within the family through inheritance. Whatever the reasons, the same glaring fact struck Simone de Beauvoir whichever way she looked: 'in every case, man put himself forward as the Subject and considered the woman as an object, as the Other'.[17] Man tends to reject a relationship of equality and reciprocity with woman, but instead is able through his privileged situation to dominate her and turn the relationship into one of oppression. Free in principle, woman is rarely given the opportunity to live her life freely and fully as a 'subject' and is refused integration into society as a human being.[18]

It is Simone de Beauvoir's contention that given the same opportunities as men, women would demonstrate the same capabilities as men. They are not inferior to men, and frequently demonstrate that they are as capable of logic, organisation, efficiency and the so-called 'masculine' qualities as men. But they are not given the chance. How can they, in their repetitive, passive existence, excluded from the real world, be capable of the sort of action that can change the face of the world? You have to be firmly rooted in the world to do that: 'To be situated at the margin of the world is not a position favourable for one who aims at creating it anew.' And so men reproach women for not achieving great heights, while deliberately imposing limits that make this impossible for all but exceptional cases: 'Women is shut up in a kitchen or in a boudoir, and astonishment is expressed that her horizons are limited. Her wings are clipped, and it is found deplorable that she cannot fly. Let but the future be opened to her, and she will no longer be compelled to linger in the present.'[19]

There are two interrelated conditions that are particularly responsible for limiting women's potential. The first is the institution of marriage which receives unqualified condemnation. Historical tradition has made women look upon marriage as their destiny, their means of existence, whereas for men it simply fills out their lives. Women are forced into it because their education has fitted them for nothing else and because they are often outcasts if they remain single. The principle of marriage itself is obscene because it turns spontaneous feelings into compulsory rights and duties. She rejects the usual argument for marriage, that it provides a protection for women, saying that in placing herself in a dependent position a woman gives up her own freedom without which she cannot exist wholly as a person. As for her role as housewife, she is obliged to seek social justification in the exercise of her functions, but the daily repetition of the same tasks is purely negative and can never lead anywhere. It is almost impossible for women to retrieve their freedom if, as almost always happens, marriage is a failure and they sink into resignation. Conjugal love is not love, because love should be free. Marriage is rarely a free relationship of equals, it is rather an oppressive condition of slavery for both partners. It is not the individuals concerned who are at fault but the institution of marriage itself, corrupt from the beginning of time.[20]

The second is maternity. She presents maternity in existentialist terms, immediately dismissing it as repetition (the perpetuation of the species) and stagnation. It therefore does not qualify as a 'project', opening up the future, but is a purely animal activity: 'For it is not in giving life but in risking life that man is raised above the animal.' While Simone de Beauvoir at moments sees that pregnancy

and motherhood can be a sort of *engagement*, and the task of mould-
ing a human being a delicate one, involving solemn obligations, her
usual view is that 'giving birth and suckling are not *activities*; they
are natural functions' and therefore cannot make women authentically free and fulfilled. In fact her existentialist argument appears to
be a rationalisation of a deeply felt disgust (the equivalent of Sartre's
nausée) at the thought of pregnancy, the foetus, childbirth. She
describes the female body as 'an obscure, alien thing', and the foetus
as a 'quivering jelly which is elaborated in the womb' which itself
evokes an image of 'the soft viscosity of carrion'. Even if a woman
deeply desires to have a child, her body revolts against the process.
This disgust, shared with Sartre, of the flesh and of biological
functions, could have its origins in the puritanical attitudes fostered
by their upbringing. Furthermore, although she admits that occasionally motherhood can be rewarding and fulfilling for the mother,
she seems to be incapable of imagining that there can be any real
love or generosity in the relationship between mother and child,
claiming that if there is, it is usually off-set by the ambivalence of the
mother's attitudes. Here a whole dimension seems to be missing
from Simone de Beauvoir's human sympathies, even if she denies it.
When discussing the question of maternal feelings and love in *La
force des choses* she says that all she had asked was that 'women should
experience them truthfully and freely, whereas they often use them
as excuses and take refuge in them'.[21] It does seem, all the same,
that her own inexperience and prejudice in this area make her treat
maternity in an altogether too idiosyncratic way.

Simone de Beauvoir argues that both marriage and motherhood
imply and encourage vicarious living, for a woman confined to these
states and accepting the conventional roles of wife and mother
necessarily lives through her husband and through her children.
Not only is this an inauthentic way of life, it is also a dangerous one:
children leave home, depriving their mother of her *raison d'être*;
husbands often leave their wives, who cannot cope with living on
their own account instead of through their men. The way out of this
is for the woman to go out to work. She insists on this as a necessity
without taking account of the reservations she or others might feel
about it: 'To earn one's living is not an end in itself, but it is the
only way to achieve securely based inner independence.' It could be
argued, as Jean Leighton has done in her book, *Simone de Beauvoir
on woman*, that going out to work does not necessarily liberate a

woman or make her an autonomous being, and that to be eco-nomically independent is not necessary in order to be emotionally independent. Conversely a woman who is economically dependent can perfectly well have and express quite independent opinions. There are also purely practical disadvantages: work outside the home may well guarantee woman 'her liberty in practice', but it often gives her twice as much work as well. Besides, Simone de Beauvoir recognises that employment can also mean oppression and exploita-tion for men as well as women: 'today, work is not in itself freedom. Only in a socialist world could women be sure of attaining freedom for themselves by gaining access to work.' Leaving aside for the moment the rosy socialist future which Simone de Beauvoir appears to envisage, it must be said that she knows perfectly well these dis-advantages but discounts them, for they seem negligible when she considers the possibilities that even the most menial job opens up for a woman: 'she regains her transcendence...she concretely affirms her status as subject'. She confirmed this opinion much later, when she asserted that if work can be tedious and humiliating for men, then women should share that experience *in the same setting*, that is, not in the home but at work.[22]

How can women become emancipated? Critical of the way Marxism treats women only as economic units, Simone de Beauvoir claims that the problem would not disappear with the revolution, although it cannot fully be resolved until then. Women differ from other oppressed groups: they are not a minority or a separate com-munity, like the blacks; they have not *lost* their freedom and power (the Marxist argument), for their situation has always been inferior to that of men; they have always existed as a group, whereas the proletariat has developed only recently as a class. So the emancipa-tion of women must be achieved by a different process. The hostility between the sexes is not 'natural', it is not a necessary corollary of the physical differences between them and must be brought to an end. The battle is to abolish the social consequences of these differences, to destroy the myths that surround women, to force men and women to consider each other as equals. For this to be possible they must be brought up in exactly the same way, so as to avoid the social conditioning that teaches men that they are superior and makes it difficult for women to 'assume' their existence, because all avenues are closed to them.

Le deuxième sexe has always been a work that Simone de Beauvoir 'would defend to the last ditch'. When she says this, she means that it is the one she would fight for the most because she still stands by all the *ideas* in it – unlike her fictional works which do not require to be defended, she says, because people have a right to differ on aesthetic or literary grounds. In fact *Le deuxième sexe* is the book she would most criticise from a literary point of view. Her only criticism of the content, as opposed to the aesthetic value, was expressed in 1963 in *La force des choses*. She had come to realise, looking at the problem now in a more Marxist light, that the relegation of woman to the role of *l'autre* had an economic basis ('the facts of supply and demand') rather than an ethical one (a 'struggle of consciences'). There are other criticisms that can be made. The book suffers from Simone de Beauvoir's usual determination not to leave unused any information that could possibly have any bearing on the subject she is investigating. Georges Hourdin rather deprecatingly remarks that she takes a thousand pages to demonstrate that woman is the equal of man but not treated as such in this alienating society dominated by men.[23] It is as if the accumulation of examples, testimonies and case histories is considered sufficient argument in itself. Moreover these examples are nearly all from literary sources, and though this has advantages in making them seem immediate and personal, it is also a drawback. She attempts through them to present a kind of sociological analysis which is, in truth, very far from scientific or balanced. They paint a very black picture of the condition of women – too black, it might be said. When one example is piled on another, extremes begin to seem like the norm. Are there *no* happy and fulfilled women in this world? It has to be said also that in her effort to prove her point, she seems to blame some women for succumbing so easily, claiming that although their situation is partly imposed on them from outside it is also partly of their own making. Seen in this existentialist light, it is their right to lead full, free and autonomous lives, but it is also their duty to do so. The complicity of women in their own oppression arises from the security offered by men in exchange for their slavery – both material protection and also the cosy risklessness of not having to use their freedom.[24] She has been accused of being a misogynist, looking down on women and unable to comprehend their suffering, although she denies this, claiming that she depicted their faults as arising out of their condition and that she gave due place to their many qualities. That may be true, but she firmly sets herself apart from these failures, believing herself to be the epitome of the emancipated woman, and she accepts unconditionally Jeanson's assessment of her: 'In short...you have understood the feminine condition in terms of someone who has escaped from it.' Jean Leighton argues that, reading between the lines of her autobiography, it looks as though Simone de Beauvoir in her own relationship with Sartre accepted for herself the subordinate role that she advises other women to reject; moreover all her female characters fall short of her ideal. Simone de Beauvoir's answer to this sort of criticism would be that if she nearly always ended up accepting Sartre's viewpoint, it was not because she was dependent or because he was a man, but because he was a more original thinker – and in debate with her usually turned out to be right! Thus she is able to reconcile her behaviour with her ideal of the independent woman. As for her characters, she argues that she does not have to choose exemplary heroines. The women in her novels all demonstrate the ambiguity that there is in all women and that is the reality.[25]

There are other criticisms that arise out of the increased consciousness today of the condition of women. For instance many of those fighting for women's liberation are convinced that society would be better if the 'feminine' virtues were to be adopted as its values. Simone de Beauvoir's notion of a sexually egalitarian society appears to be one in which the women are able to display the masculine characteristics of aggressiveness, competitiveness and action, leading to fame and power. She has refused to say that feminine qualities (gentleness, compassion, sensitivity) are better than masculine qualities, but in any case her view of woman's task as a fight to carve a place for herself in a man's world is entirely comprehensible, given the time at which the book was written. In the debates that have taken place over the last ten years it has emerged that men, too, suffer from the constraints imposed by their dominant role, which does not necessarily fulfil them.

All this said, *Le deuxième sexe* is a remarkable book for the time at which it was written. In spite of occasional assertions that sound rather too dogmatic and simplistic in the light of modern knowledge (like her claims that most miscarriages have psychological causes, or that homosexuality is due to environmental influences and not to hormonal make-up), she was both perceptive and outspoken, cutting through accepted views with honesty and an almost naïvely fresh viewpoint. She was one of the first in France to challenge the Freudian explanation of the psychology and behaviour of women and to see the importance right through history of social role-conditioning in the exploitation of women and the way they are persuaded of their own inferiority. Because of her conviction that most of the differences between the sexes were created by society, she understood that behaviour patterns would not necessarily be altered by laws but only by a completely new approach, like bringing up boys and girls in exactly the same way. Her originality in so many aspects of this whole question – take for example her passionate defence of children's rights – explains the initial reaction to a book that has now become a classic of feminist literature.

A *succès de scandale* was the last thing Simone de Beauvoir had expected, for the simple reason that in the progressive circle in which she lived she had had the impression that such views were accepted by most enlightened people. She was astounded at the violence of the reaction, and in particular when it came from friends like Camus who suddenly displayed a hitherto unsuspected concern with *machismo* and who took *Le deuxième sexe* as an affront to his masculinity. She was subjected to every kind of insult, insinuation, obscenity and proposition. Even Mauriac wrote to one of the contributors of *Les Temps Modernes*: 'Your employer's vagina has no secrets from me', showing a willingness to use in private the kind of vocabulary he publicly condemned her for using in *Le deuxième sexe*.[26] Communist reaction was distinctly cool. Their view was that all would come right with the revolution, so why bother in the meantime? There were, as well, those who defended her book, among them Mounier, and the result was a lively public debate. It was the private reactions to it that pleased Simone de Beauvoir most and that in her view amply justified the writing of it. Years afterwards she was still receiving letters from individual women whom she had helped through her book, either by making them conscious of their situation or by allowing them to see that their personal difficulties were not peculiar to them and so giving them the courage to face them. These pitiful letters from women of every social class are regarded by her as the ultimate justification of literature as communication. In an interview with Madeleine Gobeil, Sartre speaks of Simone de Beauvoir's spontaneity and gift of instant communication with the public and he differentiates between his own intellectual communication with readers and her quite different skill: 'Simone de Beauvoir, on the other hand, communicates immediately on the affective level.' She prizes her relationship with this public and does not regret that her most devoted and serious readership is made up of women: 'I have an interest in them; and I prefer having taken a limited but real hold upon the world through them to drifting in the universal.'[27]

This was all she had ever asked of the book. The question of how much influence it has had is intriguing, but almost impossible to answer. Had it not been written, would anything be different? On balance it seems unlikely that the women's liberation movement would have developed any differently. In 1963 she denied that she had ever expected to exert any real influence: 'I never cherished any illusion of changing women's condition'. However it does seem extraordinary that a book that sold 22,000 copies in the first week of its publication in France, and was an instant success when published in 1953 in the U.S.A. where nearly a million paperback copies have been sold, should not have sparked off a movement that seemed, twenty years later, to have been fermenting for a very long time. The impact of a work like this has to be seen in the wider context of the mood of the time, and the forties were not a propitious moment.[28] By the late sixties when the women's movement took off in America, the background of fairly uninhibited discussion of sexuality, protest movements (the war in Vietnam, black power), political awareness and militancy among students was conducive to its success. In England as well as in France previous political activity was often the route to the feminist movement, and many members of the Mouvement de Libération des Femmes (M.L.F.) belonged to *gauchiste* groups. *Le deuxième sexe*, in any case, is not the sort of book to persuade anyone into militant action, partly because it was never conceived as anything other than an attempt to make people conscious of the traditional role of women and rethink it. She denies that it was in any way responsible for the feminist movement of today; most feminists discovered her book only later, she declares. They became feminist because of their own experience and not because of her book, even though it described similar experiences.[29] And yet Simone de Beauvoir is a cult figure and her book compulsory reading, a sort of bible for supporters of the women's movement. This is possibly because, with its philosophical and personal approach, it has dated less than some books – a consequence, in fact, of the very approach that prevented it from being a militant work. It has been widely drawn upon by other writers on feminism, often without any acknowledgment, and she would like to think that it will continue to be read for some time yet. When asked what effect she thought it would have on future generations, she replied: 'I think that *The second sex* will seem an old, dated book, after a while. But nonetheless...a book which will have made its contribution. At least, I hope so.' It is certainly true that although the public was not ready for such a book in 1949, so much water has passed under the bridge in the last ten years that it now seems too conventional for some, and they forget how radical it was at the time. As Dorothy Kaufmann McCall puts it, there is a tendency to treat it (and her, perhaps?) 'with the distant respect appropriate for venerable ancestors'.[30]

In contrast to the marginal influence Simone de Beauvoir had on the development of the women's movement, the effect of the movement on her was traumatic. Although her theories about the feminine condition have remained remarkably static since she wrote *Le deuxième sexe*, there has been one major change in her thought: this is on the question of how to achieve the emancipation of women. There was a growing despondency during the 1960s, as she noted that things had not improved since 1949 when she had predicted that within ten years the liberation of women would be well advanced; in fact the situation, she asserted, was actually worse. The current glorification of the traditional feminine values of bourgeois society, in particular of maternity, was encouraging more women to want to stay at home and play the role of wife, housekeeper and mother. Moreover because of unemployment the climate had developed into one of hostility to the *sine qua non* of independence for women, their economic independence. There was also a fear among employers and politicians that through employment women would become politicised, a state which she defined as taking part in the social struggle through trade unions and pressure groups, and supporting others in a show of solidarity. Given the importance that Simone de Beauvoir attributes to women working and the dependence of any improvement in this area on economic factors, it is understandable that for her the only hope for French women was for France to change completely; a regime based on exploitation has every interest in maintaining discrimination between individuals, and so 'only the coming of socialism can bring equality'. Since she also believed at that time that a collective struggle was impossible for most women, and since there was no collective feminist work going on that appealed to her, her rejection of specifically feminist action comes as no surprise: 'That is why I avoided falling into the trap of "feminism".'[31]

By 1972 there was a complete reversal in her attitude: Simone de Beauvoir was now a militant feminist. *How* this happened will be recounted below, but *why* did it happen? Her own explanation is two-fold. Whereas feminist groups before 1970 were reformist and their members simply wanted to take over the world from men, 'the new feminism' was now radical and its militants wished to change the world that had been fashioned by men. Secondly, the evidence now was that socialism would not automatically solve all women's problems. She had been aware even when she wrote *Le deuxième sexe* that the coming of socialism to various countries had not resulted in the emancipation of women but she remained optimistic for the future. In the late sixties she had already begun to be sceptical of socialism as a complete answer: she had now modified her viewpoint to the extent of saying that women could only achieve equality in a socialist state but that because of the influence of traditional attitudes socialism was not enough in itself. This view has not changed since: 'socialism is necessary, if not sufficient, to ensure the equality of the sexes'. What is new is the recognition that it is possible to achieve real changes in the meantime. Whereas in *Le deuxième sexe* she stopped short of suggesting how the feminist struggle should be carried out because she was simply waiting for socialism, she now believes that women must fight for concrete improvements before the socialism of which she dreams becomes a reality. Women must take part in collective action: individual action is no longer enough. She is now, she claims, truly feminist.

In spite of the disillusion with socialism as it is, it must be understood that the feminist struggle for her is necessarily situated on the left. That is why she has taken up a position against certain feminist groups like the wealthy publishing enterprise 'Psych et po' (Psychanalyse et politique) because she believes it has displayed its capitalist colours by exploiting the women whose work it publishes. It has a very authoritarian structure and is opposed by most of the other groups, particularly since it recently copyrighted the name

'Mouvement de Libération des Femmes' for itself. Real feminists, she claims, are left wing whether they realise it or not, because they are working for absolute equality and a complete transformation of society. Because it is one way of attacking and overthrowing society as it now exists, feminism is revolutionary. However the feminist struggle is not part of the class struggle, although they are linked, and must not be subordinated to it, for the oppression of women is a major problem in its own right. Simone de Beauvoir recognises that although the corollary of all this is that working-class women ought to be closely involved in the movement, very few of them have joined and it remains the preserve of the middle classes.

If Simone de Beauvoir has changed her position in terms of practice and tactics, theoretically she retracts nothing. There have been minor adjustments only, although some of the main themes of *Le deuxième sexe* have been amplified since she became an active feminist, and it is interesting to look at those which have become recurrent and which must be assumed to be of major importance in her eyes. The first of these is maternity. She claims that she has never been opposed to maternity, only to the myths surrounding the so-called maternal instinct and the mother–child relationship, and to the conditioning of women by society to seek motherhood. Maternity *can* have a positive value, and she has seen some examples that are truly happy and enriching. She concedes the need to make maternity easier for women who work, and believes that the best solution for women who want children is to have them outside marriage. She would like to see marriage and maternity separated because she is all for abolishing the family cell, where both mother and child are treated as objects. Marriage itself is an 'alienating institution' that is also dangerous – for men who feel trapped by it, and for women who, if financially dependent on their husbands, can be thrown out when it is too late to start a new life. Typically, she does not propose an alternative: 'It's hard to say what should be put in its place, but the fact that one criticises it doesn't mean that one has to find something to replace it.' She is adamantly opposed to the notion of giving women a wage for staying at home to do the house-work and look after their children. Women at home cannot be full human beings. Indeed until society stops conditioning women for maternity, no woman should be allowed to choose it as a career because her choice would not be free. When is freedom freedom, one may ask.

For Simone de Beauvoir by far the best way to promote emancipation and equality is for women to take employment in spite of all
the practical as well as moral difficulties to which this can give rise.
Real emancipation is economic. In this area there has been some
progress made since she wrote *Le deuxième sexe* but not enough, she
claims, particularly in terms of the levels reached by women.
With very few exceptions women in France are confined to subordinate posts. Here there seems to be some ambivalence in her own
attitude. In 1975, talking to Betty Friedan, she seemed to be arguing
that it was better for the few women offered positions of power
to refuse in order not to be incorporated in the elite. They should
not play the game of this society by being 'femmes-alibis', token
women, appointed to obviate criticism of discrimination. The situation was different for her, of course, since she already belonged to
the elite: it was a problem for those who were still making their way.
She seems soon after this interview to have modified her views, and
from 1976 she has been saying that while there is the dilemma of
being used as a token, refusal to enter the power structure means
being ineffectual and giving up the possibility of promoting through
it the cause of all women.[32] In fact she talks of measuring the
progress of the feminist revolution in terms of power. Real progress
will have been made when the number of women – barristers,
doctors, politicians, for instance – at the *top* of their profession has
grown considerably.[33]

She has not substantially altered her views on the promotion of
feminine as opposed to masculine qualities. She now concedes that
feminine virtues should be developed but only provided one also
admits that there are masculine virtues that women ought to take
over. Otherwise 'la spécificité féminine' can be dangerous in that
refusal to adopt male values can be used as an excuse for being
inactive, for not taking initiatives. On the whole she does not believe
in separatism. While understanding that the various groups exclude
men, because it is at this stage important for women to rediscover
their feminine identity by discussion amongst themselves, there are
many circumstances in which men and women can work together for
the liberation of women. She is very much against the search for a
purely 'feminine' writing style. Language is admittedly a legacy
from a male-dominated society, but it is universally used, and to
adopt an esoteric, specifically feminine language is merely to cut
oneself off from most readers. She recognises that certain subjects

will be treated differently because the writer is a woman, but there should be no areas that are considered female preserves, otherwise women would simply find themselves in a ghetto. And so it is still the case that she sees the task of women to encroach upon what is otherwise a male world and to share in it as equal partners.[34]

The theory, then, has been slightly modified but remains essentially that of *Le deuxième sexe*. Recognising that 'it is not a militant book', she claims that because of its theoretical basis it is of value to militant feminists, whose movement has few theoreticians. She will not be writing a sequel to it because this would have to elaborate the practice and the volumes would then be in the wrong order because theory must arise out of practice, not the other way round. Realising that 'correct' theory is not enough for achieving emancipation, she has thrown herself into the fight in a more active and militant way than ever she pursued the socialist revolution. She makes her position clear in *Tout compte fait*: 'Now when I speak of feminism I mean the fact of struggling for specifically feminine claims at the same time as carrying on the class-war; and I declare myself a feminist.'[35]

The French feminist movement that Simone de Beauvoir joined was new of its type, but it had a predecessor in the nineteenth century. There were feminist journals as early as 1832, and the first feminist movement was started by a man, Léon Richter, in the second half of the century. The aim of this early feminism was usually an improvement in civil rights and equality in law; the right to vote was not envisaged (nor obtained until 1944). But this early flowering had faded and produced a reaction by 1914, which lasted until after the second world war. Until 1970 most self-styled feminist groups in France were, as Simone de Beauvoir claims, reformist and rather feeble, and certainly not of a type to appeal to her. The new feminism reached France later than the United States and England. The first of these new groups began to form in 1969–70, partly as a result of the desire for questioning and reappraisal in every kind of area aroused by the events of May '68 and the subsequent disillusionment with the way the *gauchiste* groups were drifting. They were clandestine, like the *gauchiste* groups, when first formed and this may have accounted for their small size and dispersion, characteristics which lasted for some years. Indeed it is still difficult to talk of 'the women's movement' in France as it consists of so many groups and factions with widely differing views about feminism. The most important of the original clandestine movements, the Mouvement de Libération des Femmes, came out into the open in January 1971.[36] This is the one that Simone de Beauvoir joined at that point, and since then the feminist struggle has been the centre of her interest and her main preoccupation. Her open activity in the movement in recent years is significant. By implication her earlier definition of *engagement* as an attitude, given literary expression or at most manifested in private, individual action, came to appear inadequate and altogether too passive. It had to be completed in a public activity in which her *engagement* was visible to all.

She claims that she was caught up in the movement more than twenty years after the publication of *Le deuxième sexe* because she felt that women had made few real gains since then. In fact her first contact with it was not initiated by herself: towards the end of 1970 certain members of the M.L.F. contacted her to talk about the new abortion bill which was to be presented to Parliament and which they considered inadequate. *Le Nouvel Observateur* suggested to the small group which was studying this question the idea of a manifesto. The result was the famous *Manifeste des 343*, published in April 1971 in both *Le Nouvel Observateur* and *Le Monde*, and in which Simone de Beauvoir's name figures. This manifesto, signed by 343 women who admitted to having had abortions, campaigned for free contraception and free abortions available to all.[37] This campaign, seen by its originators as a political battle,[38] was continued by the pressure group Choisir, formed for this purpose in June 1972 by Simone de Beauvoir, Gisèle Halimi and others. Simone de Beauvoir was its first president. Its aims were free contraception for all, changes in the laws relative to abortion to make them less repressive, and the provision of free legal aid and other assistance to anyone accused under those laws of obtaining or performing an abortion. Indeed in November 1972 she was a witness at the trial at Bobigny of a seventeen-year-old girl accused of having had an abortion; Gisèle Halimi was responsible for the defence. The group now has many branches throughout France but has changed in character partly because some of its original aims have been realised. It has become much more politicised, even presenting its own candidates at the General Election of 1978. However, Simone de Beauvoir's views and those of the more reformist Gisèle Halimi have diverged and she left Choisir some time ago; she has since claimed that an authoritarian style and internal dissension are causing the group to disintegrate. Among the other feminist activities in which she joined were: demonstrations and marches like that of 20 November 1971 which was part of a day of world-wide action for contraception and abortion; conferences like the 'Journées pour la dénonciation des crimes contre la femme' in May 1972; writing letters of sympathy to women believed to be victims of injustice; investigating incidents like that at the home for unmarried pregnant girls; messages of support when she has been unable to attend feminist events abroad; open letters and protests at specific examples of anti-feminism. Since 1974 she has been president of a group called the Ligue des droits des femmes, which fights discrimination against women, in employment for instance, and which holds itself ready to take prompt practical action in cases of such discrimination. It arose out of an idea suggested to the M.L.F. by Simone de Beauvoir herself.[39] The group would like to see legislation to forbid sexual insults, like the law that allowed people after the war to be prosecuted for insults to Jews, for sexism is equivalent to racism according to Simone de Beauvoir. Its main areas of activity today are in helping battered wives and the victims of rape, the most important issues of the day in her view. But Simone de Beauvoir herself limits her activity to 'the level of testimony, a declaration, an article', leaving it to other militants to do the field work. With other feminists she has started a journal, *Questions Féministes*, speaking out for 'an activist, Marxian feminism'. In spite of her scepticism about legislation, some of these activities have brought the issues out into the open and allowed them to be discussed and in this way they have certainly contributed towards making contraception and abortion both legal and more easily available. The text of the 1975 abortion law only went part of the way to answering their demands, but it was an important achievement and was firmly established for good and given the seal of approval by the National Assembly when the debate was reopened in December 1979. Simone de Beauvoir recognises that although the way this law is applied is far from perfect, the legal changes regarding contraception and abortion can be counted as victories. However she is still very cynical about attempts to institutionalise the feminine struggle: she dismisses government departments like the one for 'the feminine condition' as being mystifications and incapable of achieving any progress, and greater female representation in Parliament as leading to more 'femmes-

alibis', and so on. Her attitude to participation in the political
process has not really changed.

Whatever the practical results, it is clear that in feminist militancy
Simone de Beauvoir has found at last a satisfying means of trans-
lating commitment into action. It has in particular that quality
which has always been necessary before she involves herself completely in any project: working closely with other people for a
common aim. This work is essentially small-scale and individual.
While recognising that massive national action is sometimes necessary, she is adamant that there must be no organised structure for the
movement. Indeed she has said that the existence of different
tendances within the movement is a positive advantage since it
allows individuality and freedom. The rejection of bureaucratic and
hierarchical forms, however inconvenient their absence might be,
'has the advantage of trying to make each human being a *whole*
human'. Similarly, she does not believe that the women's movement
should join forces with other movements, 'but each one should do its
work in its own place, in its own way, in its own group'.[41] Thus she
justifies her own preference for working in a small, personal setting.
Nowadays she particularly likes to work with younger people, and
no praise could be higher in her view than this tribute from a
fellow member of the M.L.F. to the way she has reached across the
generations: 'across the years, we found we were fighting for the
same cause, she whose book had inspired our battle, we who turned
her theories into practice'.[42] For a time Simone de Beauvoir was convinced that this action had already achieved much and that it would
eventually be successful: in the end women would win their fight.

It has become clear that in the course of the 1970s Simone de
Beauvoir has changed her tactics, not only with regard to the
feminist struggle but also in more general terms. She has come to
believe that it is worth campaigning in order to promote not only
more compassionate treatment but also increased spending for the
old, the mentally sick, delinquents, prisoners, and all those underprivileged groups for whom she has been concerned to fight in
recent years: 'To force the system to behave in a humanitarian
manner means an undermining of all its structures.' Her idealism in
believing that this will lead to less money being spent on Concorde
or nuclear weapons is unshakable, in spite of her recognition from
time to time that the realities of the situation are otherwise. She is no

longer waiting for the revolution but is prepared to take immediate action – not, it must be stressed, by participation in politics but in small-scale, individual ways in order to improve the quality of lives and to modify society.[43] This action seems to her to produce tangible results quickly enough to make it worth pursuing and so, late in her life, there is evidence that she has adopted an attitude that is in complete contrast to the convictions she held previously. If this is so, then the reversal is understandable. Time is running out for her as for all old people: the promise of a better world which she will never see is clearly no longer enough.[44] She seems to want to retain her involvement by reaching out to a new generation – her successors – and joining in their 'projects'; she will avoid in this way that lack of purpose and the consequent inertia which she has identified as characteristic of old people. If Simone de Beauvoir has now adopted a meliorist view, has there been a reconstruction of her theoretical political position? Bearing in mind that this has always contained within itself ambiguities, ambivalences and exceptions, we must look in more detail at the way she has defined it during the 1970s in order to judge whether or not a new position has emerged.

It was in 1972 that she first confessed unequivocally that 'my high expectations of socialism. . .have not been fulfilled'. Surveying all the regimes of which she and Sartre had hoped great things in the past – Russia, Algeria, Cuba, China – she had come to the conclusion that the so-called socialist countries were not truly socialist. By this she meant that Marx's dream of 'a socialism which would change man' had nowhere been realised, that to change the relations of production was not sufficient in order to change society or man himself. This theme was to predominate later, when she drew the logical consequences from it, but until the mid-seventies her attitude was typically ambivalent. While dedicating herself to a fight for any reforms that could be achieved and to undermining the structures of society, she was still talking in terms of a global change to society to be accomplished by revolution, not reformism or revisionism, and before which certain political questions could not fall into place. Moreover she was still denying that she was pessimistic for the future: if she was 'telling the truth' about the terrible unhappiness and horror in the world today in the belief that some good would come of it, then this implied hope. Although the failure of so much that she had believed in might have made her pessimistic, it did not in fact do so, she claimed, because she was fundamentally an optimistic sort of person. By 1976 she was less sure. When asked whether she was optimistic that the changes for which she had fought would ever happen, she said that she did not know but that if they did it would not be during her lifetime or indeed for several generations. She then added that while she was certain that women would eventually win their fight, she did not know what would become of the revolution. The word 'revolution' has now almost faded from her vocabulary, and her pessimism is openly admitted. Even feminism, which in 1978 she declared to be 'well on its way', unlike socialism which had made no progress, is now seen in this light. She does not believe, she declares, that the condition of women has improved; all that has changed is that the different abuses and horrors that still exist are now openly denounced. Socialism is a dream and does not exist anywhere, and indeed the society she envisages would be so difficult to achieve in the world as we know it that it will not be realised for a long time, and perhaps even that is only a pious hope. Partly because of the inherent difficulties and partly because the whole of the left is in complete disarray, she has little hope. Perhaps, she now suggests, it is not the moment to construct, but rather to help to destroy what is unacceptable and in a modest way to create disorder, by vigilance and criticism of the police state in which we all live. Has she perhaps come the full circle to a commitment that inclines her to demystify and tell the truth, but stops short of action? We cannot be sure whether this is a serious statement of her intention to withdraw from militancy, but her pessimism could be providing an alibi for her tendency, already noted, to refuse to provide constructive alternatives for those things she wishes to see destroyed.[45]

If all this seems rather negative, it is counterbalanced by her definition of the kind of society she would like to see in the future and which clearly she is doing her best to promote, even if she does not have too much faith in the effectiveness of the possibilities open to her. It would mean an end to exploitation and inequality, and it would bring 'real' socialism, which is 'open, generous, ideal, but utopian'. If you are on the left there is something you must believe in, she claims, and indeed she puts it forward as a definition of what it means to be on the left: 'It is nevertheless the hope that history will bring about more profound changes in society than have occurred until now, changes which will really transform the relations between men – men and women, men with each other, women with each other. All of which has remained unchanged in spite of collectivisation and nationalisation of the means of production in the socialist countries.' This is something that concerns her now more than the revolution *per se* which no longer appears to be sufficient: 'That's what is really important, to change relationships between people.'[46] Not a new theory but a constant preoccupation. Preserved for ever is the profession of the Beauvoirian intellectual whom society will always need, for inspired by love for his fellow men and commitment to their well-being, he is in a unique position to be able 'to change relationships between people' – philanthropy.

Concluding remarks

Simone de Beauvoir was and is a morally committed writer with deeply held political convictions, but the very nature of these has the consequence of restricting her range of activities and thereby the possibilities open to her for exerting influence and so 'changing the world'. Furthermore this is compounded by a philosophy that exalts the value and significance of the individual and by a personal distaste – almost a psychological indisposition – for the type of action that would normally be defined as political. So while in her view the intellectual has a role to play in helping to prepare the way for the revolution, her own contribution remains circumscribed by theoretical and personal limitations.

Society must be reconstructed in its totality, she believes. The change will therefore be cataclysmic and cannot happen through a slow evolution; since any attempt to reform the system can only succeed in bolstering it and delaying the day of revolution, there must be no attempt to work within the normal democratic channels of parliament and the political parties. This means that she is uninterested in the institutions of the state, but it also means that she has little understanding of the details of the distribution of political and economic power and the use which can be made of it. It might be thought that such knowledge is a prerequisite to the successful exercise of influence for change, yet by her attitude she excludes the manipulation of the system for one's own ends. Simone de Beauvoir and her circle have sometimes been compared with an earlier literary coterie, the Bloomsbury Group. The political home of these English intellectuals was the Fabian Society, and while they were non-revolutionary their view of society was very similar to that of Simone de Beauvoir. Their methods, on the other hand, were in complete contrast, and in their limited way they were successful in securing at least some of the social engineering that they wanted, through the technique known as 'permeation' or, less nobly, 'wire-pulling'. In pluralist democracies the structure of influence depends largely on the existence of groups, official or not, which affect policy-making and opinion-changing. Pressure groups like the Bloomsbury Group operate by permeating the agencies of government, knowing the right top people – civil servants or politicians – who are in a position to influence policies and decisions, and for this a knowledge of the map of power is essential. Simone de Beauvoir and her circle had little knowledge and no interest in acquiring it, for they disdained these avenues of influence.[1]

Not only must the committed intellectual refuse to be part of 'the system', but he must also remain independent of its opponents in the form of the Communist Party or extra-parliamentary groups. This insistence on preserving one's independence puts the emphasis on individual effort and small-scale action. It not only reduces the possibilities for influence but also adds to that sense of isolation which is the corollary of being a left-wing intellectual: 'my objective condition cuts me off from the proletariat, and the way in which I experience it subjectively makes me the enemy of the middle classes'. Bitterly hating and rejecting the class from which she has come, but of which she is still professionally a member, she cannot become one of the proletariat whom she supports. This isolation is in itself a disadvantage: suspect to the Communist Party because of their origins and their independence, Sartre and Simone de Beauvoir always had to contend with the additional problem that their association with it had the effect of lessening their credibility with the political elite and even the general public.[2]

If the usual avenues of political influence are closed to him, then the left-wing intellectual can only work through his writing, or by using the name he has made for himself in a publicity exercise to give support to certain views either by his words or by his physical presence. This presupposes that the intellectual can have influence in this way. The question arises: can he? In order to evaluate the influence of French intellectuals it is necessary first to examine the rather special position accorded to them in their own country, in contrast to England where intellectuals are not taken quite so seriously.[3]

The important role of ideology in French politics, in which the debate about ideas has always taken precedence over mere programmes, and the traditional respect in which intellect and culture are held in France explain the high status enjoyed by French intellectuals. Intellectuals – and writers in particular – are assumed by virtue of their expertise in a specialised field to be fit to pronounce judgment on any subject, but especially on political or social issues of the day, and often even have their own column in the daily or weekly newspapers. The serious attention and admiration that are accorded to their opinions not only give them a sense (sometimes inflated) of their own importance, but foster in others the belief that their influence is considerable. Whether this is in fact so is very difficult to estimate. If people like Julien Benda believe that the intellectual should keep out of politics because that was never intended to be his role, others like Jean-François Revel argue the same thing simply because they believe that intellectuals are ineffective: the public indignation of leading writers carries no weight and has never had the slightest influence either on those in power or on public opinion.[4] One of the harshest critics of the French intellectuals was Nizan, but he was criticising from precisely the opposite viewpoint – that of someone who believed in political action, even if he did not trust the intellectuals to carry it out. He rejected absolutely (having just escaped being taken in himself) the cult of the thinker as saviour, offering answers to all life's problems, and the belief that thought is action. He questioned whether anything could possibly be changed by the process of verbalisation. Of course the very act of verbalisation tends to inhibit other action and it could be said of Simone de Beauvoir that her political outrage exhausts itself in rhetoric, and that the more it is literary, the less it can be defined as political.

The general consensus appears to be that their influence is much more restricted than is often believed. In this relatively small circle the phenomenon of 'cultural incest' operates to a large degree, as Nizan was profoundly aware. The impact they can have must depend on the channels of communication, and since their views tend to be expressed in a limited number of publications with a small circulation which are read by other intellectuals (as are their published works, although these are not usually intended to influence *events*), the result is, in the words of Theodore Zeldin, that 'they influenced each other most of all'.[5] Through their writings they can reach an elite who are either in government or who exercise influence in forming policy, and this is a potential source of power. On the whole they do not influence the course of events, even this way, except indirectly through ideas, changing the way people look at the important issues of the contemporary world. What often happens is that they exert an influence *after*, not before, the event, enabling people to rationalise and explain what has already taken place.[6] In terms of reaching the general public, the publicity given to them has two drawbacks. They suffer to some extent from over-exposure, which lessens the impact. The same names appear among the signatories of manifestos, the committees of associations and tribunals, and the demonstrators at marches, and these people tend to be branded as professional protesters. It is also true that their ideas can suffer from popularisation: by the time these reach a wide public, they have become distorted, and therefore cease to reflect the precise meanings and intentions of their authors.[7] Thus an impasse is reached: they need this very publicity if they are to disseminate their ideas and affect public opinion.

If this picture appears to be somewhat pessimistic, it is largely because of the contrast it presents with the popular view that the French intellectuals have immense power and influence. In reality, of course, the influence of intellectuals (and in particular of literary figures) is impossible to evaluate except in very narrowly defined areas. The whole question is such an imponderable that nothing can be concluded with any certainty. What *is* sure is that the climate of opinion changes over the years and that the ideas and views of intellectuals are one of the elements contributing to this evolution. Their effect, although it tends to be long-term and is only rarely immediate, depends upon the power of ideas to shape human consciousness and therefore social forms. If Sartre and Simone de Beauvoir always feared – rightly – that dilution of the message results from using the power structures, perhaps they were justified in believing that they could have influence, if only in the long run, by insisting on their vision.

They were nevertheless both well aware that what they were doing might not change anything. Sartre had realised by the time he wrote *Les mots* that the pen is not a sword and that the word only rarely becomes action, but still felt that even if nothing is changed by it the writer must go on making his cultural and political effort. Even though he had started to act in other ways he would never give up writing books: 'they have a use all the same'. He later (in 1975) seemed to be putting his faith in influence over the long term: 'there are some ideas that take longer to convince people'. If they had not yet had an effect at least he hoped that they would in the future.[8] Sartre is now dead. As assessments of his place in the twentieth century are beginning to be made, it is clear that here was a giant, a man of moral and intellectual stature whose honesty and integrity in living in accordance with his principles may well prove to be more powerful than his ideas. The time when he and Simone de Beauvoir were part of France's intellectual *avant-garde* has long been over: while undoubtedly they influenced a whole generation through their philosophy, existentialism is outmoded and no longer dominates current thought. In political terms what Sartre has had to say and do since the early sixties has failed to catch the popular imagination and he has remained irrelevant to the younger generation in spite of the similarities of their views on many issues, and this was already so in 1968 when the May events took place without him. It remains to be seen what the extent of his long-term reputation will be. If his ideas are to have an effect in the future it is possible that this will be through the medium of his literary works, rather than through his political pronouncements and action.

Simone de Beauvoir's view seems distinctly more cautious than Sartre's, at least about their potential impact. As early as 1948, she was already questioning the effectiveness of French intellectuals. The discussion which they undoubtedly generated appeared, she said, to imply influence and they were thus encouraged 'in an activity whose effect is perhaps more apparent than real'. These doubts about the efficacy of action – literary or any other – were part of the broader picture that can be put together from her work of the hopeless task facing a left-wing intellectual like herself. What role can she play? Conscious of her privileged position as a member of the class she rejects, unable to reach the masses whom she wishes to support, unsure that anything can be achieved by what she might do, she has every excuse for her natural instinct to shy away from those political activities which she sees as necessary, if of limited significance, and which she leaves largely to others.

If Sartre who did not abstain from action had such difficulty in influencing events and attitudes, how could Simone de Beauvoir, leaving action to others, hope to influence the course of the revolution, to change the world? In an interview in *Humanité Dimanche* on the publication of *Les mandarins*, she hotly denies that Anne is apolitical in spite of the fact that like Simone de Beauvoir herself she is not politically active: she is in total agreement with the others who *are*, and her life and thought are dominated by the same principles as theirs. Perhaps, but support for the left, vigilance and criticism of the system are really not enough to overthrow society.

If being on the left is merely to have pious hopes, then the fight for the revolution is reduced to shadow play and is purely utopian. If we use what historians call the counterfactual condition and ask whether, if she did not exist and her views were not expressed, any difference would be made to the chances of revolution, to the possibility of transforming society, then the answer must be no. She accompanies and supports revolutionary activity when it occurs, but May 1968, violent and short-lived, and the women's movement, achieving its victories more gradually and more permanently, both happened independently of her: it would be difficult to argue any causal relationship.

In fact if everyone acted like Simone de Beauvoir very few changes would ever take place in society. She wishes society to alter radically and sees that action must be taken to bring this about, but she has been happy for most of her life to leave this to other people. It does not seem to matter how little she does or whether it really corresponds to her ideas about what *should* be done. Or does it? The gap between theory and practice troubles her more than one might imagine. When asked in an interview in 1979 whether she thought that her elitist attitude as a teacher was worthy of someone on the left, she replied with characteristic honesty: 'Oh no! I don't think so at all. But after all, you know how it is, however much you try to make your life match your ideas, sometimes it won't. I'm not proud of it, but that's the way it is, and I can't do anything about it.'[9] When the theory and the practice cannot be made to correspond she does not reject, or even amend, the one or the other and this necessarily leads to contradictions that cannot be reconciled. On the other hand by keeping them separate she preserves the purity of both. No damaging compromises or qualifications are necessary, and her moral integrity is intact. On the one occasion when this might have been undermined, she was obliged to act: her position as theoretician *par excellence* of the condition of women was threatened when she was overtaken by others in the early stages of the women's movement. Possibly subconsciously regarding herself as their leader and certainly regarded by them as such, she was bound to follow. Of course this is not the whole picture and there were many other reasons for her decision to be active in this field, but this is one that she may not have admitted even to herself, honest as she is.

In political terms, everything seems to conspire to encourage her reluctance to act. There is a basic contradiction in her thinking of which she is well aware: the fact that she is fighting for a socialist society that will probably be just as hierarchical and oppressive as the one it will replace, and that is unlikely to resemble the ideal society in which, in her mind, human relationships will change for the better. Furthermore she now sees the discrepancy between what she expected and what has in fact been achieved to be so great that even her optimism has evaporated. This realisation has led her to a rejection – or at least a postponement to the distant future – of that mass action in which she was always unwilling to participate. Realising that to wait for the revolution is too lengthy a process, she has come round to the view that pressure groups can achieve certain improvements in the meantime, and to this end she has begun to act in minor ways herself. This may contradict her own previous arguments that there can be no half measures in bringing down society; on the other hand the action is still by and for individuals, society always being seen as an aggregation of persons.

This individual role is crucial. If her philosophy demands self-improvement on the part of the privileged elite who are capable of it, this is part of the work of helping others. It means that *engagement* does not require political action because it is an ethic. The opposite of political abstention is not necessarily action but can quite simply be commitment to certain attitudes and values. If that is there, then commitment is limitless and almost any action can be redefined as political, and indeed this is how Simone de Beauvoir justifies her lack of participation in politics as such. All ethical stances are in reality political stances; social action is political action for she does not differentiate between them; women's liberation is political; writing is political. This last must be considered the most important area of her *engagement*. Her view of literary activity as a testimony and a communication from writer to reader could be seen as self-indulgence: a private act of fulfilment which might, *en passant*, influence people's thinking and attitudes. Yet for her writing is valid as action (in spite of her present wish to complement it with certain public activities) and therefore has fulfilled the task to which she has devoted herself. This task is to philosophise her life and live her philosophy, an interactive personal process which is deliberately made available to the public through publications, interviews and now film. This is not mere arrogance on her part but a profession of faith and an overwhelming sense of duty, which she can never abandon, to the obligations of *engagement*.

Summaries of
Simone de Beauvoir's fictional works

Novels

L'invitée (She came to stay)

Françoise and Pierre have for eight years had a rewarding liaison, a relationship of equals. A friend of Françoise, a young girl called Xavière, living in Rouen which she hates and incapable of pursuing her studies or of finding suitable work, joins them in Paris at their invitation. They conceive the idea of forming with her a trio in which there will be a relationship of absolute reciprocity between its members, and they soon become obsessed with the girl, their lives revolving round her. The plot is simply the development of the relations of the three, the jealousies that arise, the rejection felt by one out of the three at any given time (usually Pierre or Françoise, rarely Xavière). It is the story of Françoise which is being told, and so it is the effect on her of the other two which is followed. From being a 'consciousness' in a world centred upon herself and Pierre, she is reduced to a nonentity with no individuality or inner resources in a universe peopled by other hostile individuals; then the danger becomes more threatening as Xavière invades and distorts her inner self. In the end there is only one way out: she murders Xavière.

Written 1937–41, published 1943. Although not completed until after Simone de Beauvoir's rejection of her earlier views on *l'autre*, it belongs to that first period of her life and thought. Not only did the writing of it exorcise this early attitude, but the past was being buried in another way: the murder of Xavière was a means of purging herself of all remaining resentment towards the real Xavière. Moreover she had so identified with Françoise that a way out of mental isolation had to be found for the character in order for the author herself to escape.

Le sang des autres (The blood of others)

Jean Blomart, while at the bedside of the dying Hélène, is turning over in his mind the problem of whether to authorise the next operation of his Resistance group. He relives episodes from his past. The son of a rich industrialist, he cannot accept his privileged position, joins the Communist Party and goes to work in a factory. A friend follows him into the Party and is killed at a

demonstration. Blomart, feeling responsible, withdraws from political involvement, although he becomes active in a trade union which has no political
affiliations. He gives way to the pressing attentions of Hélène, but when war
is declared and he joins up, she uses her influence to have him moved away
from the front line against his will and he breaks with her. He forms a
Resistance group: he has finally realised that both action and inaction can hurt,
and avoiding bloodshed is as sinful as shedding the blood of others. Hélène,
until the occupation totally self-centred, recognises her responsibilities and
joins the group, but during a rescue operation she is mortally wounded.
At the end of the novel she dies, and Blomart makes the decision to go ahead
as planned.

Written 1941–3, published 1945. Because of its Resistance setting
and the time of publication it was very well received, although in
her view it has many faults: the construction is good, but it is too
didactic and moralistic and the characters lack depth. It belongs to
the 'moral period' of her writing and reflects her own changed
viewpoint. Hélène's concern with her personal salvation gives way
to a more responsible attitude; Blomart, already conscious of his
responsibilities, learns that he cannot preserve his peace of mind by
abstention and that violence, although to be avoided if possible, is
sometimes necessary as a means to an end.

Tous les hommes sont mortels (All men are mortal)

Fosca, prince of Carmona in fifteenth-century Italy, has ambitions for the
glory of his town, but he also wishes to exert political influence on a grander
scale to possess the world, with the universal good of mankind as his aim.
Believing that it will enable him to achieve his ambitions, he drinks an elixir
to make himself immortal. He then journeys through history, taking part in
the Holy Roman Empire, the discovery of the New World, the French
Revolution of 1848. His immortality destroys his relations with his fellow
human beings and with women in particular, and eventually it becomes clear
that without death his life has no meaning: he is not like other men.
His quest only brings misfortune and misery in its wake, and in any case
the world is made up of individuals who must each find their own way.
As history repeats itself he sinks into indifference and pessimism: through
the centuries he has seen no evidence of progress. The only character who
affirms the validity of human effort and sacrifice is his great grandson,
Armand, a revolutionary who is totally involved in the drama of his time.
The story of Fosca's life is told by him in retrospect to Régine, an actress who
had hoped to conquer the world through an association with an immortal:
at the end she is in despair.

Written 1943–6, published 1946. It was not a success, although
Simone de Beauvoir thought at the time that it was better than her

previous novels. She did not intend to put forward a particular thesis, and here there is a direct contrast with *Le sang des autres*: she does not commit herself to optimism or pessimism, for although the latter predominates, it is balanced by the optimism of the final chapter. This ambivalence reflects her feeling that those who died in the Resistance might have been sacrificed in vain, while at the same time she recognises that life and therefore hope is renewed with each generation.

Les mandarins (The mandarins)

The novel follows the relationships of a group of left-wing intellectuals in Paris between 1944 and 1947, seen against the contemporary background. At the centre of the group are Henri Perron, a writer who runs a newspaper, *L'Espoir*, Robert Dubreuilh, also a writer, and his wife Anne, a psychoanalyst. 'Gratuitous' writing is relegated to second place as Henri concentrates on his paper and Dubreuilh creates an independent left-wing political group, the S.R.L. Reluctantly Henri gives in to pressure from Dubreuilh to align his nearly bankrupt *Espoir* politically with the S.R.L., on the promise of financial help without strings, but finds he has been misled. This leads to a quarrel between the two men which comes to a head when *L'Espoir* publishes information about the Soviet labour camps against Dubreuilh's wishes, and breaks with the political group. The S.R.L. folds, and Henri resigns from *L'Espoir* after differences with his co-editors. Running parallel there are the psychological problems and the personal relationships of the characters, particularly the women. Paule, in love with Henri who no longer loves her, has played the role of the woman in love for so long that she now has no resources to fall back on and comes near to madness. Nadine, the Dubreuilhs' daughter, aggressive and selfish, gradually softens and grows up. Anne meets Lewis Brogan, a writer, while on a visit to the States, and has an affair with him which ends when Lewis will not accept her on a part-time basis and she will not leave Paris or the people to whom she belongs. At the end, Henri and Robert are reconciled and start planning a new project; Paule reaches some sort of equilibrium by throwing herself into society life; Nadine appears to find happiness with Henri in marriage and motherhood; and Anne, overcome by the horrors of the world and an empty existence, is momentarily tempted by suicide but refrains because it is others who will suffer by her death. She is thus choosing the path of hope: perhaps they will help her to live again.

Written 1951–4, published 1954. Won the Prix Goncourt. She started writing it at the end of that heady postwar period which had begun with such hopes of rebuilding a just and happy society. Now all this had gone: bourgeois domination had been re-established, the warm friendships which had sprung up after the occupation had died together with the shared hopes. It had been a failure, and

Simone de Beauvoir felt it as a personal defeat which she must redeem in words, much as she had done with another failure by writing *L'invitée*. The title was not intended to imply a criticism of the group as has sometimes been thought; it was used ironically and affectionately of intellectuals who found themselves in a difficult situation and who tried to accept and use it to the best of their ability.

Les belles images

Laurence works in advertising, her husband Jean-Charles is an architect. Laurence's parents are separated: her father, to whom she is very close, takes refuge in culture and the past, her mother Dominique has a high-powered job on the radio and lives with Gilbert, one of the richest men in France. The novel is a succession of scenes which are mostly conversation pieces, in the course of which Laurence decides to end a half-hearted affair, Gilbert leaves Dominique, Jean-Charles is furious with his wife for damaging his car in order to avoid a cyclist. Laurence and her father go to Greece, and her impatience with his concern for the aesthetic and for the past to the exclusion of the realities of the present is compounded by the news that he and her mother have made it up. Her ten-year-old daughter Catherine, tormented by a friend's revelation of the misery and poverty in the world, has been sent to a psychiatrist who advises separation from the friend. Laurence has a sudden nervous collapse, takes to her bed and cannot eat. She only emerges from the crisis when promised that Catherine will not be prevented from seeing her friend. At least they will not turn the child into 'une belle image', even if for Laurence it is too late.

Written 1965–6, published 1966. Simone de Beauvoir wanted to evoke the atmosphere of a particular milieu, that of the technocratic society in which she lives but to which she feels so hostile, and in particular to let the reader listen in to the inanities of its idle talk. Some readers have expressed surprise that she concerned herself with such people; she concludes that they have failed to read between the lines. She cannot identify with any of the characters, and neither Laurence who connives at the attitudes of this society, nor her father who takes refuge in the past, expresses Simone de Beauvoir's own views.

Short stories

La femme rompue (*The woman destroyed*)

L'âge de discrétion (*The age of discretion*). Two intellectuals growing old face the fact in different ways. André accepts the coming of old age and the fact that he no longer has new ideas, his wife is upset by her physical decline and by criticism of her new book for repeating her earlier ones. An estrangement between them arises out of her quarrel with their son. She joins her husband in the country where he is staying with his mother, an ideal example of how to grow old. As they talk they grow closer, her anger is dissipated, misunderstandings are explained, dialogue is re-established, and a reconciliation with the son is envisaged.

Le monologue (*The monologue*). Murielle, twice married and now separated from her second husband who has custody of their son, is alone on Christmas Eve. She defends and justifies herself in an incoherent monologue, but she knows in spite of what she says that she is guilty of her daughter's suicide by her possessiveness and domination, and that she is largely responsible for her other failed relationships. The monologue is one long expression of loneliness and hatred.

La femme rompue. Monique is in her forties. She gave up her career to marry Maurice and prides herself on being a devoted housewife and mother. Both their daughters have now left home. Maurice has long since ceased to love her although she is unaware of the fact; he is now in love with a successful barrister, Noëllie, and gradually detaches himself from his wife. Her diary gives her account of what is happening and is an exercise in self-deception. The past was built on the myth that by living only for her family she justified her life; now she is clutching at every straw in order to deceive herself that Maurice will give up Noëllie. Maurice's efforts to avoid hurting her only encourage this. Eventually he moves out and she is left to face the future alone.

Written 1966–7, published 1968. The reader is asked to decipher for himself the reality between the lines. The stories have in common two central subjects, isolation and failure, and they reflect Simone de Beauvoir's constant preoccupation with the problems of the passage of time, approaching old age and the iniquities of bourgeois marriage. Critics saw them as pitiful proof of her own horror at growing old. Feminists saw as a betrayal her concentration on women who are failures, but she has always claimed the right to portray such women: they have her sympathy but also her criticism for their total dependence on their husbands and their attempts at domination over their children.

Quand prime le spirituel

Each story centres round one of five young women who are connected in one way or another. *Marcelle* has a taste for self-sacrifice. This leads her eventually to marry a penniless aspiring poet who turns out to be a parasite. He lives on her earnings, deceives her and leaves her. *Chantal* is proud of having discarded bourgeois values. In the provincial town where she teaches she delights in dazzling her colleagues and pupils with her elegance and her progressive views, but when put to the test she turns out to be as bourgeois as the rest. *Lisa* is a student in a Catholic establishment in Paris. Poor and plain, and conscious that the future holds nothing for her, she proudly resigns herself to her condition. We follow her on a day out when she meets her friend Marguerite, Marcelle's younger sister, and Pascal their brother, whom she adores from a distance. But Pascal is in love with *Anne*, who met him through Chantal. Pascal is unacceptable to Anne's family and Anne is torn between love and filial duty. About to be despatched to England for a year, she succumbs to a mysterious disease of the brain and dies. *Marguerite* attempts to free herself from her bourgeois background by losing herself in her studies and by frequenting bars at night in a search for vice and bohemian adventure. She takes over her brother-in-law, seeing herself as Marcelle did as his saviour. It is only when he decides to return to Marcelle and settle for a safe, ordinary life that she is brought back to earth, finally discarding her fantasy existence.

Written 1935–7, published 1979. It was rejected by Gallimard and by Grasset as lacking originality; it was an interesting view of a decaying world but left the reader with no clear indication of what was to take its place. Both criticisms astonished her at the time since she had not meant to depict a particular period but to make subtle psychological studies. She has now been persuaded to publish it since friends have discerned in it certain qualities, and she herself finds it 'sympathetic' because it was her first literary work.

Play

Les bouches inutiles

The town of Vauxcelles is besieged by the Burgundians. Jean-Pierre Gauthier has crossed the enemy lines with the message that the King of France will relieve the town in the spring, but the food supplies will not last until then. The leader of the town council, Louis d'Avesnes, asks Gauthier to take charge of provisions but he refuses to take on such an onerous responsibility, just as he has always refused to participate in governing the town. It is when the council takes the decision to throw out all the 'useless mouths' – the women and children, the infirm and the old – to die in the ditches outside the town walls that he realises that abstention is now impossible. He tries to persuade the townsfolk to refuse the order. Louis sees growing evidence that the rule of tyranny is infectious and destructive, and calls upon the council to change its mind. Convinced finally by evidence of treason and by Jean-Pierre's persuasive arguments that it has the right and duty to reverse its decision, the council agrees to a mass exodus from the town: all together they will win or be massacred. The outcome is left undecided.

Written 1944, published 1945, first performed 31 October 1945. This is another work from the 'moral period' and displays, in Simone de Beauvoir's view, the same faults as *Le sang des autres*: political problems are treated in abstract moral terms, the characters are merely a set of ethical attitudes, the whole is too idealistic and didactic. One could add that the dialogue is littered with rather facile expressions of existentialist philosophy, although one of her reasons for attempting a play was that so many people had commented on the excellent dialogue in her novels. She recognised later that she did not have a gift for the theatre and never tried again.

Abbreviations

The following abbreviations have been used in the notes for works by Simone de Beauvoir:

Age	*Old age*
All men	*All men are mortal*
All said	*All said and done*
Ambiguity	*The ethics of ambiguity*
America	*America day by day*
Blood	*The blood of others*
Bouches	*Les bouches inutiles*
Circumstance	*Force of circumstance*
'Idéalisme/réalisme'	'Idéalisme moral et réalisme politique'
Images	*Les belles images*
Mandarins	*The mandarins*
March	*The long march*
Memoirs	*Memoirs of a dutiful daughter*
'Merleau-Ponty'	'Merleau-Ponty et le pseudo-sartrisme'
'Œil'	'Œil pour œil'
'Pensée/droite'	'La pensée de droite aujourd'hui'
Prime	*The prime of life*
Pyrrhus	*Pyrrhus et Cinéas*
'Sagesse'	'L'existentialisme et la sagesse des nations'
2nd sex	*The second sex*
She came	*She came to stay*

Notes

1. From apoliticism to involvement

1 See for instance Paul Roubiczek, *Existentialism for and against*, p. 124.
2 Sartre, interview with Madeleine Gobeil, quoted in Serge Julienne-Caffié, *Simone de Beauvoir*, p. 38.
3 *Memoirs of a dutiful daughter* (*Mémoires d'une jeune fille rangée*), pp. 42, 131, 135 and 139. This will be referred to henceforward as *Memoirs*.
4 *Ibid.*, p. 139. It is interesting to note that Sartre's faith was lost in exactly the same way. Suddenly one day he said to himself: ' "Well, fancy that! God doesn't exist." It happened just like that – and for good' (Alexandre Astruc and Michel Contat, *Sartre par lui-même*, p. 27).
5 Not to be confused with Mounier's *Esprit* (see pp. 47 and 102). On the *Philosophies* group, see n. 7.
6 *Memoirs*, p. 239; *All said and done* (*Tout compte fait*), p. 19. This will be referred to henceforward as *All said*.
7 Raymond Aron, *The opium of the intellectuals*, p. 213. The E.N.S. is one of the prestigious *grandes écoles*, specialised institutions of advanced training, entrance to which is gained by competitive examination. It trains the elite of the teaching profession, preparing them for the extremely difficult agrégation, also competitive. The successful candidates, *agrégés*, are then nominated to posts in lycées and universities. Aron claims that the attitudes of intellectuals are to be explained by the social origins of each of them, and in these he includes the different faculties with their different 'climates'. Theodore Zeldin, while agreeing that certain faculties and *grandes écoles* were associated with certain political attitudes, believes that although the assumption is often made that the E.N.S. was left wing, it was not really so until after the second world war: the school produced just as many supporters of the right or extreme right in the thirties (*France 1848–1945*, vol. II, p. 1122). It does seem that between the wars the E.N.S. typified the tendency to polarisation into extremes of right and left which was characteristic of many French intellectual groups of the time.
   On the left was a Marxist core in the *Philosophies* group, which no doubt exercised influence in orientating some students towards the left. For details of the personalities involved, their activities and the background to them, see Walter Redfern, *Paul Nizan. Committed literature in a conspiratorial world*.
8 *Memoirs*, pp. 339 and 344.

9   *Force of circumstance* (*La force des choses*), p. 644. This will be referred
    to henceforward as *Circumstance*.
10 Georges Hourdin, *Simone de Beauvoir et la liberté*, p. 160.
11 *The prime of life* (*La force de l'âge*), p. 30. This will be referred to
    henceforward as *Prime*.
12 *Ibid.*, pp. 18, 112 and 116; Aron, *Opium*, pp. 210 and 212. 'Le désordre
    établi' is Mounier's phrase.
13 *Prime*, pp. 32 and 114; *Memoirs*, p. 34; interview with Madeleine
    Chapsal in Claude Francis and Fernande Gontier, *Les écrits de Simone
    de Beauvoir*, p. 393. Sartre felt the same way about politics and writing:
    in the film about his life he talks of the 'fascist' riots of 1934 as being
    for him at that time 'an area you didn't write about' (Astruc and
    Contat, p. 44).
14 *Prime*, pp. 18, 45, 127, 93 and 132.
15 *Ibid.*, pp. 175 and 211–12. One is struck by similar reactions in her later
    life. When she reads of horrors like the starvation of Biafran children or
    atrocities in Vietnam: 'the reaction is one of fury at one's impotence'
    (*All said*, p. 143).
16 In fairness to Blum, he had agreed to send aid and had been forced by
    pressure both from the British and from the Radicals in his government
    to join in a non-intervention agreement. He did, however, send aid
    officially in the form of clothing, food and medical supplies, and secretly
    (in 1936) in the form of planes. Moreover the French government also
    shut its eyes to the passage of arms through the frontier. (Hugh Thomas,
    The Spanish civil war)
17 *Prime*, pp. 220–1, 231 and 283; *All said*, p. 23.
18 *Prime*, pp. 119, 256 and 285. Alfred Cobban confirms that the French
    left did indeed share Simone de Beauvoir's belief that fascism would
    fail (*A history of modern France*, vol. III, p. 163).
19 *Prime*, pp. 26–8 and 49.
20 *Memoirs*, p. 70; *All said*, p. 114; *Prime*, p. 290. The 'trio' originated in
    Rouen, when Olga Kosakiewicz, a former pupil of Simone de Beauvoir's
    at Rouen, who could not settle to any career or further studies, was taken
    over by her and Sartre and given a place in their lives as the third
    member of a triangle whose relationships with each other would all be
    equal. Infatuated by her, they saw her as the incarnation of the *enfant
    terrible*, whose youth and enthusiasm would invigorate their lives. The
    equality was a myth: as adults they had control and had annexed her;
    moreover it soon became apparent that the relationship between Olga
    and Sartre was beginning to exclude Simone de Beauvoir. The situation
    was happily resolved by Olga becoming involved with a young man who
    was another friend of theirs, not by a murder as in *L'invitée* where
    Xavière (Olga) is murdered by Françoise (Simone de Beauvoir).
21 *Prime*, pp. 28, 122, 268 and 474; *All said*, p. 23.
22 Francis Jeanson, *Simone de Beauvoir ou l'entreprise de vivre*, p. 85.
    In fact, with every journey abroad her awareness was increased by
    experience and the American visit was not such an important turning-
    point.

23 *Prime*, pp. 18 and 289; *Circumstance*, p. 658 (partly author's translation); interviews with Caroline Moorehead, Francis Jeanson and Madeleine Gobeil.

24 *Memoirs*, pp. 59–60 and 294; *Prime*, pp. 19–22 and 78.

25 As when Sartre was given a teaching post in Le Havre, to allow him to be near Simone de Beauvoir in Rouen.

26 *Prime*, pp. 285, 296 and 373; *Memoirs*, p. 170; *Circumstance*, p. 4. The impossibility of avoiding such commitment became a basic element of her philosophy, and her own change of attitude is detailed in the person of Jean Blomart in *The blood of others* (*Le sang des autres*). This will be referred to henceforward as *Blood*.

27 Aron, *Opium*, p. 290; Pierre Bourdieu and Jean-Claude Passeron, *Reproduction in education, society and culture*, pp. 169–70.

28 *Prime*, p. 288. Nizan's view of the E.N.S. is given in Walter Redfern, p. 23, and also in a paper presented by him at the University of Warwick, 6 February 1978.

29 Michel-Antoine Burnier, *Choice of action: the French existentialists on the political front line*, pp. 3–4, using in part phrases culled from *Prime*; Sartre, preface to Nizan's *Aden–Arabie* in *Situations*, p. 166.

30 *Prime*, p. 309. It is a view supported by Redfern, p. 185.

31 *Memoirs*, p. 240. In Sartre's *Crime passionnel* (*Les mains sales*) Georges accuses Hugo of the same crime of never having experienced hunger.

32 *Mauvaise foi* is hypocrisy, primarily aimed at oneself; that is, it is often self-deception, usually deliberate. It is a device which man often uses to pretend to himself that he is not free and that he must therefore passively accept the situation in which he finds himself.

33 Sartre, *Situations*, pp. 134 and 166; *Prime*, pp. 31, 295 and 342; Burnier, p. 7.

34 *All said*, p. 28.

2. Freedom and responsibility

1 *Circumstance*, pp. 4 and 644; interview with Madeleine Gobeil, quoted in Julienne-Caffié, p. 38. One example of her understanding of Sartre's work is to be found in 'Merleau-Ponty et le pseudo-sartrisme'. This will be referred to henceforward as 'Merleau-Ponty'.

Although she sees her relationship with Sartre as one between equals, in intellectual terms it resembled that between disciple and master. As Julien Cheverny comments in his admittedly hostile review of the film *Simone de Beauvoir*, this was in evidence to the last: 'And always in his presence she behaves like a good pupil looking for approval; she doesn't allow herself to smile at any shared jokes and she replies to the teacher's questions diligently but with a certain gaucheness' (*Le Figaro Magazine*, 17 February 1979, p. 57).

2 *Memoirs*, p. 59; *Prime*, pp. 433 and 435; *Circumstance*, p. 38.

3 For a more detailed discussion of what she hoped to achieve by her writing, see chapter 4.

4 *Les bouches inutiles, She came to stay* (*L'invitée*), *The blood of others*

(*Le sang des autres*), *All men are mortal* (*Tous les hommes sont mortels*), *Pyrrhus et Cinéas* and *The ethics of ambiguity* (*Pour une morale de l'ambiguïté*). These will be referred to henceforward as *Bouches*, *She came*, *Blood*, *All men*, *Pyrrhus* and *Ambiguity*.

5 Sartre, *Existentialism and humanism* (*L'existentialisme est un humanisme*), pp. 26–8. Simone de Beauvoir herself states it explicitly in *The second sex* (*Le deuxième sexe*), p. 264; 'essence does not precede existence'. This will be referred to henceforward as *2nd sex*.

6 *Blood*, p. 68; *Ambiguity*, p. 16. Like Sartre in *Existentialism and humanism* (p. 33) Simone de Beauvoir attributes the words 'si Dieu n'existe pas, tout est permis' to Dostoevsky. Strictly speaking, the sentiments are expressed on more than one occasion by Ivan Karamazov in *The brothers Karamazov*. In fact it would appear that for Dostoevsky too the non-existence of God would mean total responsibility laid on man's shoulders, and would set the highest possible moral standards (see, for example, *The possessed*).

7 Sartre, *Existentialism and humanism*, p. 34; *Blood*, p. 179. Or, in a variation on Sartre's words, 'An existant *is* nothing other than what he does' (*2nd sex*, p. 264). For Sartre it is the same: 'Man is nothing else but what he purposes, he exists only in so far as he realises himself, he is therefore nothing else but the sum of his actions, nothing else but what his life is' (*Existentialism and humanism*, p. 41). See also Sartre, *Literary and philosophical essays*, p. 227: 'Thus freedom is to be discovered only in the act, and is one with the act.'

   The question of making choices is sometimes seen as the weak point in the existentialist argument. Every act involves a choice, even the mere act of perception, and this reduces free choice to a rather arbitrary level. Inaction is in itself a choice, because freedom is freedom to choose, but not freedom not to choose; however, to act in an authentically existentialist way man must make a *conscious* choice which is then an expression of his own will. The outcome will then be different – and by implication better – if only in psychological terms.

8 *Ambiguity*, pp. 28–30. She herself had been guilty of rebelling against the vicissitudes of fortune, but had begun to realise during the war that life must be a compromise and that 'you had either to find a way to get around them, or else put up with your lot' (*Prime*, p. 385).

9 *Bouches*, p. 98. This is a recurrent platitude of the period, to be found in such disparate writers as Genet, Céline, Guilloux and Malraux.

10 *Ambiguity*, pp. 27, 74–8 and 157; *Pyrrhus*, pp. 11, 28 and 60; *2nd sex*, p. 27 (author's translation). The use of 'indéfiniment' needs qualification. Simone de Beauvoir makes a clear distinction: the future, like human enterprise, is neither finite nor infinite but indefinite (see also *Circumstance*, p. 66).

11 *Prime*, p. 435; *Pyrrhus*, p. 119.

12 'L'existentialisme et la sagesse des nations' (which will be referred to henceforward as 'Sagesse'), p. 397; *Pyrrhus*, pp. 70–4 and 88. Elisabeth in *She came*, Denise in *Blood* and Paule in *The mandarins* (*Les mandarins*, which will be referred to henceforward as *Mandarins*) are all

guilty of the first, and André's wife in *The age of discretion* (*L'âge de discrétion*, in *La femme rompue*) of the second.

13 *Ambiguity*, pp. 138–9; *Prime*, p. 434.

14 *Prime*, pp. 22 and 27–8; Jeanson, pp. 251–2 (interview with Simone de Beauvoir); Astruc and Contat, p. 32. See also Sartre, *Words* (*Les mots*), p. 169: 'I was running away; external forces shaped my flight and made me.' According to Carol Evans (Le problème de l'autre dans l'œuvre de Simone de Beauvoir', p. 210) Simone de Beauvoir told her in an interview that she had come to believe to a large extent in psychological determinism, and was much more in agreement with Freud than she had been in the past.

15 It is appropriate to define this total freedom. In part IV, chapter I, section II, 'Freedom and facticity: the situation', of *Being and nothingness* (*L'être et le néant*), Sartre discusses the limits which might appear to reduce man's freedom, but dismisses them. For instance, man exercises his liberty *en situation*, that is, in the situation in which he finds himself in this world and which might be said to impose limitations. But, Sartre argues, to be free is *not* to choose the world in which he finds himself but to choose himself in that world. Similarly although the existence of *l'autre* does really limit man's freedom because he exists for others in a way he has not freely chosen, this limitation cannot come from the actions of others (man can even freely allow himself to be tortured) but resides simply in the fact that other people's freedom also exists. Even so man is free to accept another's view of himself as an object or to reject it and himself to treat others as objects.

16 *Prime*, pp. 434–5; *Existentialism and humanism*, pp. 41–2. Simone de Beauvoir tells us that when Sartre was writing *Saint-Genet*, in 1952, he had begun to see that 'the possibilities of any individual were strictly limited by his situation; the individual's liberty consisted in not accepting his situation passively but, through the very movement of his existence, interiorising and transcending it in order to give it meaning. In certain cases the margin of choice left to him came very close to zero' (*Circumstance*, p. 199).

17 Astruc and Contat, pp. 75–6. See also Sartre, *Between existentialism and Marxism*, p. 35: 'This is the limit I would today [1970] accord to freedom: the small movement which makes of a totally conditioned social being someone who does not render back completely what his conditioning has given him.' One example of Simone de Beauvoir's less categorical attitudes is to be found in *Les belles images*, p. 89 (this will be referred to henceforward as *Images*). Laurence's father is one of those people who can be authentically free, but he sees this as normal: ' "As for you, you can cope with anything, dominate any situation, but that's not within everybody's reach." "What I can do everyone can do. I'm not exceptional." "I think you are," said Laurence affectionately.'

18 She notes that on re-reading Hegel she began to realise the extent to which her own thought now diverged from his; she was too sensible now of being bound up with her contemporaries to ignore the two-fold bond of dependence and responsibility (*Prime*, pp. 372–3).

19   *Prime*, pp. 433 and 435; *Circumstance*, p. 67.
20   Sartre, *Being and nothingness*, p. 429. The theory here is Sartre's, as
     expounded in that work; the examples quoted from *She came* show to
     what extent Simone de Beauvoir was in agreement with him.
21   Sartre, *Being and nothingness*, p. 429; *Prime*, pp. 54 and 428; *She came*,
     pp. 7–9, 12–13, 300–1 and 304–5; *2nd sex*, pp. 347–8.
22   Simone de Beauvoir knows that this was no answer to the problem, but
     she needed to 'murder' Olga, Xavière's original, through her book in
     order to rid herself vicariously of this past episode (*Prime*, p. 270).
23   Colette Audry, *Connaissance de Sartre*, p. 69; Burnier, p. 23; Adereth,
     Commitment in modern French literature, p. 142. As Adereth points out
     (p. 142, n.), Marx stated that a classless society would do away with
     social conflicts, but not necessarily human ones.
24   'And in thus willing freedom, we discover that it depends entirely upon
     the freedom of others and that the freedom of others depends upon our
     own. Obviously, freedom as the definition of a man does not depend on
     others, but as soon as there is a commitment, I am obliged to will the
     liberty of others at the same time as mine. I cannot make liberty my aim
     unless I make that of others equally my aim' (Sartre, *Existentialism and
     humanism*, pp. 51–2). This humanism represents a development in his
     view of relationships since *Being and nothingness*.
25   *Existentialism and humanism*, pp. 29–30; *Situations III*, pp. 13–14.
     Similarly he says: 'in choosing for himself he chooses for all men'
     (*Existentialism and humanism*, p. 29).
26   Orestes achieves his own freedom by the positive act of taking upon
     himself the crimes of the people of Argos, thus disobeying the laws of the
     Gods: but when he leaves them *they* are still in a state of subservience to
     the Gods. According to Simone de Beauvoir, 'The contrast between
     Orestes's departure at the end of *The flies* and Goetz's final stance
     illustrates the distance Sartre had covered between his original anarchistic
     attitude and his present commitment.' Sartre himself states quite clearly:
     'I made Goetz do what I was unable to do' (*Circumstance*, pp. 242–3,
     including unpublished notes by Sartre written in 1951); Philippe Gavi,
     Jean-Paul Sartre and Pierre Victor, *On a raison de se révolter*, p. 171.
27   *Ambiguity*, pp. 71 and 73; *Pyrrhus*, pp. 96 and 115.
28   See Linda Hansen, 'Pain and joy in human relationships. Jean-Paul
     Sartre and Simone de Beauvoir', pp. 343–6.
29   *Ambiguity*, p. 82; *Pyrrhus*, p. 101. She sees the extreme case of the
     Marquis de Sade as exemplifying a dilemma which is fundamental to the
     human condition. *Must we burn Sade?* ('Faut-il brûler Sade?'), p. 11.
30   *Pyrrhus*, p. 90. These words, put by Dostoevsky into the mouth of the
     Elder Zossima in *The brothers Karamazov*, were also used by Simone
     de Beauvoir as the motto for *Blood*. See also *Ambiguity*, p. 72.
31   *Ambiguity*, p. 38; *All men*, pp. 201, 203 and 319; *Pyrrhus*, p. 79.
32   *Pyrrhus*, p. 90; *Bouches*, pp. 91–2.
33   Sartre's image, in *Being and nothingness*, p. 553.
34   Jeanson, pp. 290–1; *Circumstance*, p. 284. She also refers to 'my
     puritanical upbringing' (*Prime*, pp. 55 and 62). Her characters often

reflect this 'puritanical' attitude: Françoise in *She came*, Anne in *Mandarins*. Sartre's puritanism could be explained by his Protestant background, but Simone de Beauvoir's is less easy to understand in religious terms. It could be that the vocabulary ('puritan', 'puritanical') was simply her way of designating certain moral attitudes which have less to do with a confessional background than with her personality. Yet it can be argued that her mother's strict moral code influenced Simone de Beauvoir and was itself derived from the Catholic Church, with which it became connected in Simone de Beauvoir's memory.

35 With the possible exception of *Pyrrhus*, p. 88.
36 Emmanuel Mounier, *Personalism*, pp. xiii, 22, 24, 32, 59–60 and 82 (author's translation).
37 *Prime*, pp. 25 and 54.
38 Malebranche, quoted in Mounier, p. 67.
39 *Prime*, p. 479; *Ambiguity*, pp. 7–9 and 11; 'Sagesse', p. 404. She says of the philosophy of existentialism: 'it has faith in men'. Sartre himself tried to stress the optimistic side of existentialism in *Existentialism and humanism*.
40 *Prime*, pp. 478–9; *2nd sex*, pp. 36–7; 'Sagesse', p. 397. See also Laurent Gagnebin, *Simone de Beauvoir ou le refus de l'indifférence*, pp. 87–8.
41 Gagnebin, p. 103.
42 *Ambiguity*, p. 70; 'Sagesse', p. 399; *Pyrrhus*, pp. 17 and 105. It is Laurent Gagnebin who makes this point when arguing the profoundly Christian tendency of Simone de Beauvoir's thought. Both he and Georges Hourdin see her work from the point of view of the believer. The inhumanity of Marxism is a major criticism of hers and is one of the great divides that separate her from the Communist Party.
43 Astruc and Contat, pp. 100–2.

3. Where ethics and politics meet

1 *Circumstance*, pp. 256 and 645.
2 *Mandarins*, p. 165; 'Idéalisme moral et réalisme politique' (which will be referred to henceforward as 'Idéalisme/réalisme'), pp. 249, 260 and 268.
3 Astruc and Contat, pp. 100–2; *Sartre in the seventies*, pp. 169–71.
4 Interview with Mo Teitelbaum; *Sartre in the seventies*, pp. 204–7. This is what Ernest Gellner calls 'the Fraud theory of democracy...the elections, the show of consultation and consent, in the so-called Liberal democracies are but a fraud' (*Contemporary thought and politics*, p. 27).
5 *Sartre in the seventies*, p. 210; Gavi, Sartre and Victor, p. 356. In fact, *Les Temps Modernes* did not in the end take any line on this matter.
6 Raymond Aron, *Marxism and the existentialists*, pp. 79 and 167–8; Philip Thody, *Sartre: a literary and political study*, pp. 233–4; interview with Catherine David, p. 83.
7 Pierre Domaize, quoted in Julienne-Caffié, p. 233; Jean-Marie Domenach, 'Une politique de la certitude'; Anne-Marie Lasocki, *Simone de Beauvoir ou l'entreprise d'écrire*; interview in Jeanson, pp. 276–7. The Manichees

were a sect which believed the world was governed by the twin powers of good and evil.

8   Gellner, *Contemporary thought*, e.g. pp. 9–10 and 80. An example of this is the contrast between their action over Algeria, compared with that of Francis Jeanson (see chapter 5).

9   *Circumstance*, p. 5; *Mandarins*, p. 500; interview with John Gerassi, 1976, in Francis and Gontier, pp. 547–65. See also Bourdieu and Passeron, *The inheritors*, for the way such privileges operate in the world of education.

10 Gellner, *Contemporary thought*, p. 179; Herbert Marcuse, 'Repressive tolerance'; 'Merleau-Ponty', pp. 2117–18. In lighter vein, Professor Coe relates that in 1970 the students of Monash University (Melbourne) had as their revolutionary slogan: 'We are oppressed by permissiveness!' A similar complaint is made by a radical student in Malcolm Bradbury's *The history man*: 'Why don't they repress us the way they used to?'

11 *Sartre in the seventies*, p. 83; *Ambiguity*, pp. 131–2.

12 Aron, *Marxism*, p. 87; Gellner, 'Ernest Gellner on sandcastles and the search for certainty', p. 568; *Existentialism and humanism*, pp. 40–1; *Sartre in the seventies*, pp. 83–4.

13 *All said*, pp. 406–20 and 462–3; interviews with Alice Schwartzer, 1972, and with Pierre Viansson-Ponté, 1978, in Francis and Gontier, pp. 482–7 and 583–92.

14 Mark Poster (*Existential Marxism in postwar France*) is one of the former. Those who do not see it as a success include Aron (*Marxism*), Gellner ('Sandcastles'), Herbert Read (*Existentialism, Marxism and anarchism*), Alfred Stern (*Sartre: his philosophy and existential psychoanalysis*), John Mander (*The writer and commitment*), and Thody. Aron says that Sartre tried to show that political commitment could not be separated from his philosophy, whereas *he* tried to show 'there is no necessary connection between the two' (*Marxism*, p. 8). Gellner sees the difficulty in philosophical terms, as being the uneasy mix of *a priori* existentialism and 'the concrete empirical context of his social observations' (p. 569). His view is that Sartre's philosophy depends on an *a priori* psychology: it tells you how you feel and think, or ought to, not by asking or observing but by deducing it from certain premises about your general situation.

15 Germaine Brée, *Camus and Sartre. Crisis and commitment*, p. 50; *Prime*, p. 38. Henry Stuart Hughes in *Consciousness and society*, sees Sartre as the last of the intellectuals who in the first half of this century have attempted to create a vast synthesis to explain the world and man's actions within it.

16 Aron, *Marxism*, pp. 9–10; *Circumstance*, pp. 7 and 261; Sartre, interview with Olivier Todd (1957), quoted in Adereth, p. 145; Sartre, *Critique de la raison dialectique*, p. 111. The passage in question appears at the end of 'Questions de méthode'. See also James O'Rourke, *The problem of freedom in Marxist thought*.

17 She accuses herself of being guilty of the latter fault in the *Temps Modernes* articles of the 1940s.

18 These arguments are all contained in *Ambiguity*. The refusal of the French Communist Party to allow its members to make individual decisions according to their conscience was the main deterrent to Sartre's and Simone de Beauvoir's ever joining the party.

19 'Idéalisme/réalisme', p. 258; *Ambiguity*, pp. 28 and 87–9.

20 *Ambiguity*, pp. 42–67.

21 *Ibid.*, p. 91.

22 'Idéalisme/réalisme', p. 263; *Ambiguity*, p. 122. This political implication of the importance of the individual finds its first expression in *Blood*, p. 65: 'The masses are made up of people who exist as individuals.'

23 *Ambiguity*, p. 108; *Blood*, p. 55; 'Idéalisme/réalisme', p. 267.

24 For the whole question of means and ends, see 'Idéalisme/réalisme', pp. 256, 260–2; *Blood*, p. 180; *Ambiguity*, pp. 110–15, 124–5, 133–4, 145, 147–8 and 151–2.

25 'Idéalisme/réalisme', pp. 253–4 and 266; *Ambiguity*, p. 148.

26 The seeking out and punishment or elimination of people who had been collaborators during the occupation.

27 'Œil pour œil' (which will be referred to henceforward as 'Œil'), p. 828; Julienne-Caffié, p. 166.

28 *Circumstance*, pp. 20 and 68. That is why she refused to sign a plea for indulgence for Robert Brasillach, sentenced to death for his war crimes, in spite of her being moved by his court appearance. She, Sartre and Camus shared the view that generally speaking a middle course should be taken between the unconditional pardoning of all collaborators and the application of extreme measures in every case. At first Camus thought, as she did, that the worst offenders must not be pardoned (see, for instance, *Combat*, 30 August 1944), but when asked to sign the plea for clemency in Brasillach's case he decided after a sleepless night that he must sign because of his opposition to the death penalty. Brasillach was executed.

29 *Circumstance*, p. 68. Yet in 1957 she was still using the same vocabulary, if with a different emphasis: 'to be free to eat meat is to have the money to buy some...one is not free to enjoy the sunshine today if one is gnawed by anxiety about tomorrow...Above all for the younger generation, this new freedom is a very concrete reality.' *The long march* (*La longue marche*), p. 496. This will be referred to henceforward as *March*.

30 Compare Genet, who steadfastly refused to jettison aesthetic values and adopt the materialistic values of revolution, in spite of rejecting the present system and admiring certain individuals who revolt against it (Richard N. Coe, *The vision of Jean Genet*, p. 255). Simone de Beauvoir managed to overcome the antipathy she felt towards seeing life in material terms.

31 *Circumstance*, p. 317.

32 'La pensée de droite, aujourd'hui', pp. 1539–43, 1549 and 2231–2. This will be referred to henceforward as 'Pensée/droite'. It could of course be said that Simone de Beauvoir herself was insulated from the realities of life, even if she was aware of them.

33 This was not Sartre's forte either. Michel Crozier notes that 'Sartre

became paradoxically naïve each time he dealt with institutions, political parties, techniques of organisation or social structure' (quoted in Henry Stuart Hughes, *The obstructed path*, p. 225).

34 Astruc and Contat, p. 126.

4. Possibilities for action: I The theory

1   *The great betrayal*, pp. 29–33.
2   Zeldin, vol. II, in particular pp. 1042–4, 1074–6, 1083 and 1151: John Flower, *Writers and politics in modern France*, p. 8.
3   Paul Clay Sorum, *Intellectuals and decolonization in France*, pp. 13 and 17–20; Zeldin, vol. II, p. 309; François Mauriac, 'L'engagement de l'écrivain', *Le Figaro*, 8 April 1953, quoted in Sorum, p. 13.
4   Victor Brombert, *The intellectual hero*, pp. 143–4; Herbert R. Lottman, *Albert Camus: a biography*, p. 381; Jean Blomart in *Blood*, pp. 110–15; Anne in *Mandarins*, p. 85 ('The misfortunes you don't actually share... well, it's as if you were to blame for them.'); *Circumstance*, pp. 369, 384 and 408.
5   *Pyrrhus*, p. 117; *Blood*, p. 57 (author's translation). See also Sartre: 'I have always believed that silence, even when it passes unnoticed, is commitment' (*L'Observateur*, 9 March 1953); and more positively Mounier, asserting that non-intervention in the thirties caused the war: 'for whoever will "have nothing to do with politics" passively furthers the politics of the *de facto* power' (p. 92); and Paul Guth: 'To abstain from politics is to support the policies of the right' (*Le naïf aux quarante enfants*, Paris, Livre de Poche, 1954, p. 62).
6   Lottman, p. 89. Lottman details many examples of intervention by Camus. An article in *Révolution Prolétarienne* at the time Camus was awarded the Nobel prize shows that not everyone was ignorant: 'What we know of Camus is his solidarity...towards the militants of Spain, Bulgaria, Hungary. Not only at the occasion of meetings or of manifestos...but when there are no other witnesses than anonymous ones' (quoted in Lottman, p. 608). To the list could be added Greece and Algeria.
7   *Circumstance*, p. 262; Hughes, *Path*, p. 223. This conclusion is seen by Georges Hourdin as 'the practical inference which she draws from her philosophy of freedom' (p. 159).
8   Aron, *Marxism*, p. 16; Mander, pp. 12–13; Adereth, p. 132.
9   Sartre interview with Jean-Claude Garot, 1968, in *Politics and literature*; Simone de Beauvoir, interview with John Gerassi, 1976.
10 Sorum, p. 12; Astruc and Contat, pp. 125–6; Sartre, interview with Jean-Claude Garot; Aron, *Opium*, p. 210. This was exactly the line followed by *Les Temps Modernes*, a policy agreed by the editorial board of which Simone de Beauvoir was and is a member. The rule was occasionally broken, as at the beginning of 1955 when Péju defined a realistic programme of very precise policies for Mendès-France's government to follow.

11 *Circumstance*, p. 405 (author's translation).
12 Hughes, *Path*; Burnier. Burnier argues that because they are often alone in their protest the verbal violence sometimes appears both exaggerated and ineffectual, but that at any rate their words serve as a warning.
13 Cogniot, *L'avenir de la culture*, quoted in David Caute, *Communism and the French intellectuals*, p. 54; Caute, pp. 34–48, 54, 360 and 367.
14 Astruc and Contat, p. 81; Gavi, Sartre and Victor, p. 17; Sartre, *What is literature? (Qu'est-ce que la littérature?)*, pp. 189 and 196; *Circumstance*, p. 131. See also Adereth and Flower.
15 See chapter 5.
16 Astruc and Contat, p. 121; *Sartre in the seventies*, p. 53.
17 *Circumstance*, pp. 46 and 652–3; *Blood*, p. 25.
18 *All said*, pp. 405–6; Madeleine Descubes, *Connaître Simone de Beauvoir*, pp. 75–6.
19 *Circumstance*, p. 131 (the period referred to is 1946, when he was writing *What is literature?*); Jean-François Revel, *En France. La fin de l'opposition*, p. 53; Astruc and Contat, p. 83.
20 *Clarté* was the organ of the communist student group, the U.E.C.F. The debate was later published as a book under the same title.
21 *Que peut la littérature?*, pp. 34 and 87; Adereth, p. 58; *Circumstance*, p. 622.
22 Astruc and Contat, pp. 81–2; *What is literature?*, pp. 12–13, 205–6 and 220; *Situations II*, p. 30; Adereth, p. 29; Brée, *Camus and Sartre*, p. 194.
23 *Memoirs*, pp. 344–5; Sartre, 'A long, bitter, sweet madness', interview in *Encounter* (1964), pp. 61–3; Adereth, p. 225.
24 *What is literature?*, p. 141; Thody, pp. 169–70; 'A long, bitter, sweet madness', p. 62.
25 Nizan's phrase.
26 Astruc and Contat, pp. 11–12 and 128–9; interview in *L'Idiot International* (1970) in *Between existentialism and Marxism*, pp. 286–98; *Sartre in the seventies*, pp. 54, 179 and 184. See chapter 5, on the episode of *La Cause du Peuple*.
27 *Circumstance*, p. 365; *Prime*, pp. 18 (partly author's translation), 67, 290 and 431; *All said*, p. 114; *Que peut la littérature?*, p. 24.
28 *Prime*, pp. 26, 52 (author's translation) and 178; *Memoirs*, p. 143; *All said*, pp. 29, 134 and 463; Josée Dayan and Malka Ribowska, *Simone de Beauvoir*, pp. 76–7 and 92.
29 *Que peut la littérature?*, pp. 76–9, 80–2 and 92; *All said*, p. 115; lecture in Jerusalem on the role of literature in the contemporary world, 1967, summarised in Francis and Gontier, pp. 227–8.
30 See p. 88.
31 *Circumstance*, pp. 4, 47–8 and 131; Julienne-Caffié, p. 210; *Que peut la littérature?*, p. 73 (author's italics); *Memoirs*, p. 347. See chapter 5, for the aims of *Les Temps Modernes*.
32 *Mandarins*, pp. 225–6 and 255; *Prime*, pp. 431, 435–6 and 479; *Circumstance*, pp. 263, 267, 270–1; Francis and Gontier, pp. 227–8. Sartre believed that the world could be perceived and fixed in words, and she relates a discussion of this subject with him in *Prime*, pp. 37–8.

The imperative of ambiguity, she asserts in 'La littérature et la métaphysique' (pp. 1160-3), can be carried out to perfection in the philosophical novel, and that is one reason why existentialist thought is expressed through the medium of fiction as much as through theoretical treatises. Unfortunately if the author does not make his position clear it can give rise to misunderstandings. To her disgust she has been credited, for instance, with holding the same views as Laurence's father in *Images*. His statements about the happiness of the poor and the beauties of frugality were even quoted in an examination question for the baccalauréat as expressing her viewpoint (*All said*, pp. 123-4).

33   *Prime*, pp. 26-7, 67 (author's translation), 119 and 479; *Circumstance*, pp. 13, 134, 274, 650 and 655; *All said*, pp. 119 and 134.

34   *Circumstance*, p. 649; *All said*, pp. 29 and 209.

35   Towards the end of the Algerian war, about the time when she was feeling about her own writing: 'All writing, my own as well as that of others, seemed so meaningless, I couldn't bring myself to bother with it' (*Circumstance*, p. 620).

36   *All said*, pp. 462-3.

37   Gavi, Sartre and Victor, p. 26; *Sartre in the seventies*, p. 54.

5.   Possibilities for action: II The practice

1   Sartre, interview with Madeleine Gobeil in Julienne-Caffié, p. 41; *Mandarins*, p. 55; interview with J.-F. Rolland, 1954, Francis and Gontier, p. 359; interview with Caroline Moorehead.

2   Astruc and Contat, p. 68; Dayan and Ribowska, p. 48; *Prime*, pp. 383, 396, 424-5 and 479.

3   Comité National des Ecrivains. A classic communist front organisation originating in the Resistance (see Caute on its activities).

4   *Prime*, pp. 425 and 445; *All said*, p. 24.

5   Over Socialisme et Liberté she was sceptical; she thought he was wasting his time when he wanted to set up the Rassemblement Démocratique Révolutionnaire (see p. 107); she was worried that in moving so much closer to communism in 1953 he might be going too far away from 'his own truth' (*Circumstance*, pp. 289-90).

6   *All said*, p. 27; *Circumstance*, pp. 256 and 263.

7   *Circumstance*, pp. 4, 369 and 407.

8   *Ibid.*, pp. 13-14, 48 and 107; Gavi, Sartre and Victor, p. 14; Sartre, 'Merleau-Ponty' (1961) in *Situations*, p. 244; *Les Temps Modernes*, vol. 1, no. 1, pp. 7-8. *Esprit*'s connections with the Catholic Church were not as strong as they appeared to be and it more than once fell foul of orthodox Catholicism.

9   *Circumstance*, pp. 38 and 42-8; Sartre, *Situations*, p. 238; Gavi, Sartre and Victor, pp. 27 and 46.

10   Dayan and Ribowska, p. 61.

11   *Situations*, p. 252.

12   Merleau-Ponty had always argued that the U.S.S.R. would never resort to

aggression and now he had been proved wrong; Sartre took the view that the North Korean forces had been tricked into attacking South Korea. They both, together with Simone de Beauvoir and many others, were convinced that this was the start of another world war and that France would soon be invaded by the Soviet Union – not a prospect any of them envisaged with equanimity. Simone de Beauvoir even talked of their being forced to emigrate rather than stay in France, although she and Sartre did not subscribe to the view of some people that he would have to commit suicide.

13 *All said*, p. 137; *Sartre in the seventies*, pp. 79–81. According to Sartre this homogeneity is deep and is clear from the choice of texts published, when these are seen as a whole – even though they might appear incompatible at first sight.

14 *All said*, pp. 134–5; *Sartre in the seventies*, pp. 81–2; Astruc and Contat, p. 86; *Les Temps Modernes*, vol. xxxv, no. 406, May 1980, editorial.

15 She played a part by acting as interpreter for Richard Wright at a vast meeting in December 1948 to which the R.D.R. had invited various French and foreign personalities to speak (*Circumstance*, p. 172; Burnier, p. 61).

16 *La Gauche*, February 1949, p. 1; *Circumstance*, p. 146.

17 *La Gauche*, 15–30 May 1948, p. 1; *Circumstance*, pp. 147–9; *Entretiens sur la politique*, p. 41.

18 There is no exact record. See Burnier, p. 60. Simone de Beauvoir puts the figure at 5,000 (*Circumstance*, p. 171) but Burnier's estimate is probably closer to the truth.

19 Burnier, especially pp. 60, 70 and 75; *Circumstance*, pp. 171 and 176; Julienne-Caffié, pp. 116–17; *Sartre in the seventies*, p. 49. For a detailed account of the R.D.R., see Burnier, part 1, chapter iv.

20 The phrase 'la troisième voie', it will be remembered, originated with *Esprit* and La Troisième Force.

21 *Circumstance*, pp. 198–9, 233 and 255.

22 She compresses the period (even going so far as to transpose certain real events) to 1944–7 (*Circumstances*, p. 269).

23 *Ibid.*, p. 263. Henri Perron comes to the same conclusion in the book. He has always believed that the purpose of literature is 'to show the world to others as you yourself see it', but he failed at first to realise that 'the truth of one's life is outside oneself, in events, in other people, in things; to talk about oneself, one must talk about everything else' (*Mandarins*, p. 314).

24 Brombert calls it 'a central document concerning the psychology of the French intellectual' (p. 145). Julienne-Caffié believes that if it were not for *The mandarins* nobody would now remember this early postwar progressivism and its attempts to mould the future (pp. 116–17).

25 Hourdin, p. 153; Hughes, *Path*, pp. 165–7.

26 *Mandarins*, pp. 15, 25, 48 and 276; *Circumstance*, p. 269. Henri's hesitations about the value of literature reflect Simone de Beauvoir's ambiguous attitude at the time she was writing the book (*Circumstance*, pp. 264–5).

27 *Mandarins,* pp. 135, 469 and 673. Mounier saw very clearly much earlier than this the difficult balance between committed action and the pursuit of truth. Action demands choices and sacrifices, and if he is to achieve anything the intellectual must compromise. If he pursues perfection then he is condemned to immobility (*Traité du caractère,* [1943], quoted in Domenach, *Emmanuel Mounier*).

28 *Mandarins,* pp. 161, 409, 436 and 455. It should be said that, according to Simone de Beauvoir, Sartre himself had no hesitation in publishing the facts about the camps (*Circumstance,* p. 269).

29 *Mandarins,* p. 275. Lambert (and one suspects Simone de Beauvoir agrees) sees all politics in this light: 'The trouble is that in politics you never come down from the high plateau of history to the problem of the lowly individual... You get lost in generalities and no one gives a damn about particular cases' (*ibid.,* p. 165).

30 *Ibid.,* pp. 59, 213, 274–5 (author's translation) and 334.

31 De Gaulle's *rassemblement,* the R.P.F. (Rassemblement du Peuple Français) started in exactly the same way, purporting not to be a party but a movement, or 'rally', and allowing dual membership. When reconstituted in the Fifth Republic as the U.N.R. (Union pour la Nouvelle République), it did not take long to become effectively a powerful political party, although the fact that it is now a political party like any other is still not conceded in its name, as witness its latest title, the Rassemblement pour la République.

32 *Mandarins,* pp. 493 and 592. According to Simone de Beauvoir, Sartre never for a moment considered giving up his writing; indeed after the failure of the R.D.R., as after his rejection by the Communist Party at the end of the war, he took refuge in literary activity.

33 See Germaine Gennari, *Simone de Beauvoir,* p. 11.

34 Note that *Ambiguity* was published in the same year as her visit.

35 *America day by day* (which will be referred to henceforward as *America*), Preface and p. 178. There is a long discussion on the problem of the blacks on pp. 183–92.

36 *Ibid.,* p. 295 is the context, but the passage is omitted; author's translation.

37 *Ibid.,* pp. 209 and 237.

38 Burnier, p. 38, n. 3.

39 Sartre was just the same. The enthusiasm is partly explained by the vision of America which they had in their minds before either of them visited the country. Not only had it contributed to their cultural education through its jazz, cinema, literature – all held in great esteem by them – but it promised so much: 'America was also the country which had sent our deliverance; it was the future on the march; it was abundance, and infinite horizons; it was a crazy magic lantern of legendary images; the mere thought that they could be seen with one's own eyes set one's head whirling' (*Circumstance,* p. 28). Many years earlier, in the early thirties, they had been attracted by America while condemning its regime, whereas they had no interest in the U.S.S.R. while admiring the social experiment which was taking place there (*Prime,* p. 116).

40 *Circumstance*, p. 346; interview in Jeanson, p. 288; *March*, p. 419; *All said*, p. 415.

41 *Circumstance*, pp. 323–4; *All said*, pp. 292 and 341.

42 Sorum, p. 159. This is Jeanson's account of Sartre's first reactions (interview with Sorum).

43 *Circumstance*, pp. 369–71, 442–3 and 461; *Djamila Boupacha*, pp. 11–13.

44 In contrast in 1940, when she was still unknown and teaching at the Lycée Camille-Sée in Paris, she ended up by signing a declaration that she was neither a Freemason nor a Jew, although she found this repugnant: there was 'no possible alternative' (*Prime*, p. 369).

45 For details, see Brée, *Camus and Sartre*, and Lottman.

46 For the whole of this section on Algeria the reader may refer to *Circumstance*, pp. 326–7, 336–41, 349, 368–71, 382–4, 393–5, 400–3, 407–8, 442–3, 448, 456, 461, 506, 572–4, 584–5, 610–14, 616 and 652–3.

The research of Sorum (e.g. pp. 173–5 and 177) makes it quite clear that although people like Jeanson and Sartre changed the attitude of other intellectuals, they did little to end the war. The general public was not swayed until de Gaulle began to argue for independence. Even then it was more because they were heartily sick of the whole thing than from a sense of moral outrage at torture or a sympathy for the claims of Algeria to independence.

47 *All said*, p. 421.

48 *Ibid.*, pp. 423–5 and 430–1.

49 *Sartre in the seventies*, p. 23; Axel Madsen, *Hearts and minds*, pp. 219 and 259.

50 Susan M. Roberts, 'Simone de Beauvoir: a study of her life and work', p. 103.

51 Madsen, pp. 275 and 280.

52 *Libération*, special holiday edition, August 1973; Gavi, Sartre and Victor, p. 336.

53 Dayan and Ribowska, p. 78.

54 *Ibid.*, p. 64.

55 *Circumstance*, p. 645.

56 Dayan and Ribowska, pp. 62–3 (author's italics).

57 *Circumstance*, pp. 528–30.

58 *Mandarins*, p. 56.

6. *Engagement* as philanthropy

1 *Memoirs*, pp. 41 and 239. This was reflected in her conversation with Simone Weil, recorded above.

2 An example is the case (on which Genet's *Les bonnes* was modelled) of the Papin sisters of Rouen, who had murdered their employer and her daughter. At first Sartre and Simone de Beauvoir saw the two sisters, orphaned and put into service, as victims of their circumstances: it was small wonder that they had rebelled against harsh treatment by their

employer, and that the system had turned them into murderers who had taken justice into their own hands. She describes years later how she and Sartre were put out to discover on reading the details of the trial that one of the sisters was paranoid and the other influenced by her paranoia; they were forced to admit that the crime was carried out blindly by two people who were confused and frightened, so that it hardly constituted a conscious gesture for liberty against society (*Prime*, pp. 108–9).

3   Canabis, quoted in Julienne-Caffié, p. 225; Hourdin, p. 160. *Le dévouement* is her prime target, but charity is included by implication in her attack on all forms of moral and social rescue.

4   Benda, pp. 61–3.

5   *Ambiguity*, p. 50; interview with Mo Teitelbaum, 1973. Sartre took part in one of these tribunals, investigating a mining accident at Lens, in which 16 miners died (*All said*, pp. 437–9).

6   'La Syrie et les prisonniers', *Le Monde*, 1973; interview with Pierre Viansson-Ponté, 1978.

7   *Old age* (this will be referred to henceforward as *Age*); *All said*, p. 141.

8   *Circumstance*, p. 185; *All said*, pp. 130–1.

9   *Prime*, p. 168; *Circumstance*, pp. 254, 285 and 656; interview in Jeanson, p. 274; interview with Madeleine Gobeil in Julienne-Caffié, p. 217.

10   Interview with Caroline Moorehead, 1974; *All said*, p. 131; *Age*, p. 10.

11   Interview with Caroline Moorehead; *Age*, pp. 10, 215–16, 261–2, 276, 539 and 542–3.

12   Madsen, p. 271.

13   *All said*, p. 132.

14   'The old feminism' as Martin Seymour-Smith calls it, as opposed to the new feminism which started with Simone de Beauvoir's *2nd sex* (*Sex and society*).

15   *Esprit*, 1 June 1936. Mounier takes up the problem of women in society yet again in *Personalism*: 'It is nevertheless true that our social world is one that man has made for men...woman also is a person' (p. 109).

16   *Prime*, p. 54; *Circumstance*, pp. 185 and 189; *Sartre in the seventies*, p. 97. Sartre always thought of her as an equal, but was ambivalent generally in his attitude to women, whom he regarded as both equal and unequal.

17   *2nd sex*, pp. 60 and 273; *Prime*, p. 291; *Circumstance*, p. 185.

18   Simone de Beauvoir cites Brigitte Bardot as the epitome of the conscious being, a free woman, the very opposite of 'the woman as object' (*Brigitte Bardot and the Lolita syndrome*). Woman's freedom depends not on laws but on the attitudes of society: she compares ancient Greece where women were legally in an excellent position but in fact were kept in a state of semi-slavery, with Rome where they had few rights but enjoyed a very privileged position (*2nd sex*, History, chapter III).

19   *Ibid.*, pp. 152, 567–8 and 574.

20   Interestingly enough, Caroline Moorehead quotes friends of theirs as saying that Simone de Beauvoir's relationship with Sartre was just like a bourgeois marriage, even if they did live apart, and that Simone de

Beauvoir was as careful as any married woman to steer away rivals. It also has to be said that her views on the family are probably based on a rather restricted social sample; moreover the family in France is an institution that has no equivalent elsewhere. It is not difficult to understand her loathing of conventional marriage when one looks at some of the examples of the established wisdom of the period of her childhood and adolescence in the section on marriage and morals in Zeldin, vol. 1.

21 *2nd sex*, pp. 57, 88-9, 165 and 500; interview in Jeanson, p. 283; *Circumstance*, p. 191. The influence of their puritanism is convincingly argued by Dorothy Kaufmann McCall in 'Simone de Beauvoir, *The second sex*, and Jean-Paul Sartre', pp. 215-16.

22 *Prime*, pp. 291-2; *2nd sex*, pp. 641-2 (part of sentence omitted: author's translation).

23 Interview with Nina Sutton, 1970; interview in Jeanson, p. 286; *Circumstance*, p. 192; Hourdin, p. 116.

24 In *Age*, the situation is seen as being imposed by society, and in no way the fault of old people themselves. The evolution between the two books reflects the evolution in her conception of freedom. Jean Leighton remarks that the book is a 'lamentation about women's woes but a diatribe against the female sex' (*Simone de Beauvoir on woman*, pp. 118-19).

25 Interview in Jeanson, p. 253; Dayan and Ribowska, p. 75; *All said*, p. 128.

26 The article in question appeared in *Le Figaro Littéraire* and was about pornographic literature, in which category he included *2nd sex* (*Circumstance*, p. 187).

27 Julienne-Caffié, p. 42; *Circumstance*, p. 193.

28 Professor Margaret Stacey of the University of Warwick points out that, conversely, after the war there was an attempt to persuade women back into the home (private letter, 27 February 1978); in France the postwar *politique familiale* (giving financial aid to large families) was in reality a *politique nataliste* (to encourage a rise in the birth rate), thus reinforcing the family unit; later in England there was the young Queen and her family which 'reinforced the idyll of love and marriage' (Sheila Rowbotham, quoted in Anna Coote, 'In the beginning was the unburnt bra').

29 Interview with John Gerassi, 1976; interview with Claude Francis, 1976, in Francis and Gontier, pp. 568-76.

30 Interviews with Alice Jardine, 1977, in *Signs*, p. 236, and Caroline Moorehead, 1974; McCall, p. 223.

31 'La condition féminine', Francis and Gontier, pp. 401-9; 'Situation de la femme d'aujourd'hui', lecture given in Japan in September 1966, Francis and Gontier, pp. 422-38; interview in Yugoslavia, 1968, Francis and Gontier, pp. 234-6; *Circumstance*, p. 192.

32 This is precisely the point made by Betty Friedan in her interview with Simone de Beauvoir in *It changed my life*. One suspects a tendency on the part of Simone de Beauvoir during this somewhat acrimonious interview to disagree for the sake of it.

33 For the evolution of her views on feminism in the 1970s, see *All said*, p. 448; 'Situation de la femme d'aujourd'hui', 1966; interviews with Alice Schwartzer, 1972; John Gerassi, 1976; Claude Francis, 1976; Caroline Moorehead, 1974; Alice Jardine, 1977; and Pierre Viansson-Ponté, 1978.

34 Interviews with Claude Francis, John Gerassi and Alice Jardine; preface to Anne Ophir, *Regards féminins*.

35 *All said*, pp. 455 and 459; interview with Claude Francis.

36 See Nicole Benoît and Bernard Paillard, 'L'offensive néo-féministe du Mouvement de Libération des Femmes' in Benoît, Morin and Paillard, *La femme majeure*, pp. 108–29; Catherine Bodard Silver, 'Salon, foyer, bureau: women and the professions in France' in Joan Huber, *Changing women in a changing society*, pp. 74–89; Zeldin, vol. 1.

37 Simone de Beauvoir has admitted to having had an abortion herself, in her evidence at the Bobigny trial in 1972 (Francis and Gontier, pp. 510–13). She was characteristically ambiguous, however, about her signing of the manifesto. This was a deliberate provocation to the authorities to prosecute her for having had an abortion if this was true, or for perjury if not. In the event, of course, nothing happened (interview with Madeleine Gobeil, 1973, quoted in Francis and Gontier, p. 253).

38 Annie Pisan and Anne Tristan, *Histoires du M.L.F.*, p. 68. The movement itself is regarded by its members as political. Anne Tristan writes: 'for us, the movement was obviously primarily political, because in challenging exploitation it went to the very root of the problem: the relationship of man to woman' (p. 72). They claim that their previous apoliticism was an advantage in that they approached the liberation of women as though it were in itself a subversive political activity (p. 9).

39 This is spelt out in her preface (*Les Temps Modernes*, vol. xxix, no. 329, December 1973) to the first appearance of the 'Sexisme ordinaire' pages which she edits for the review. She also edited a special issue of *Les Temps Modernes* devoted entirely to the condition of women, entitled 'Les femmes s'entêtent' (vol. xxix, nos. 333–4, April 1974). See also interview with Alice Jardine, p. 226.

40 *Ibid.*, pp. 225–6, and introduction to the interview.

41 Friedan, pp. 163 and 169. The concern for preserving individual autonomy and the consequent rejection of a large, organised movement is reminiscent of the R.D.R. episode and must surely reduce the effectiveness of the women's movement.

42 Pisan and Tristan, p. 96.

43 Interview with Mo Teitelbaum; Friedan, pp. 168–9. When asked by Betty Friedan what women should do if men decided to make nuclear war, given that they must not take part in politics, Simone de Beauvoir replied: 'That becomes a much too complicated question...Before all these questions that you raise can fall into place, society has to change.' Refusing to say how, she merely claims: 'We are already moving it.'

44 *Age*, p. 412.

45 *All said*, pp. 406–20 and 462; interviews with Alice Schwartzer, 1972, Mo Teitelbaum, 1973, Caroline Moorehead, 1974, Betty Friedan, 1975,

John Gerassi, 1976, Pierre Viansson-Ponté, 1978, and Catherine David, *Nouvel Observateur*, 22 January 1979.
46 Interviews with Pierre Viansson-Ponté, Catherine David and Caroline Moorehead.

Concluding remarks

1 Mo Teitelbaum calls them examples of the 'gentle, self-deceptive, in-effectual niceness of Anglo-Saxon liberalism' (interview with Simone de Beauvoir). Their style of thought 'pre-supposed a rather sharp division of society into two classes: the weak, who suffered oppression and needed succour; and the strong, who had the choice between being either oppressors of the weak, or champions of them' (Arnold Toynbee, quoted in Gilbert Murray, *An unfinished autobiography*).

   Rejecting normal political activity now as in the past ('I think that politics as it exists does not interest me'), she admires the decision of certain feminist and young revolutionary groups to 'sap this regime but not play their game', by refusing to take part in politics (interview in Friedan, p. 168).

2 *Circumstance*, p. 653; Sorum, p. 239. Aron's view in 1955 was that the products of the E.N.S. saw political issues in Marxist or existentialist terms, and that although they took sides with the proletariat, which they wished to emancipate, against capitalism, which they wished to destroy, they knew little of either (*Opium*, p. 213). Genet, whose views on the bourgeoisie corresponded with those of Simone de Beauvoir, had the advantage of an intimate knowledge of that section of society which he supported, since he had come out of it himself (Coe, pp. 162–3).

3 For a sceptical view of the importance and influence of French intellectuals, see Zeldin, Aron, Caute and Revel.

4 Revel does not believe that in postwar years any more serious notice was taken of the left than of 'fifty small shopkeepers, hairdressers and plumbers calling for a reform of the *agrégation*' (p. 55).

5 Redfern, paper given at the University of Warwick (1978); Zeldin, vol. II, p. 1128. For a long time now, Simone de Beauvoir has preferred to live in the close, intimate circle of a few old friends, like-minded people, known as 'the family'.

6 Burnier (pp. 170–1) believes that Sartre's political influence is exerted through certain of his books, purely literary works in which politics is only one dimension of the world we live in. Redfern (p. 119) questions whether books like the political novel can do anything more than confirm views which are held already. See also Sorum, p. 15. In *Intellectuals and decolonisation in France*, one of the few pieces of detailed research on the influence of intellectuals in a very specific area, Sorum claims that 'even if they have little influence on immediate policies, they can still prepare the ways in which people will eventually conceptualise their experiences. When the external situation has changed, people must find a means of integrating the new situation into their world view and,

therefore, may have to accept ideas they formerly rejected' (p. 242). What influenced decolonisation in general and the outcome of the Algerian war in particular were the practical and financial arguments of the 'realist' intellectuals (who in fact were misconstrued as arguing for abandonment of the colonies, and whose influence did not lead to the result they had intended), and the pragmatic stance eventually taken by de Gaulle, rather than the revelations about torture.

7 See previous note. Witness also the popularised versions of 'existentialism' in the postwar period which reflected badly on the integrity of Sartre and on his political views as well as his philosophy (see chapter 2).

8 *Words*, p. 172; *Sartre in the seventies*, pp. 89–90.

9 *America*, p. 265 (part of sentence omitted: author's translation); interview with J.-F. Rolland, Francis and Gontier, p. 359; interview with Catherine David, p. 84.

Bibliography

The works of Simone de Beauvoir

The reader is referred to Claude Francis and Fernande Gontier, *Les écrits de Simone de Beauvoir*, for a comprehensive bibliography of her works. The less important minor items have been omitted from the list below unless referred to in the notes, as have extracts from her books before publication and preliminary material later developed in books. Some of the *Temps Modernes* articles were subsequently regrouped into the two volumes, *L'existentialisme et la sagesse des nations* and *Privilèges*; the references in the notes are to the original articles.

Works published in book form

The French title is given first, with details of the first edition; it is followed by details of the English translation (if one exists) in the edition referred to in the notes.

L'invitée. Paris (Gallimard) 1943. *She came to stay*. Transl. Yvonne Moyse and Roger Senhouse. London (Penguin/Secker & Warburg) 1966
Pyrrhus et Cinéas. Paris (Gallimard) 1944
Le sang des autres. Paris (Gallimard) 1945. *The blood of others*. Transl. Yvonne Moyse and Roger Senhouse. London (Secker & Warburg/Lindsay Drummond) 1948
Les bouches inutiles. Play in two acts. First performed 31 October 1945, Théâtre des Carrefours, Paris. Paris (Gallimard) 1945
Tous les hommes sont mortels. Paris (Gallimard) 1946. *All men are mortal*. Transl. Leonard M. Friedman. Cleveland (World Publishing Company) 1956
Pour une morale de l'ambiguïté. Paris (Gallimard) 1947. *The ethics of ambiguity*. Transl. Bernard Frechtman. New York (Philosophical Library) 1948
L'Amérique au jour le jour. Paris (Morihien) 1948. *America day by day*. Transl. Patrick Dudley. London (Gerald Duckworth) 1952
L'existentialisme et la sagesse des nations. Paris (Nagel) 1948
Le deuxième sexe. 2 vols. I *Les faits et les mythes*. II *L'expérience vécue*. Paris (Gallimard) 1949. *The second sex*. Transl. H. M. Parshley. London (Jonathan Cape) 1953
Must we burn Sade? ('Faut-il brûler Sade?'). Transl. Annette Michelson. London (Peter Nevill) 1953

Les mandarins. Paris (Gallimard) 1954. 52nd Prix Goncourt. *The mandarins.*
    Transl. Leonard M. Friedman. London (Collins) 1957
Privilèges. Paris (Gallimard) 1955
La longue marche. Paris (Gallimard) 1957. *The long march.* Transl. Austryn
    Wainhouse. London (André Deutsch/Weidenfeld & Nicolson) 1958
Mémoires d'une jeune fille rangée. Paris (Gallimard) 1958. *Memoirs of a
    dutiful daughter.* Transl. James Kirkup. London (André Deutsch/
    Weidenfeld & Nicolson) 1959
La force de l'âge. Paris (Gallimard) 1960. *The prime of life.* Transl. Peter
    Green. London (André Deutsch/Weidenfeld & Nicolson) 1962
Brigitte Bardot and the Lolita syndrome. London (André Deutsch/Weidenfeld
    & Nicolson) 1960
La force des choses. Paris (Gallimard) 1963. *Force of circumstance.* Transl.
    Richard Howard. London (André Deutsch/Weidenfeld & Nicolson) 1965
Une mort très douce. Paris (Gallimard) 1964. *A very easy death.* Transl.
    Patrick O'Brian. London (André Deutsch/Weidenfeld & Nicolson) 1966
Que peut la littérature? A symposium, ed. by Yves Buin, under general editor-
    ship of Jean-Edern Hallier and Michel-Claude Jalard. Paris (Union
    Générale d'Editeurs: Collection L'Inédit) 1965. Contributions by Simone
    de Beauvoir, Yves Berger, Jean-Pierre Faye, Jean Ricardou, Jean-Paul
    Sartre and Jorge Semprun
Les belles images. Paris (Gallimard) 1966. *Les belles images.* Transl. Patrick
    O'Brian. London (Fontana/Collins) 1969
La femme rompue, followed by *Monologue* and *L'âge de discrétion.* Paris
    (Gallimard) 1968. *The woman destroyed,* followed by *The monologue*
    and *The age of discretion.* Transl. Patrick O'Brian. London (Collins) 1969
La vieillesse. Paris (Gallimard) 1970. *Old age.* Transl. Patrick O'Brian.
    London (André Deutsch/Weidenfeld & Nicolson) 1972
Tout compte fait. Paris (Gallimard) 1972. *All said and done.* Transl. Patrick
    O'Brian. London (André Deutsch/Weidenfeld and Nicolson) 1974
Quand prime le spirituel. Paris (Gallimard) 1979

Articles and other minor items

'Quatre jours à Madrid', *Combat-Magazine,* 14–15 April 1945, pp. 1–2
'Le Portugal sous le régime de Salazar' (under the pseudonym of Daniel
    Secrétan), *Combat,* 23 April 1945, pp. 1–2, and 24 April 1945, pp. 1–2
'Idéalisme moral et réalisme politique', *Les Temps Modernes,* vol. 1, no. 2,
    November 1945, pp. 248–68. Later published in *L'existentialisme et la
    sagesse des nations*
'*La phénoménologie de la perception* de Maurice Merleau-Ponty' (book
    review), *Les Temps Modernes,* vol. 1, no. 2, November 1945, pp. 363–7
'L'existentialisme et la sagesse des nations', *Les Temps Modernes,* vol. 1,
    no. 3, December 1945, pp. 385–404. Later published in the book of the
    same title
'Œil pour œil', *Les Temps Modernes,* vol. 1, no. 5, February 1946, pp. 813–
    30. Later published in *L'existentialisme et la sagesse des nations*
'La littérature et la métaphysique', *Les Temps Modernes,* vol. 1, no. 7, April

1946, pp. 1153–63. Later published in *L'existentialisme et la sagesse des nations*

'Pour une morale de l'ambiguïté', *Les Temps Modernes*, vol. II, nos. 14–17, December 1946–February 1947, pp. 193–211, 385–408, 638–64 and 846–74. Later published in book form

'Faut-il brûler Sade?', *Les Temps Modernes*, vol. VII, nos. 74–5, December 1950 and January 1951, pp. 1002–33 and 1197–1230. Later published in *Privilèges*

'La pensée de droite, aujourd'hui', *Les Temps Modernes*, vol. X, nos. 112–13 and 114–15 May and June–July 1955, pp. 1539–75 and 2219–61. Later published in *Privilèges*

'Merleau-Ponty et le pseudo-sartrisme', *Les Temps Modernes*, vol. X, nos. 114–15, June–July 1955, pp. 2072–2122. Later published in *Privilèges*

'Pour Djamila Boupacha', 'Libres opinions' column, *Le Monde*, vol. XVII, no. 4,779, 2 June 1960, p. 6

Preface to Gisèle Halimi, *Djamila Boupacha*. Paris (Gallimard) 1962

'Méru. En France aujourd'hui on peut tuer impunément', *J'accuse*, 15 February 1971, pp. 24–5

'La Syrie et les prisonniers', *Le Monde*, vol. XXX, no. 8996, 18 December 1973, p. 2

Preface to *Le sexisme ordinaire*. First published in *Les Temps Modernes*, vol. XXIX, no. 329, December 1973, introducing the first appearance of the feminist section in the review, from which the articles collected together in the book were taken. Paris (Editions du Seuil) 1979

Interviews

The only interviews listed are those relevant to this book; those which have appeared in books included in the bibliography are not listed separately, but in each case the first note reference indicates the book title.

Nina Sutton. 'Simone de Beauvoir faces up to mortality', and 'Sartre and the second sex', *Guardian*, 16 February 1970, p. 9, and 19 February 1970, p. 11

Mo Teitelbaum. 'Women against the system', *Sunday Times Magazine*, 29 April 1973, pp. 28–31

Caroline Moorehead. 'Simone de Beauvoir: "Marriage is a very dangerous institution"', and 'Happiness is a snare when the world is a horrible place', *The Times*, 15 May 1974, p. 9, and 16 May 1974, p. 11

Catherine David. 'Beauvoir elle-même', *Le Nouvel Observateur*, 22 January 1979, pp. 82–5 and 88–90

Alice Jardine (1977). *Signs*, vol. V, no. 2, Winter 1979, pp. 224–36

Works devoted wholly or in part to Simone de Beauvoir

For a comprehensive bibliography of works on Simone de Beauvoir up to 1970, the reader is referred to Claire Cayron, *La nature chez Simone de Beauvoir*. The following list attempts to be comprehensive from 1970 onwards

but omits both theses and book reviews unless they have been referred to in
the text.

L'Arc, no. 61, 1975, 84 pp. 'Simone de Beauvoir et la lutte des femmes'.
Special issue devoted to Simone de Beauvoir and the women's movement. Includes: Catherine Clément and Bernard Pingaud, 'Une femme
pour d'autres', p. 1; a discussion between Simone de Beauvoir and
Sartre later published in *Situations X* and translated in *Sartre in the
seventies*, pp. 3–12; 'Des femmes en lutte', interview with Simone de
Beauvoir, pp. 19–31; and Sylvie Le Bon, '*Le deuxième sexe*. L'esprit et
la lettre', pp. 55–60

ARMOGATHE, Daniel. *Le deuxième sexe: Beauvoir*. Paris (Hatier) 1977

AUDET, Jean-Raymond. *Simone de Beauvoir face à la mort*. Lausanne (L'Age
d'homme) 1979

BEIBER, Konrad. *Simone de Beauvoir*. Boston (Twayne's World Author Series)
1979

BOISDEFFRE, Pierre de. 'L'entreprise de Simone de Beauvoir', in his *Où va le
roman?*, Paris (Del Duca) 1972, pp. 123–41

BREE, Germaine. *Women writers in France*. New Brunswick (Rutgers University Press) 1973

BRUEZIERE, Maurice. *Histoire descriptive de la littérature contemporaine*,
vol. I, pp. 375–84. Paris (Berger-Levrault) 1975

CAYRON, Claire. *La nature chez Simone de Beauvoir*. Paris (Gallimard) 1973.
Detailed bibliography

CHEVERNY, Julien. 'Une bourgeoise modèle: Simone de Beauvoir', review of
film *Simone de Beauvoir*, *Le Figaro Magazine*. 17 February 1979, p. 57

CISMARU, Alfred. 'Enduring existentialists. Sartre and Simone de Beauvoir in
their golden age', *Antioch Review*, vol. XXXI, 1971–2, pp. 557–64

'Simone de Beauvoir's "All said and done" – but not quite', *American
Society Legion of Honor Magazine*, New York, no. 48, 1977, pp. 87–100

COTTRELL, Robert D. *Simone de Beauvoir*. New York (Fr. Ungar: Modern
Literature Monographs) 1975

CUENAT, Paul. 'Commentaire d'un passage de *Tout compte fait*', *Humanités
Classiques*. *L'Information Littéraire*, Paris, no. 485, April 1973, pp. 6–12

DAYAN, Josée and RIBOWSKA, Malka. *Simone de Beauvoir*. Text of a film
portrait of Simone de Beauvoir. Paris (Gallimard) 1979

DESCUBES, Madeleine. *Connaître Simone de Beauvoir*. Paris (Editions Resma)
1974

DOMENACH, Jean-Marie. 'Une politique de la certitude', *Esprit*, vol. XXXII,
no. 3, March 1964, pp. 502–6

DUCHENE, Roger. 'Simone de Beauvoir à Marseille. Le temps d'un exil?',
Marseille, no. 102, 1975, pp. 55–8

ECHARD, Martine. 'Approche des principaux écrivains féminins contemporains
1945–1970', in *Bibliographie de la France*, Chronique CLXIV, 1975,
pp. 834–45

EPSTEIN, Cynthia Fuchs. 'Guineas and locks', *Dissent*, vil. XXI, no. 4 (no. 97),
Fall 1974, pp. 581–6

EVANS, Carol. 'Le problème de l'autre dans l'œuvre de Simone de Beauvoir'.
M.A. thesis, University of Wales at Cardiff, 1964

FRANCIS, Claude (ed.). *Simone de Beauvoir et le cours du monde*. Photographs of Simone de Beauvoir with connecting text. Paris (Klincksieck) 1978

FRANCIS, Claude and GONTIER, Fernande. *Les écrits de Simone de Beauvoir*. Paris (Gallimard) 1980

GAGNEBIN, Laurent. *Simone de Beauvoir, ou le refus de l'indifférence*. Preface by Simone de Beauvoir. Paris (Editions Fischbacher) 1968

GENNARI, Geneviève. *Simone de Beauvoir*. Paris (Editions Universitaires) 1958

HANSEN, Kirsten Lund. 'Crêpage de chignon', *(Pré)Publications*, no. 42, July 1978, pp. 15–30

HANSEN, Linda. 'Pain and joy in human relationships. Jean-Paul Sartre and Simone de Beauvoir', *Philosophy Today*, vol. XXIII, no. 4/4, Winter 1979, pp. 338–46

HARTH, Erica. 'The creative alienation of the writer: Sartre, Camus and Simone de Beauvoir', *Mosaic*, University of Manitoba, Canada, vol. VIII, no. 3, 1975, pp. 177–86

HOURDIN, Georges. *Simone de Beauvoir et la liberté*. Paris (Editions du Cerf) 1962

HUVOS, Kornel. *Cinq mirages américains. Les Etats-Unis dans l'œuvre de Georges Duhamel, Jules Romains, André Maurois, Jacques Maritain et Simone de Beauvoir*. Paris (Didier) 1973

JEANSON, Francis. *Simone de Beauvoir ou l'entreprise de vivre*. Paris (Editions du Seuil) 1966

JULIENNE-CAFFIE, Serge. *Simone de Beauvoir*. Paris (Gallimard) 1966

KEEFE, Terry. 'Beauvoir's *La femme rompue*. Studies in self-deception', *Essays in French Literature*, University of Western Australia, vol. XIII, November 1976, pp. 77–97

'Marriage in the later fiction of Camus and Beauvoir', *Orbis Litterarum*, Copenhagen, vol. XXXIII, 1978, pp. 69–86

KRISHNAMURTHY, R. 'The world of books. The two Simones of France', *Thought*, Delhi, vol. XXVII, no. 25, 21 June 1975, pp. 14–15

LABAT, Joseph. 'Le concept de la mort pour Simone de Beauvoir', *Proceedings of the Pacific Northwest Conference on Foreign Languages*, vol. XXVII, no. 1, 1975, pp. 33–6

LASOCKI, Anne-Marie. *Simone de Beauvoir ou l'entreprise d'écrire*. The Hague (Nijhoff) 1971

LE DŒUFF, Michèle. 'Operative philosophy. Simone de Beauvoir and existentialism'. *Ideology and Consciousness*, no. 6, Autumn 1979, pp. 47–57

LEIGHTON, Jean. *Simone de Beauvoir on woman*. London (Associated University Presses) 1975

LIKAVSKA, Eva. 'L'invitée de Simone de Beauvoir', *Etudes romanes de Brno*, Prague, vol. IX, 1977, pp. 51–64

McCALL, Dorothy Kaufmann. 'Simone de Beauvoir, *The second sex*, and Jean-Paul Sartre', *Signs*, vol. V, no. 2, Winter 1979, pp. 209–23

MADSEN, Axel. *Hearts and minds. The common journey of Simone de Beauvoir and Sartre*. New York (William Morrow) 1977

MARCOTTE, Gilles. 'Simone et Jean-Paul à cinquante ans', in his *Les bonnes rencontres. Chroniques littéraires*, Montreal (H.M.H. Reconnaissances) 1971, pp. 32–7

MARKS, Elaine. *Simone de Beauvoir. Encounters with death.* New Brunswick (Rutgers University Press) 1973

'The dream of love. A study of three autobiographies', in STAMBOLIAN, George (ed.), *Twentieth century French fiction. Essays for Germaine Brée,* New Brunswick (Rutgers University Press) 1975, pp. 73–88

MERCIER, Michel. *Le roman féminin.* Paris (Presses Universitaires de France) 1976. Section on Simone de Beauvoir

MŒLLER, Charles. 'Simone de Beauvoir et la "situation" de la femme', in his *Littérature du XXe siècle et le christianisme,* vol. v, *Amours humaines,* Paris and Tournai (Casterman) 1975, pp. 135–200

MOORTGAT, Pierre. 'Lou Andréas-Salomé et Simone de Beauvoir', *Revue d'Allemagne,* vol. v, 1973, pp. 938–43

MOROT-SIR, Edouard. 'La critique existentialiste. 4. Simone de Beauvoir', in his *La pensée française d'aujourd'hui.* Paris (Presses Universitaires de France) 1971, pp. 38–9

MOUBACHIR, Chantal. *Simone de Beauvoir.* Paris (Seghers) 1972

MUNSTER, G. J. 'En route to existentialism', *Nation,* Sydney, no. 22, 18 July 1959, p. 21

OPHIR, Anne. 'La femme rompue', in her *Regards féminins. Condition féminine création littéraire,* Paris (Denoël/Gonthier) 1976, pp. 13–87. Introduction by Simone de Beauvoir, Christiane Rochefort and Claire Etcherelli

PAGES, Irène. 'Beauvoir's *Les belles images,* "desubstantification" of reality through narrative', *Forum for Modern Language Studies,* University of St Andrews, Scotland, no. 11, 1975, pp. 133–41

ROBERTS, Susan M. 'Simone de Beauvoir: a study of her life and work in an existentialist context'. Ph.D. thesis, University of Reading, 1973

STRAUSS, David. 'In quest of America. Six French resistants in the United States, 1945–47', *Contemporary French Civilisation,* Columbia, U.S.A., vol. i, no. 1, 1976, pp. 1–18

TUCKER, William R. 'Simone de Beauvoir: from existentialism to Marxism', *Lamar Journal of the Humanities,* vol. iv, no. 1, pp. 6–26

VAN DEN BERGHE, Christian Louis. *Dictionnaire des idées dans l'œuvre de Simone de Beauvoir.* Paris and The Hague (Mouton) 1966

VERCIER, Bruno. 'Les livres qui ont marqué notre époque', *Réalités,* no. 307, August 1971, pp. 11–17

Background material

In the case of French works, the details given are of the English edition referred to in the notes, with the French title and date of publication in brackets.

ADERETH, Maxwell. *Commitment in modern French literature.* London (Victor Gollancz) 1967

ARON, Raymond. *The opium of the intellectuals* (*L'opium des intellectuels,* 1955). Transl. Terence Kilmartin. London (Secker & Warburg) 1957

Marxism and the existentialists (five essays previously published in various places and at different times since 1946). Transl. Robert Addis, Helen

Weaver and John Weightman. New York, Evanston and London (Harper & Row) 1969

ASTRUC, Alexandre and CONTAT, Michel. *Sartre par lui-même*. Text of a film portrait of Sartre. Paris (Gallimard) 1977

AUDRY, Colette. *Connaissance de Sartre*. Paris (Julliard) 1955

BENDA, Julien. *The great betrayal (La trahison des clercs.* 1927). Transl. Richard Aldington. London (George Routledge) 1928

BENOIT, Nicole, MORIN, Edgar and PAILLARD, Bernard. *La femme majeure.* Paris (Club de l'Obs'/Editions du Seuil) 1973

BORNE, Etienne. *Mounier*. Paris (Seghers) 1972

BOURDIEU, Pierre and PASSERON, Jean-Claude. *Reproduction in education, society and culture (La reproduction,* 1970). Transl. Richard Nice. London and Beverly Hills (Sage Publications) 1977

  The inheritors (Les héritiers, 1964). Transl. Richard Nice. Chicago (University of Chicago Press) 1979

BREE, Germaine. *Camus and Sartre. Crisis and commitment.* London (Calder & Boyars) 1972

BROMBERT, Victor. *The intellectual hero.* London (Faber & Faber) 1960

BURNIER, Michel-Antoine. *Choice of action: the French existentialists on the political front line (Les existentialistes et la politique,* 1966). Transl. Bernard Murchland. New York (Random House) 1968

CABAUD, Jacques. *Simone Weil. A fellowship in love.* London (Harvill Press) 1964

CAUTE, David. *Communism and the French intellectuals (1914–1960).* London (André Deutsch) 1964

COBBAN, Alfred. *A history of modern France*, vol. III, 1871–1962. London (Penguin) 1965

COE, Richard N. *The vision of Jean Genet.* London (Peter Owen) 1968

COOTE, Anna. 'In the beginning was the unburnt bra', *Sunday Times Magazine*, 1 October 1978, pp. 34–48

CRUICKSHANK, John. *Albert Camus and the literature of revolt* (1959). New York (Oxford University Press) 1960

DOMENACH, Jean-Marie. *Emmanuel Mounier.* Paris (Editions du Seuil) 1972

Esprit, no. 45, 1 June 1936. 'La femme aussi est une personne'. Special issue on women

FLOWER, John E. *Writers and politics in modern France.* London (Hodder & Stoughton) 1977

FRIEDAN, Betty. *It changed my life.* London (Victor Gollancz) 1977

La Gauche R.D.R., nos. 1–13, 15–30 May 1948–11 March 1949

GAVI, Philippe, SARTRE, Jean-Paul and VICTOR, Pierre. *On a raison de se révolter.* Paris (Gallimard) 1974

GELLNER, Ernest. *Contemporary thought and politics.* Vol. II of his collected papers. London (Routledge & Kegan Paul) 1974

  'Ernest Gellner on sandcastles and the search for certainty', *Listener*, 4 May 1978, pp. 567–70

GINSBOURG, Ariel. *Paul Nizan.* Paris (Editions Universitaires) 1966

HUGHES, Henry Stuart. *Consciousness and society* (1958). London (MacGibbon & Kee) 1967

The obstructed path: French social thought in the years of desperation 1930–60. New York (Harper & Row) 1966

JEANSON, Francis and Colette. *L'Algérie hors la loi*. Paris (Editions du Seuil) 1955

LOTTMAN, Herbert R. *Albert Camus, a biography*. London (Weidenfeld & Nicolson) 1979

MANDER, John. *The writer and commitment*. London (Secker & Warburg) 1961

MARCUSE, Herbert. 'Repressive tolerance', in WOLFF, Robert Paul, MOORE Jr, Barrington and MARCUSE, Herbert. *A critique of pure tolerance*, London (Jonathan Cape) 1970, pp. 43–137

MEAD, Margaret. *Sex and temperament* (1935). New York (William Morrow) 1963

MOUNIER, Emmanuel. *Personalism* (*Le personnalisme*, 1949). Transl. Philip Mairet. London (Routledge & Kegan Paul) 1952

MURRAY, Gilbert. *An unfinished autobiography with contributions by his friends*. Jean Smith and Arnold Toynbee (eds.). London (Allen & Unwin) 1960

O'ROURKE, James J. *The problem of freedom in Marxist thought*. Dordrecht and Boston (D. Reidel) 1974

PISAM, Annie de and TRISTAN, Anne. *Histoires du M.L.F.* Paris (Calmann-Lévy) 1977. Preface by Simone de Beauvoir

POSTER, Mark. *Existential Marxism in postwar France. From Sartre to Althusser*. Princeton, New Jersey (Princeton University Press) 1975

READ, Herbert. *Existentialism, Marxism and anarchism*. London (Freedom Press) 1949

REDFERN, Walter D. *Paul Nizan. Committed literature in a conspiratorial world*. Princeton, New Jersey (Princeton University Press) 1972

REVEL, Jean-François. *En France. La fin de l'opposition*. Paris (Julliard) 1965

ROUBICZEK, Paul. *Existentialism for and against*. Cambridge (Cambridge University Press) 1964

ROUSSET, David, ROSENTHAL, Gérard and SARTRE, Jean-Paul. *Entretiens sur la politique*. Paris (Gallimard) 1949

SARTRE, Jean-Paul. *Being and nothingness* (*L'être et le néant*, 1943). Transl. Hazel E. Barnes. London (Methuen: University Paperback) 1969

  Existentialism and humanism (*L'existentialisme est un humanisme*, 1946). Transl. Philip Mairet. London (Methuen) 1949

  What is literature? (*Qu'est-ce que la littérature?*, 1948). Transl. Bernard Frechtman. London (Methuen) 1950

  Words (*Les mots*, 1964). Transl. Irène Cléphane. London (Hamish Hamilton) 1964

  'A long, bitter, sweet madness', interview, *Encounter*, vol. XXII, no. 6, June 1964, pp. 61–3

  'Entretien avec Jean-Paul Sartre', interview with Madeleine Gobeil, *Vogue*, American edition, July 1965

  Situations II (1948) and *Situations III* (1949). Paris (Gallimard)

Collections of English translations of essays, articles and interviews taken from *Situations I to X*:

> *Literary and philosophical essays* (from *Situations I and II*). Transl. Annette Michelson. London (Rider) 1955
>
> *Situations*. Transl. Benita Eisler. London (Hamish Hamilton) 1965
>
> *Politics and literature*. Transl. John Calder and J. A. Underwood. London (Calder & Boyars) 1973
>
> *Between existentialism and Marxism* (from *Situations VIII and IX*). Transl. John Matthews. London (New Left Books) 1974
>
> *Sartre in the seventies* (from *Situations X*). Transl. Paul Auster and Lydia Davies. London (André Deutsch) 1978

SEYMOUR-SMITH, Martin. *Sex and society*. London (Hodder & Stoughton) 1975

SILVER, Catherine Bodard. 'Salon, foyer, bureau: women and the professions in France', in HUBER, Joan (ed.), *Changing women in a changing society*, Chicago and London (University of Chicago Press) 1973, pp. 74–89

SORUM, Paul Clay. *Intellectuals and decolonization in France*. Chapel Hill, North Carolina (University of North Carolina Press) 1977

STERN, Alfred. *Sartre. His philosophy and existential psycho-analysis*. London (Vision Press) 1967

Les Temps Modernes, vol. XXIX, nos. 333–4, April 1974. 'Les femmes s'entêtent'. Special issue on the condition of women, edited by Simone de Beauvoir

THODY, Philip. *Sartre: a literary and political study*. London (Hamish Hamilton) 1960

THOMAS, Hugh. *The Spanish civil war* (1961). 3rd edition (revised). London (Hamish Hamilton) 1977

ZELDIN, Theodore. *France 1848–1945*. I *Ambition, love and politics*. II *Intellect, taste and anxiety*. Oxford (Clarendon Press) 1973 and 1977

Index